Anonymous

A Collection of Memorials Concerning Divers Deceased Ministers

and Others of the People Called Quakers

Anonymous

A Collection of Memorials Concerning Divers Deceased Ministers and Others of the People Called Quakers

ISBN/EAN: 9783337402150

Printed in Europe, USA, Canada, Australia, Japan

Cover: Foto ©Suzi / pixelio.de

More available books at **www.hansebooks.com**

A

COLLECTION

O F

MEMORIALS

CONCERNING

Divers deceafed Minifters and others
of the People called QUAKERS,

I N

Pennfylvania, New-Jerfey, and Parts adjacent, from nearly the firft Settlement
thereof to the Year 1787.

With fome of the laft Expreffions and
Exhortations of many of them.

Not by works of righteoufnefs which we have done, but according to his mercy, he faved us, by the wafhing of regeneration, and renewing of the Holy Ghoft. Titus iii—5.

PHILADELPHIA:

PRINTED BY JOSEPH CRUKSHANK, IN MAR-
KET-STREET, BETWEEN SECOND
AND THIRD-STREETS.

M DCC LXXXVII.

PREFACE.

ALTHOUGH they who are departed hence in the Lord, can receive no addition to their happinefs by any teftimonial of their furviving friends, however juft; yet to the wife in heart, precious is the memory of the truly pious and upright, whofe humble walking in the fear of God has livingly witneffed againft the appearance of evil in its various transformations; their conformity in fpirit and practice to the holy law of the Lord, evincing the delight and benefit to be found therein; for " Verily there " is a reward for the righteous, verily he is " a God that judgeth in the earth." Pfalm lviii, verfe 11.

" What fcene in this life more dignifies " humanity? what fchool is more profita- " bly inftructive than the death-bed of the " righteous, impreffing the underftanding " with a convincing evidence, that they " have not followed cunningly devifed fa- " bles, but folid fubftantial truth; that " there is a meafure of divine light and " grace in man, which if duly minded and " obeyed, is fufficient to preferve thro' all the " viciffitudes in life, to give him the vic-

" tory

" tory over his fpiritual enemies, and in the
" end over death, hell, and the grave?" *

It is right therefore, that the remembrance
of thofe fhould be preferved, whofe lights
have fo fhone before men as to excite the
beholders of their good works to glorify
God, the original, and fource from whom
all good is derived, that tho' being dead, the
luftre of their pious example through life,
and on the approach of death, may continue to fpeak the inviting language, " *Fol-*
" *low us as we have followed Chrift.*"

With this view, our yearly-meeting confidering that many memorials of our departed friends lay dormant on the records, directed a Collection to be made of fuch of
them as were moft likely to be of general
benefit by publication, which the committee
appointed for the fervice having performed
to the beft of their judgment, it is now pre-
fented to the readers, fome of whom will be
reminded of the fincere piety and virtue of
their anceftors, who through the dangers and
difficulties to which they were fubjected, in
their removal from their native land, and
forming a new fettlement in a wildernefs,
were happily preferved in a fteady attention
to their religious duty, and many of them
faithfully engaged in promoting the caufe of
truth and rightcoufnefs among mankind,
to whom others fucceeded, who through
obedience to the powerful influence of Divine grace, became alike eminent in their
day, and ferviceable in the church.

The

* Life of James Gough, page 53.

- The following Collection is affectionately recommended to the defcendants of thofe worthies, to the readers in general, and particularly to the youth, who may derive profitable inftruction by a ferious obferva- tion of the happy effects of an early devoti- on of heart, and the inexpreffible advant- ages of embracing the merciful vifitation of the Moft-High, to fecure their true comfort in this life, and enduring felicity in that which is to come.

Though the language and ftyle of thefe memorials may not be calculated to pleafe fuch curious readers who in their eftimate of the value of a Book, are too much amuf- ed by the difplay of wit and literary accom- plifhments in the compofition, to give due attention to the inftructive import of an art- lefs account of the chriftian experiences of thofe, who have not been fo folicitous for the approbation of men, as to be found humble followers of Chrift, their meek and lowly pattern and redeemer; but it is hop- ed, that there are many to whom the con- tents of this Collection will afford informa- tion, edification, and encouragement in the purfuit of their moft fubftantial intereft, a life of true wifdom, piety, and virtue; and that the number of fuch may increafe is the defign of the following publication.

Philadelphia, 12th Month, 1787.

A N

A COLLECTION

A
COLLECTION

O F

MEMORIALS or TESTIMONIES

C O N C E R N I N G

Divers MINISTERS and ELDERS deceafed.

An abſtraƈt of Nicholas Waln's *Teſtimony, concerning that faithful Jervant of the Lord,* CUTHBERT HAYHURST, *who departed this life, at his own houfe in the county of* Bucks, *in* Pennſylvania, *about the 5th of the firſt month,* 1682-3, *near the fiftieth year of his age.*

H E was born at Eafington, in Bolland in the county of York, in Old England, and was one of the worthies in Ifrael. My fpirit is comforted in a fenfe of that power, which did attend him in our meetings, for many years in the land of our nativity, and alfo after he came into thefe parts; having been a valiant foldier for the truth, and bore a faithful teftimony to the fame, in

B word,

word, life and converſation. He went through many great exerciſes and impriſonments, and was a comfort unto the faithful and true believers, who *follow the Lamb through many tribulations.* He was a worthy inſtrument in the Lord's hand, againſt the falſe teachers and hirelings, going ſeveral times to their ſteeple-houſes, and teſtifying againſt their deceiving the people. He alſo went to ſeveral market towns, and at their croſſes, declared and publiſhed the truth as it is in Jeſus: I accompanied him and his dear wife at one of them, where he faithfully warned the people and exhorted them to repentance; the divine power and preſence eminently attending him, which my ſoul was made ſenſible of to my comfort and ſatisfaction. I can ſay he was of great ſervice to me and many others, being inſtrumental in bringing us near unto the Lord, whoſe name over all we have cauſe to bleſs on his behalf; and although his body is gone to the earth, his memorial liveth among the righteous, and I am perſuaded his ſoul is in the enjoyment of peace with the Lord. I was often with him in the time of his ſickneſs, and beheld his meek, innocent and lamb-like deportment; being alſo by his bed-ſide when he departed, which was in a quiet and truly reſigned frame, like one falling into a ſweet ſleep; ſo that I have great cauſe to believe he is one of thoſe *that died in the Lord, and is at reſt with him forever.*

NICHOLAS WALN.

William Yardley's *Teſtimony concerning* CHRI-
STOPHER TAYLOR, *who died about the
year* 1686.

H E was one of the Lord's worthies,
ſtrong and ſteadfaſt in the faith, very
zealous for the truth and careful for the
church; his life being hid with God in Chriſt.
His miniſtry ſtood not in the wiſdom of the
fleſh, but in the power of God. It was the
birth born from above, that could receive
him and was refreſhed by him. In a word,
he was a Jew inward whoſe praiſe is not
of men but of God. And foraſmuch as he
was a man thus qualified, I could not well
be ſatisfied that ſo worthy a man as dear
Chriſtopher Taylor, ſhould be buried in oblivion. His chiefeſt joy was to feel friends in
the inviſible life; and although many exerciſes did attend him for the truth's ſake, he
was *faithful unto the death, and ſo has received a crown of life*; and though his departure
from us is our loſs, yet it is his gain; for
*bleſſed are the dead which die in the Lord, they
reſt from their labours and their works do follow them.*

WILLIAM YARDLEY.

It appears our ſaid friend came from Old
England, his native country, on a religious
viſit to New England, in the year 1675; af-
terwards into Pennſylvania, among the firſt
Engliſh, and ſettled at Philadelphia. He was
B 2 of

of confiderable fervice in public affairs, and very active in fettling meetings for difcipline in thofe early times; the firft of that fort for the women, being held at his houfe in 1683.

William Yardley *and* Phineas Pemberton's *Teſtimony concerning* ROGER LONG-WORTH.

H E was born at Longworth, near Bolton in Lancaſhire. We were well acquaint-ed with him almoſt from the time of his convincement, being a man of a peaceable difpofition, gentle and mild, ready and willing to ferve his friend to the utmoſt of his ability, and a very diligent labourer in the work of the Lord, willing to ſpend and be ſpent, not counting any thing in this world too dear to part with, for the fame. The Lord did eminently blefs his miniſtry, where-unto he was called about the year 1672, and travelled fometimes in that work, in his own country until 1675; after which time he was wholly given up and devoted to the fervice of the Lord, travelling much in England, where he ſuffered impriſon-ment in feveral places; fix times he paſſed through Holland, and ſome others of thofe provinces; alſo part of Germany and there-about, feveral times as far as Dantzick, where he laboured much for the releafe of

friends,

friends, who then were prifoners there, writing to the king, magiftrates and officers on their behalf. At Embden, where friends were fufferers, he laboured for their freedom, and it being a time of hot perfecution, went through the ftreets, warning the people to repent of their wickednefs, where they kept him two nights a prifoner: At another time in the faid place, he delivered a paper to the council, relating to the liberty of friends; after the reading whereof, he was called in to the council room and received in a friendly manner, with promifes of freedom to the people called Quakers, in matters of faith and worfhip; he alfo had good fervice with magiftrates, lawyers, priefts and collegians, and was feveral times a prifoner in thofe parts. Five times he paffed through Ireland, vifiting friends, where he had good fervice, fometimes among the Irifh when at mafs. Once he paffed through part of Scotland, twice at Barbados, once through New England and Virginia, twice in Maryland and the Jerfeys, and twice at Pennfylvania; having travelled by land above 20,000 miles, his travels by water, not being much lefs: And though he was often in ftorms and tempefts at fea, perils by land, and met with bad fpirits and exercifes of divers kinds, yet the Lord ftood by him and made him a fuccefsful inftrument in his hand: Cheerfully paffing through them all, by the power of him that called him thereto, not being flack to labour in word and doctrine,

trine, wherever he came, to the edifying of
the brethren, and reconciling things where
he found them amifs: Settling and eftablifhing meetings in many parts where he
came, to the great comfort and refrefhment
of the upright in heart, by which he got a
name amongft the ancients, and is recorded
among the worthies of the Lord. Not long
after his arrival in Pennfylvania, he was
taken ill with a fever; his diftemper was
violent upon him, yet he bore it patiently
and paffed away like a lamb, leaving a good
favour. And though *the name of the wicked
fhall rot, yet the righteous fhall be had in everlafting remembrance.*

WILLIAM YARDLEY.
PHINEAS PEMBERTON.

He died the 7*th* of the fixth month 1687,
about the fifty-feventh year of his age.

John Hayton's *Teftimony concerning* THOMAS
LANGHORNE, *who died at his own habitation in* Bucks *county,* Pennfylvania, *the
6th of the* eighth *month* 1687.

I KNEW him 14 years, he having been
made inftrumental in the hand of the
Lord, to turn me from the evil of my ways,
and from darknefs to his marvellous light;
and I am a witnefs that he held his integrity until the finifhing of his courfe, according

ing to the faying of David, " Mark the perfect man and behold the upright, for the end of that man is peace", And therein he laid down his head. Having experienced the work of regeneration in himfelf, he became qualified to ftrengthen the brethren, and went forth in the miniftry and word of life, preaching the everlafting gofpel of Chrift Jefus; having freely received he freely gave, not fearing man but obeying God, who had committed a large meafure, and clear manifeftation of his fpirit unto him, not only for his own profit and benefit, but many others received comfort thereby; for his doctrine dropped as the rain, and his fpeech diftilled as the dew, to the renewing and refrefhing the feed and plant of God.

Thus he went forth in the name of the Lord, and was valiant for truth upon earth; and though many weapons were formed, and many tongues rofe up againft him, yet the divine power which ftopped the mouths of lions, and quenched the violence of fire, girded him with ftrength and valour, whereby he was enabled to encounter all his enemies, and fuch as endeavoured to ftop the work which God has begun in the earth. After fome time, he with his wife and two children came into this country, and whilft here, he bore a living, found and faithful teftimony for the Lord God, to the great fatisfaction and comfort of the faithful in this wildernefs, where his lot did fall. For having had the opportunity of being with

him

him here in this folitary country, as well as
in our native land, both in private and public places; I am a witnefs according to my
meafure, that the power and prefence of the
Lord did greatly attend him in preaching
the everlafting truth. After he was taken
fick, he grew weaker until his departure,
faying " The will of the Lord be done."
His fhort continuance here caufed many to
mourn when he was taken from them, yet
not as thofe that mourn without hope, for
tho' he be dead, yet he lives, and tho' his
removal is our lofs, it is his gain.

JOHN HAYTON.

William Yardley *and* Phineas Pemberton's
Teftimony concerning JAMES HARRISON.

THAT the righteous may not be buried
in oblivion, we give forth this fhort
teftimony concerning our well beloved friend
James Harrifon, who was born near Kendal,
in Weftmoreland, and in the breaking forth
of the truth in thofe parts he was early
convinced thereof, and in a fhort time after,
came forth in a public teftimony for the
fame. His miniftry was not " *In the wifdom
of this world, but in the demonftration of the
fpirit and power of God*", By which many
were convinced, the ferpent's head was broken, the wifdom of the flefh confounded,
and

and feveral came forth in a living teftimony
for God, who were begotten to the Lord by
by him, and ftill remain feals of his miniftry. As he was inftrumental in *turning-
ing many to God*, fo he was helpful in the
eftablifhing of fuch as were converted, being a good pattern, as well in converfation
as doctrine, *walking uprightly as in the day-
time*, being bold and valiant for the truth,
in oppofing its enemies, whether profeffors
or profane, tho' they often raged fore againft
him, fo that his fufferings were very great,
both by imprifonment and fpoil of goods;
yet he always with great courage fteadily
kept his ground againft all thofe that rofe
up againft him for the truth's fake, which
was of more worth to him than all outward
enjoyments. In the year 1682, he removed
with his family into Pennfylvania, and as
his teftimony was in the power of God,
when in the land of his nativity, fo it was
when here; he being likewife ferviceable
many ways. And tho' he had great concerns in this world, yet he earneftly laboured to keep a confcience void of offence, being a man of a peaceable fpirit, and the
Lord's power kept him a fweet favour to the
end. He bore his ficknefs with much patience, tho' often greatly bowed down therewith to the time of his departure, laying
down his head in peace, and paffing away in
much ftillnefs, the fixth of the eighth month,
1687, in the fifty-ninth year of his age: His
removal

removal being our lofs but his gain, for, *blef-* *fed are the dead which die in the Lord, they reft from their labours and their works do follow them.*

WILLIAM YARDLEY.
PHINEAS PEMBERTON.

Jane Atkinfon's *Teftimony concerning her late husband* THOMAS ATKINSON.

HE was born at Newby in the County of York, being the fon of John Atkinfon, of Thrufh-Crofs, was convinced of the truth and had received a gift of the miniftry before I knew him. We were joined in marriage in the year 1678, and lived together in love and unity. He was a zealous man for the truth, and according to the gift which he had received, bore a faithful teftimony unto it, of which many were witneffes in that country from whence we came. In 1682 we came into this country, with one confent, and in the unity of our dear friends and brethren, who gave a good teftimony for us, by a certificate from their monthly meeting; and my foul hath good caufe to blefs the Lord, and to prize his mercies, whofe prefence was with us by fea and land. Since we came into this part of the world, he retained his love and zeal for God and his truth, his treafure not being in this world, and as it often opened in his

heart,

heart, did exhort others to ſtand looſe from things which are here below, and diligently ſeek after thoſe things that are above. He was a tender huſband, ready to encourage and ſtrengthen me in that which is good. About the latter end of the fifth month 1687, he was taken with the ague and fever, which much weakned his body, in which he continued a conſiderable time; being well content with the dealings of the Lord: His heart was often opened in prayer and ſupplication unto his God, to preſerve him in patience unto the end of his days, and that none of us might think hard of any of thoſe exerciſes that he is pleaſed to try us withal. At times he would look upon me and ſay, *my dear wife, the Lord preſerve thee and take care of thee, for I muſt leave thee and go to my reſt*; with many more ſweet and heavenly expreſſions and exhortations, in the time of his great weakneſs, which continued until the 31ſt of the eighth month, when he once more exhorted me to be content, and that I would deſire his brother (who was then abſent) to be content alſo: After which he paſſed away as one falling into a quiet ſleep. And as the Lord hath hitherto been my ſtrength and my ſtay in the time of my great diſtreſs, ſo the deſire of my heart is, that I, with my brethren and ſiſters, who yet remain behind, may alſo finiſh our courſe in faithfulneſs, that in the end we may receive the ſame reward with the righteous that are gone before.

JANE ATKINSON.

Samuel Jennings's *Teſtimony concerning* JOHN
ECKLEY, *of* Philadelphia *in* Pennſylvania,
who died about the year 1690.

I AM perſuaded it is a juſtice due to the
righteous, and a duty upon us, to con-
tribute ſomething to perpetuate the names
of ſuch who have left a fragrancy behind
them, and *through faith have obtained a good
report.* Tho' their bodies ſleep in the grave,
and by divine appointment, they die like
other men, yet this ſignal difference hath
the Lord declared, *the memory of the juſt is
bleſſed, but the name of the wicked ſhall rot,*
Pro. 10, 7. And to give teſtimony to thoſe
that die in the Lord, is not only juſt to
them, but is very uſeful to the living; as
many under great conflicts of ſpirit have
experienced, that it hath been to their comfort and ſtrength, to hear or read of the
faithfulneſs and conſtancy of God to his
own in all ages, and how he hath in due time,
made them more than conquerors, and crowned their end with peace and dominion. Theſe
conſiderations, together with the ſincere affection I had for this our dear friend, hath
prevailed with me, in truth and ſoberneſs,
to give the following teſtimony concerning
him. As a man he was pleaſant, courteous,
diſcreet and grave, and in public ſervices
accompanied the foremoſt. *The word of wiſdom was in his mouth, and he had received the
tongue of the learned, to ſpeak in due ſeaſon.*
                                                    I might

I might truly fay much of his innocency,
love and zeal for truth, which hath left a
lively impreffion upon the hearts of many.
His laft ficknefs was the fmall pox, a diftemper often known to be very afflicting;
notwithftanding which, he cheerfully and
contentedly fubmitted to the providence of
God in it, upon all occafions expreffing a free
and hearty refignation to his will; and was
frequently filled with praifes to God, and
inftructions to his people.

SAMUEL JENNINGS.

Mary Radcliff's *Teſtimony concerning her late
husband* JAMES RADCLIFF, *who died in
or about the year* 1690.

HE was an innocent man, and one that
did truly fear the Lord, and wifhed
the welfare of all. It was his chiefeft care,
faithfully to ferve the Lord, and obey him
in whatfoever he required; and it was often
in his heart to exhort others to faithfulnefs,
and to improve the gift which the Lord had
committed to them. I knew him when he
was young, we both belonging to the fame
meeting. He was a prifoner upon truth's account, when about fifteen years of age;
after which his mouth was opened to bear
a public teftimony for the Lord and his
bleffed truth, travelling many miles, and
undergoing many hardfhips, imprifonments
and

and other exercifes: And after we were married, he alfo paffed thro' many deep fufferings and imprifonments, but the Lord preferved him through them all: And as he
was of a mild lamb-like difpofition, and
lived an innocent harmlefs life, fo he ended his days in innocency, and being redeemed from the earth, laid down his head
in peace. And tho' his body be gone to the
duft, from whence it came yet his fpirit
is afcended to God who gave it, and his
living teftimony and good favour that he
hath left, are comfortable memorials upon
my mind, defiring I may fo live and fo finifh
my courfe as he hath done.

MARY RADCLIFF.

Thomas Janney's *Teftimony concerning*
WILLIAM YARDLEY.

HE was born near Leek, in the north
part of Staffordfhire, of honeft parents, who brought him up in the employment of a farmer. In his youth he fought
more after the knowledge of God and the
things of his kingdom, than the fading vanities or momentary pleafures of this world,
and therefore joined himfelf in fociety with
a people that were then the higheft in profeffion in thofe parts, who called themfelves,
the family of love, among whom he walked
for fome time; but when it pleafed the Lord

to

to fend two of his faithful meffengers, called
in fcorn Quakers, out of the north of England into the parts where William lived,
he received their teftimony, as did alfo feveral others of the aforefaid fociety. But this
my friend received the truth with a ready
mind and gladnefs of heart, and thought
nothing too dear to part with for it, yea it
was precious to him as *the pearl of great
price*, and it wrought effectually in him,
not only in opening his underftanding, but
alfo in its various operations, both to wound
and to heal, to purge out the old leaven and
to leaven anew into its holy nature and qua-
lity: And as the Lord had made him a
living witnefs of the power and life of truth
in himfelf, he called him to bear a teftimony to the truth as he had received it, and
alfo againft the falfe ways and worfhips that
were then extant in the world; for which
he fuffered feveral imprifonments, bearing
the burden and heat of the day, being one
of the firft that received and bore witnefs
to the truth in thofe parts. He was very
ferviceable in his public teftimony, not only in convincing but alfo to the edification
of many; yea he was a great ftay and fupport to friends in the parts near where he
lived: For he was an inftrument of great
fervice in the Lord's hand, being much
efteemed for his works fake, not only at
home but in other places where he travelled
in truth's fervice.

In the year 1682, being in the fiftieth year
of

of his age, he removed himſelf and family into America, and ſettled according to his intention in Pennſylvania, where he continued
very ſerviceable amongſt us, in his miniſtry, and ſometimes viſited places adjacent:
He was alſo uſeful in ſome other ſervices in
our firſt ſettlement here. In ſhort, as he
was a ſenſible, ſo he was a ſerviceable member of the body, having a ſenſe of and
ſhare in whatever tended to the ſtrength and
benefit thereof; as on the other hand, if
any thing happened that cauſed grief or
trouble, he bore his part of it.

He was a man of ſound judgment and
good underſtanding, not being drawn aſide
by any falſe ſpirit that hath riſen in our
day, nor joined with any that broke forth
into ſeparation, or ſought to divide or make
ſchiſms in the body, either in England or
America. He dearly loved the ſociety of
his brethren, and much prized unity, as
one who knew the comfort and benefit thereof. He had a high eſteem for all who were
of a right ſpirit and of ſervice in the church,
although his younger brethren. His miniſtry was with a good underſtanding, not
only of what he ſpoke from, but alſo what
he ſpoke unto; and the things which he
teſtified were *what he had learned of the
Lord, and had himſelf ſeen, heard and taſted
of in the good word of life, not boaſting in
other men's lines.* In the latter part of his
days he grew weak in body by ſome infirmities which increaſed upon him, nevertheleſs,

lefs, he was often raifed in meetings by the
power of the Lord, and thereby carried on
in his teftimony, to our refrefhment and
comfort.

What I have here written concerning this
my dear friend and brother, is from my
own certain knowledge, we having been intimate friends, from our youth up, and
fince we came into America, we have had
the advantage of frequent opportunities together, it being our lot to live near to each
other, which now makes my lofs in the
want of him to be the greater, altho' I am
fatisfied *his removal is his gain.*

From my houfe in Makefield, in the county of Bucks, 26*th* of the fixth month 1693.

THOMAS JANNEY.

James Dickinfon's *Teftimony concerning* JOHN
DELAVAL, *who died in* Philadelphia, *about
the year* 1693, *fuppofed to have been written
when on one of his vifits to* America.

MY heart is opened by the power of
truth, to give forth a teftimony to
the Lord's power, that hath wrought effectually in this latter age of the world, for
the bringing many fons unto glory; of the
number of whom I do believe was this my
dear friend John Delaval, whofe memory
lives among the faithful that knew him,
and needs not thefe characters, to fet forth

C   that

that comelinefs which the Lord put upon
him, but his name is recorded in Heaven,
and fhall never be obliterated. Altho' he
was one called in at the eleventh hour, yet
he was faithful and zealous for the truth, a
man of a tender broken fpirit, and loved
the power of truth and the operation of it,
which helped him through and over what
was contrary to it. My foul loved him and
was drawn near him the firft day I faw
him, becaufe of the fincerity that I beheld
in him; and as our familiarity increafed, fo
I found the bent of his mind was to ferve
the Lord in uprightnefs of heart. The
Lord gave him a gift in the miniftry, and
bleffed him in it, and enabled him to get
his days work done in his day, whofe example I pray God, we that remain may follow; who was valiant for the truth upon
earth, and turned not his back to the op-
pofers of it, nor would fpare the backfli-
ders from it, but ftood faithful to the end.
His bow abode in ftrength, and tho' many
archers fhot at him, yet he kept the fhield
of faith, by which the fiery darts of the
wicked one were quenched, and his foul
preferved in communion with the Lord, and
in the faith of Chrift he finifhed his teftimony, with a heart full of love to God
and his people: The Lord took him away
from evil to come. And my defire is that
we who remain, may keep to the fame power by which he was vifited; and love the
operation of it, that thereby all may be

prepared

prepared for their latter end, which haſtens upon us; ſo obtain the crown that is laid up in ſtore, for all them that fight the good fight and keep the faith, and keep their eyes ſingle to Chriſt Jeſus the author of it, and keep the word of patience; theſe will be kept in the hour of temptation, and know an overcoming: And unto him that over-cometh, faith Chriſt, will I grant to ſit with me in my throne, even as I alſo overcame, and am ſat down with my father in his throne. Theſe ſhall not be hurt of the ſecond death, but know a part in Chriſt, the firſt reſurrec-tion, and know that they are the ſons of God, as was anciently ſaid, " Now are we the ſons of God, and it doth not yet ap-pear what we ſhall be." But " When Chriſt, who is our life ſhall appear, then ſhall we alſo appear with him in glory." Let all keep to Chriſt and know him to be their life, ſo ſhall they be made partakers of the better reſurrection, even that unto life; when the ſentence will be paſſed upon all, either come ye bleſſed, or go ye curſed, by the juſt Judge of the whole earth, who will do rightly to every man, and give to every one according as their works ſhall be: To whom all muſt give an account, and happy will they be who keep to God's power, they will be kept by it to his glory, and their eternal ſalvation.

JAMES DICKINSON.

Elizabeth

Elizabeth Walker's *Teſtimony concerning her husband* WILLIAM WALKER.

T HE love of God to him was great, in calling him out of the broad way to labour in his vineyard; and tho' it was late in the day, I believe he received his penny. Great was the care and awe that was on his mind, left he ſhould do any thing to hinder his religious growth and ſervice; for having no trade, and we poſſeſſing little but what my dear huſband earned by hard labour, he was adviſed to learn a trade, to which he anſwered, " I dare not let out my mind to learn one, but can freely follow my preſent calling, if the Lord will enable me; becauſe it is no incumbrance to my mind, and thro' God's goodneſs we do not want." However, in an unexpected time, way was made for our getting into a ſmall buſineſs, which ſuited our capacities, and the Lord gave a bleſſing unto our endeavours. He often viſited the ſick, and his ſoul ſympathized with the afflicted, being alſo willing to adminiſter to the neceſſities of the poor as objects of charity preſented. He was a tender huſband unto me, and one whom my ſoul had true unity with in the life of Jeſus; his delight and meditations being in the law of the Lord. Many were the ſeaſons of divine love we enjoyed the little time we were together, which often tendered our hearts before the Lord, in our private retirements, ſo that

that praifes have been returned to his pure name, in a fenfe of the aboundings of his love and life. And altho' his body is re- moved from me, I am well fatisfied he hath obtained the recompence of reward with the redeemed of the Lord.

ELIZABETH WALKER.

The aforefaid William Walker, was born in Yorkfhire, but removed to Pennfylvania, where he was convinced. In the latter end of the year 1693, he went to England on a religious vifit, and died at London the 12th of the fourth month 1694. A further account of him and fome of his laft expreffions, are inferted in the 2d part of the book, called piety promoted.

A Teſtimony from the Monthly-Meeting of Haverford in Pennfylvania, concerning THOMAS LLOYD.

THE love of God and the regard we have to the bleffed truth, conftrains us to give forth this teftimony, concerning our dear friend Thomas Lloyd, many of us having had long acquaintance with him, both in Wales, where he formerly lived, and alfo in Pennfylvania, where he finifhed his courfe, and laid down his head in peace with the Lord, and is at reft and joy with him for- evermore.

He

He was by birth of them who are called
the gentry, his father being a man of a
confiderable eftate and of great efteem in
his time, of an ancient houfe and eftate
called Dolobran, in Montgomeryfhire in
Wales. He was brought up at the moft
noted fchools, and from thence went to one
of the univerfities; and becaufe of his fuperior, natural and acquired parts, many
of account in the world had an eye of regard towards him: Being offered degrees
and places of preferments, he refufed them
all: The Lord beginning his work in him,
and caufing a meafure of his light to fhine out
of darknefs, in his heart, which gave him
a fight of the vain forms, cuftoms and tra-
ditions of the fchools and colleges: And
hearing of a poor defpifed people called
Quakers, he went to hear them, and the
Lord's power reached unto him and came
over him, to the humbling and bowing his
heart and fpirit; fo that he was convinced
of God's everlafting truth, and received it
in the love of it, and was made willing,
like meek Mofes, to choofe rather to fuffer
affliction with the people of the Lord, than
the honours, preferments and riches of this
world. The earthly wifdom came to be of
no reputation with him, but he became a
fool, both to it and his former affociates,
and through felf denial, and taking up the
daily crofs of Chrift Jefus, which crucified
his natural will, affections and pleafures,
he came to be a fcholar in Chrift's fchool,

and

and to learn the true wifdom which is from above. Thus by departing from the vanities and iniquities of the world, and following the leadings, guidance and inftructions of the divine light, grace and fpirit of Chrift, he came more and more to have an underftanding in the myfteries of God's kingdom, and was made an able minifter of the everlafting gofpel of peace and falvation; his acquired parts being fanctified to the fervice of truth.

His found and effectual miniftry, his godly converfation, meek and lamb-like fpirit, great patience, temperance, humility, and flownefs to wrath; his love to the brethren, his godly care in the church of Chrift, that all things might be kept fweet, favoury and in good order; his helping hand to the weak, and gentle admonitions, we are fully fatisfied have a feal and witnefs in the hearts of all faithful friends who knew him, both in the land of his nativity and in thefe American parts. We may in truth fay, he fought not himfelf, nor the riches of this world, but his eye was to that which is everlafting, being given up to fpend and be fpent for the truth and the fake of friends.

He never turned his back on the truth, nor was weary in his travels Sion-wards, but remained a found pillar in the fpiritual building. He had many difputes with the clergy and fome called peers in England, and alfo fuffered imprifonments and much lofs of outward fubftance, to the honour of
truth,

truth, and ftopping in meafure, the mouths
of gainfayers and perfecutors. Yet thefe exercifes and trials in the land of his nativity,
which he fuftained through the ability God
gave him, were fmall and not to be compared to the many and great exercifes, griefs
and forrows he met withal and went thro'
in Pennfylvania, from that miferable apo-
ftate George Keith and his deluded company. Oh the revilings, the great provocati-
ons, the bitter and wicked language, and
rude behaviour which the Lord gave him
patience to bear and overcome. He reviled
not again, nor took any advantage, but
loved his enemies, and prayed for them that
defpitefully abufed him. His love to the
Lord, his truth and people was fincere to
the laft. He was taken with a malignant
fever, the 5th of the feventh month 1694, and
tho' his bodily pain was great, he bore it
with much patience. Not long before his
departure, fome friends being with him, he
faid, " Friends, I love you all, I am go-
" ing from you, and I die in unity and
" love with all faithful friends: I have
" fought a good fight and kept the faith,
" which ftands not in the wifdom of words,
" but in the power of God: I have fought,
" not for ftrife and contention, but for the
" grace of our Lord Jefus Chrift, and the
" fimplicity of the gofpel. I lay down my
" head in peace and defire you may all do fo;
" friends, farewell all." He further faid to
Griffith Owen, a friend then intending for
England,

England, " I defire thee to mind my love to
" friends in England, if thou lives to go over
" to fee them ; I have lived in unity with
" them, and do end my days in unity with
" them; and defire the Lord to keep them all
" faithful to the end, in the fimplicity of the
" gofpel." On the 10th day of the feventh
month aforefaid, being the 6th day of his ficknefs, it pleafed the Lord to remove him from
the many trials, temptations, forrows and
troubles of this world, to the kingdom of everlafting joy and peace; but the remembrance
of his innocent life and meek fpirit lives with
us, and his memorial is, and will remain to
be fweet and comfortable to the faithful.

He was buried in friends burial-ground
in Philadelphia, aged about forty-five years,
having been feveral years prefident and de-
puty governor of Pennfylvania.

The followng epiftle, which appears to
have been written foon after his arrival in
Pennfylvania, is thought not improper to be
here fubjoined.

Philadelphia, 2d of fixth Month 1684.

*My dear and well beloved friends, of and be-
longing to* Dolobran *Quarterly-Meeting.*

THE warm and tender falutation of my
love is unfeigned to you, with whom
I have converfed and walked fome years, in
unity, zeal, concord, and endeavoured fer-
viceablenefs :

viceablenefs: You are, becaufe of our
nearnefs, familiar, yet honourable in my
thoughts and efteem. The truth as it is in
Jefus, profper and increafe daily in your
minds, and reft bountifully on your habi-
tations. My heart is affected with the remembrance of you, and efpecially of the
virtue and operation of that living principle which traverfeth the deeps, and though
it bounds the feas, yet cannot be bound
thereby, but continues its being and intire-
nefs through and over all diftances, and
makes us of many, one people to himfelf.
The God of Ifrael and the excellency of
Jacob is with us, and the prefent days are
as the former, days of glad tidings, days
of humility, days of holy fear, obedience
and refrefhment, increafe and growth to the
faithful. We and you are under refpective
exercifes, the way of your trial may be in
a more fevere manner at prefent. The Lord
in his wonted tendernefs bear you up, and
grant you a rejoicing in fimplicity and godly fincerity before him. That is no new thing
to you, to fuffer joyfully in your perfons
and goods; the Lord gave us ftrength, courage, fatisfaction and honours thereby.
Whilft he is in our eyes, and his holy fear
in our hearts, whether in bonds or free, in
that or this part of the world, our prefervation we fhall witnefs.—Our meetings are
very full: I guefs we had no lefs number
than eight hundred laft firft day; we are
glad to fee the faces of ferviceable friends
here,

here, who come in God's freedom, who are perfons of a good underftanding and converfation, and will difcharge their ftations religioufly; fuch will be a bleffing to the province. The favourable revolution of Providence hath founded the government fo here, that a man is at liberty to ferve his Maker without contempt, difcouragement, or reftraint. Truth indeed makes men honourable, not only here, but in moft places at laft; but here truth receives a good entertainment at firft. Our governor is embarking for England; our well wifhes go with and attend him. He hopes to have an opportunity by teftimony or writing, to exprefs his love and remembrance to the feveral churches of Britain. Our friends from the neighbourhood are generally well, and tolerably fettled. In love I lived with you, in love I took my leave of you, and in love I bid you a chriftain and brotherly farewel.

Your friend and brother

THOMAS LLOYD.

A Teftimony from the Falls *Monthly-Meeting in* Bucks *county,* Pennfylvania, *concerning* THOMAS JANNEY.

H E fettled with us at his firft coming into thefe parts, labouring amongft us in word and doctrine divers years. We loved

loved and highly efteemed him for his works
fake, being an able minifter of the gofpel,
found in doctrine, endowed with wifdom
and a ready utterance; and favour'd with
openings into the myfteries of the things of
God's kingdom. He was not forward to
offer his gift, having a true regard to the
giver, who faid formerly, " Caft the net on
the right fide of the fhip:" Therefore his
" Bow abode in ftrength." And tho' the
Lord had furnifhed him with fuch excellent
qualifications, he had fo learned felf-denial
as not to glory therein; but was ready to
prefer his friends before himfelf, and give
them the right hand of fellowfhip; being
careful to keep the teftimony of truth clear
on all accounts, faying, " Thofe that appear in public, are doubly bound fo to do."
He was of a cheerful and peaceable temper,
and innocent and blamelefs in life. As the
Lord had beftowed on him a gift of the
miniftry, beyond many of his fellows, fo
he was careful to improve it to his honour
and the comfort of his people, labouring
therein, not only here in Pennfylvania and
New-Jerfey, but he alfo feveral times vifited the churches in New-England, Rhode-
Ifland, Long-Ifland and Maryland, and
laftly he went on that fervice to Old-England, where he finifhed his courfe. And
tho' our lofs of him is great, we are fatif-
fied he hath his portion, among *thofe that
turn many to righteoufnefs, and fhine as the
ftars forever and ever.*

There

There are other accounts concerning Thomas Janney, from which it appears, that he was born in Chefhire, and received the truth about the year 1654, and the twenty-firft year of his age. In 1683 he came with his family into Pennfylvania: And in 1695 he went in company with Griffith Owen, to vifit his brethren in England; where, in the courfe of his travels, he was taken ill at Hitchin; and two of his relations from Chefhire, going thither to vifit him, he faid to one of them, " It is fome exercife to " think of being taken away fo far from " my home and family, and alfo from my " friends and relations in Chefhire. My " care hath been for my fons, that they " may be kept in the fear of God: I have " been a good example to them. I have a " care upon me, that they may be kept " humble while they are young, that they " may bend their necks under the yoke of " Chrift. If I am taken away, I am very clear " in my fpirit, I have anfwered the requir- " ings of God. I have been faithful in my " day, and I have nothing that troubles " my fpirit; my fpirit is very clear." He alfo expreffed his concern for his brethren of the miniftry, efpecially the young, that they might obferve the leadings of God's fpirit in their miniftry, and not lean upon their own natural parts. After this, he recovered

covered fo as to be able to get down into
Chefhire; but after fome time his diforder
returning, he faid to his fifter, " If it be
" the will of God, that I be taken away
" now, I am well content." He departed in
much quietnefs of mind, the 12*th* of the
twelfth month 1696, and was buried the
15*th* of the fame month, in friends burying place in Chefhire. Aged fixty-three years.
A public minifter 41 years.

Hugh Roberts's *Teftimony concerning his brother* ROBERT OWEN.

HE was one that feared the Lord from
his youth, being convinced of the
truth, when about feventeen years of age;
he loved the company of fuch of his acquaintance as were moft fubftantial in religion, and
was alfo beloved by them and all fort of
people that knew him, being greatly helpful to his brethren, and made a caufe of
gladnefs to thofe that were his fathers in
the truth. The Lord not only opened his
heart like Lydia's formerly, but he likewife
opened his mouth to publifh his name and
truth amongft many, travelling feveral times
through his native country Wales, where
he was of good fervice. In 1690, he came
into Pennfylvania, where he lived about
feven years, vifiting this and the adjacent
provinces, and was alfo very ufeful in the
meeting

meeting where he refided, both in doctrine and difcipline; he was indeed a ftrong pillar in the church: I never faw him take part with a wrong thing: Oh the want of him which I feel! his place is yet empty, I pray God, if it be his will, to fill it up. Oh my brother, my dear companion! how can they that knew thy faithfulnefs to truth, do lefs than leave a memorial to fucceeding generations? for thy name is worthy to be recorded in Ifrael. He was a man of peace and hated all appearance of contention, and indeed he was a fkilful peacemaker, being endued with wifdom and authority, yet full of mercy and compaffion unto every appearance of good. His removal is a great lofs unto us who are left. Well my dear brother, in the remembrance of thee, and the many good and precious opportunities we have had together, my foul is bowed and ready to fay, I fhall never have the like companion, fo fitted and knit together in every refpect; the more I confider my lofs of thee, the greater it appears; therefore conclude this my teftimony, and return to my own work and fervice, that I may be prepared to follow after thee.

HUGH ROBERTS.

He died the 8*th* of the fifth month, 1697, and was interr'd the 10*th* of the fame, in friends burying ground at Merion in Pennfylvania.

Rowland

Rowland Ellis's *Teſtimony concerning* ROBERT OWEN *before mention'd, and* JANE *his wife.*

WHEN I think of former times and days that are over and gone, wherein the Lord viſited a remnant by the gathering hand of his power, in the land of our nativity, to wait for the renewing of his love from one meeting to another, to our great refreſhment and daily encouragement, to run our race through many trials within and without: The Lord whom we waited for, hath been the ſtrength of his people in this our age and generation, as in all by paſt ages. So the remembrance of thoſe days and times, and that near fellowſhip which was between the little remnant in that part of the country, is at preſent brought to my view; tho' moſt of the ancients that bore the heat of the day are now removed, yet methinks their names and worthy acts ſhould be had in remembrance, that generations to come might ſee and underſtand, by what inſtruments the Lord was pleaſed to carry on his work, by making a clear diſcovery of the good way once loſt in the night of apoſtacy; amongſt whom were my dear friends Robert Owen and Jane his wife. And altho' we are not to ſet up or praiſe that in man or woman which periſheth, but becauſe they made choice of the better and moſt durable ſubſtance, therefore their names ſhall be had in remembrance.

He

He was defcended of a very ancient and (according to the worlds account) one of the greateſt families in thoſe parts, having by his father a competent inheritance, and in all his time had the right hand among his equals; brought up a ſcholar, quick in apprehenſion, and whatever he took in hand he did it with all his might. He was zealouſly devoted to religion, and a great ſearcher for the pearl of great price; being one of the firſt in our parts who ſought after it; and having found it, he ſold all to purchaſe the ſame.

After King Charles II came to the crown, he ſuffered five years cloſe impriſonment, for not taking the oath of allegiance and ſupremacy, being confined at the town of Dolgelly, in Merionethſhire, North Wales, within about a mile from his dwelling houſe, to which he was not permitted to go during the ſaid time: And it was obſerved, that the perſon who had the greateſt hand in proſecuting him, was viſited with ſicknefs, when remorſe of confcience feized fo hard upon him, that he could find neither reſt nor eaſe, until he ſent a ſpecial meſſenger to releaſe him.

And concerning his wife Jane Owen. She was daughter of a juſtice of peace, a man of great integrity and exceeding moſt of his rank at that time. She was a woman rarely endowed with many natural gifts, being an help-meet to her huſband in his exercifes, ſolid in her deportment, and not given to

D   many

many words. In all their exercifes together
for the truth's fake, they did not fhrink nor
give way for fear or flattery; not only their
hearts, but their houfe was open to all upon
truth's account; meetings being held therein for many years. They were ferviceable
in their places and much beloved in their
native land, where having borne their fhare
of the heat of the day, they embark'd therefrom in the fifth month 1690, and came
into Pennfylvania, where they finifhed their
courfe, and were buried within a few days
of each other.

John Bevan's *Teflimony concerning* H u g h
R o b e r t s.

TRUTH in the inward parts God loves,
and thofe that love it and give way to
the operation thereof, are made precious
and lovely in the fight of God, and he
makes them inftrumental in his hand for
the good of others; among whom was my
dear friend and brother Hugh Roberts deceafed, who was qualified by God's power,
to be a ferviceable inftrument to the churches of Chrift in our parts of America. He
came to this country about 18 years fince;
we were near neighbours and entirely loved
each other, not having had a crofs word,
nor I believe an hard thought one of another, at any time fince our firft acquaintance.

ance. Having paffed through many trials and exercifes, he could by experience fpeak a word in feafon for the encouragement of weary travellers; his doctrine often " dropping as the dew, and diftilling as the fmall rain upon the tender plants," for in the openings of life, " things new and old" came forth of the treafury of wifdom, which gladned our hearts and comforted our fpirits in a fenfe of God's love, who is the author of all good to his people. He was zealous for good order in the church, ferviceable in the difcipline, and fkilful in accommodating differences. And it is my defire, that we, efpecially of that meeting he belonged to, and the adjacent meetings, which moftly received the benefit and advantage of his labour of love, may lay to heart and confider our lofs of him, and in the fenfe thereof, may breathe and cry unto the Lord, who is the repairer of breaches, to raife up inftruments in his room, for carrying on of his great work that he hath begun in the earth, to his own praife, who is alone worthy of the fame forever.— I was twice with him over fea, and in many places in our native land, alfo in Maryland, and in his laft journey to vifit friends on Long-Ifland, Rhode-Ifland and New-England, where he had good fervice. And though he was often very weakly, yet his heart was bent to accomplifh the work the Lord laid upon him, which he was enabled to perform to his great comfort and fatisfaction.   D 2   On

On our return homeward, being sick and in much pain, at the house of our friend John Rodman, on Long-Island, he said *nothing lies in my way as an obstruction to hinder my peace and well being with God.* He afterwards came home, and a few days before his departure, a dear friend taking leave of him said, " I believe thy deep trials and exercises are near at an end, and that peace and joy everlasting will be thy portion from the Lord." In much brokenness of heart and sense of the sweet presence of God upon his spirit, he answered, *I am satisfied thereof, and can bless my God for it.*

He died the 18*th* of the sixth month 1702, and on the 20*th* was interred at Merion, after which a large meeting was held, wherein the Lord's presence was sweetly enjoyed, and several living testimonies borne concerning his faithfulness to God and friends satisfaction of his eternal well-being.

JOHN BEVAN.

Margaret Minshell's *Testimony concerning* J O H N S I M C O C K.

H E was a nursing father in Israel, tender over the seed of God, and wherever he saw it in the least appearance he was a cherisher of it without respect of persons; but he abhorred deceit and hypocrisy. I have known him

him near forty years, and may fay that his miniftry was found, edifying and helpful to myfelf and many others, he being endued with a fpirit of difcerning, and wifdom beyond many in fpiritual things. He was a great fufferer in Old England, for truth's fake, both by imprifonments and lofs of goods. He travelled pretty much in truth's fervice, and notwithftanding all his fufferings, he was no ways chargeable to any, but rather helpful to thofe that ftood in need.

MARGARET MINSHELL.

In Jofeph Beffe's hiftory of friends fufferings, are fome accounts of thofe fuftained by the aforefaid John Simcock, and of his pious, meek difpofition towards his oppreffors. Once he was imprifoned a year and three months, for accompanying his wife to a fteeple houfe, for a fign and teftimony againft their falfe ways and worfhips. His perfecutors at different times, diftrained from him to the amount of feveral hundred pounds fterling, for preaching; taking nineteen cattle at one time, and twelve at another, befides corn, cheefe, and other goods; all which he bore patiently. Once when they were driving away his cows, his fervant maid, who did not profefs amongft friends, faid to him, " Mafter, how can you ftand by and fee them drive away fo many cattle?" He replied, it did not trouble him any more than if they had drove away fo many geefe.   He

He removed to Pennſylvania in early times, and ſettled in Cheſter county; and when the ſpirit of diviſion began to appear in George Keith, he was active in viſiting him, to endeavour to recover him; and when the labour of friends in that reſpect proved ineffectual, he joined ſteadily with faithful friends in teſtifying againſt the ſaid George Keith and his party.

In the time of his laſt ſickneſs, he appear'd to be in a heavenly frame of mind, and utter'd many lively expreſſions: At one time he ſaid, " I have had many hard beſet-
" ments with the enemy of my ſoul ſince
" I knew the truth, and have been in many
" ſtraits, and great combats and buffetings
" for the trial of my faith; but the keeper
" of Iſrael is near to all them that wait up-
" on him, and truly put their truſt in him,
" and their faith is made ſtrong in him,
" whereby they are enabled to make war
" againſt the adverſary of ſouls, and to
" fight the good fight of faith, for whom
" is laid up a crown of eternal and endleſs
" joy, peace and heavenly comfort and glo-
" ry. And now I may ſay in truth, that
" I have kept this living faith, in which
" my ſoul hath renewed cauſe to magnify
" the name of my holy Redeemer, and
" powerful Saviour Chriſt Jeſus, in whom
" my faith hath been made ſtrong at this
" time." The day before his departure, his wife and ſon, with ſome other friends being preſent, he bore a living teſtimony to the

neceſſity

neceffity of dwelling in love, even that holy
love which labours for the peace, welfare
and everlafting good of all; concluding in
thefe words, " And now I defire my love
" may be remembred to friends in general,
" and it is the defire and earneft prayer of
" my foul, that the heavenly fpring of true
" love and ftream of divine life, may ever
" be known to fpring and run amongft
" thofe who would be accounted children
" of God, and followers of Chrift Jefus
" our bleffed Lord and eternal Saviour, who
" laid down his life to be a ranfom for fall-
" en man, and to be an atonement for all
" them that would come to God by him,
" who is the living word and promifed feed
" of the covenant."
He died the 27*th* of the firft month, 1703.

A *Teftimony from* Derby *Monthly-Meeting*, in
Pennfylvania, *concerning* E L E A N O R
S M I T H, *wife of* John Smith.

SHE was born at Harborough, in Lei-
cefterfhire, Old England, her maiden
name was Eleanor Dolby. She received the
truth about the age of thirteen years, and
lived and died therein, being a religious exemplary woman, and fome years before her
death was concern'd in a public teftimony.
A little before her departure, defiring that
her hufband and children fhould come and
fit

fit down by her, fhe fpoke as follows, " I
" entreat you my children to walk foberly,
" plainly and keep to the truth, and the
" Lord will provide for you every way be-
" yond your expectation. I am clear of
" you, having done the part of a tender
" mother to you: I leave and commit you
" to the Lord, who is able to keep you to
" the end of your days."—She defired them
not to mourn if it fhoud pleafe God to remove
her from amongft them, faying, " It will be
" my great gain." Often repeating her full
affurance of future happinefs, adding, " I
" can praife thy name O Lord in the midft of
" affliction, for furely thou art worthy of all
" praife, honour and glory, and that forever
" more; for thou neither leaveft nor forfakeft
" thofe that put their truft in thee." Then
faid, " Dear children be content, for I fhall
" die in favour with God, and true love and
" unity with his people." She defired to be
diffolved, faying, " I can freely give up huf-
" band and children and all this world, to be
" with the Lord, whofe prefence I feel flow-
" ing as a river into my foul."

She died the 10*th* day of the feventh month
1708, aged fifty-five years.

In the time of her laft illnefs, fhe wrote
the following epiftle to the monthly-meeting
of women friends at Derby, viz.

Dear Sifters,

Herewith I fend you the laft falutation of
my love, with whom I have been many
times

times refreſhed and truly comforted. I ſay
I have travelled with you through various
exerciſes and difficulties, when the Lord
has been ſometimes pleaſed to give us (as it
were) the bread of adverſity to eat, and the
water of affliction to drink; yet bleſſed be
his name, he has ſweetened our cups many
times as with honey, and ſuſtained us as
with the oil of the cruſe; and by his ſweet
preſence cauſed our cups to overflow, to the
praiſe of his great name. Wherefore, dear
ſiſters, I entreat you to dwell in the love of
God, which love is the bond of peace. Let
charity be found to dwell amongſt you, and
then I do believe, you will be neither barren nor unfruitful, but your branches laden
with good and weighty fruit, which will
find acceptance with God. So no more, but
my tender love to you in the bleſſed truth.
I take my leave and bid you farewell in the
Lord. The laſt from your loving ſiſter,

ELEANOR SMITH.

The following Teſtimony concerning HENRY
WHITE, *is from the committee of the Yearly
Meeting in* North Carolina.

HE was a miniſter of the goſpel and a
faithful friend, whoſe chriſtian conduct and loving behaviour towards the Indians, who were numerous in theſe parts at
that time, was ſuch, as we have been credi-
bly

bly informed, not only procured him great
efteem and refpect from them, but for his
fake they fhewed great love and tendernefs
towards others in the infant fettlement of
thefe parts.

He dwelt in Pafquotank county, and died
the 3*d* of the eighth month 1712, aged
about feventy-feven years.

A Teſtimony from Derby *Monthly-Meeting, in*
Pennfylvania, *concerning* JOHN SMITH.

HE was born in Licefterfhire, in Old
England in 1645, and was convinced
of the truth at the age of fourteen years,
and being faithful thereto, after fome time
he came forth in the miniſtry. He was an
early fettler in Pennfylvania, where he was
well beloved. Being taking fick, he was
vifited by many friends; and about two days
before his departure, being afked how he
did, he anfwered, " I am very poorly and
" weak indeed, but much eafier than I have
" been, for I was extreme ill, fo fick and
" full of pain, fuch as I never had under-
" gone before; fo that I could not retire in
" my mind to God, my extremity was fo
" great; but now the Lord has been pleaf-
" ed to give me eafe, fo that I can ſtay my
" mind on him, for which I am truly thank-
" ful: And now I feel the frefh remem-
" brance or renewings of the love of God,
" flowing

" flowing into my heart, which is of much
" more comfort to my foul than all tranfi-
." tory things that are here below. Now I
" feel his living divine prefence is with me,
" which bears up my fpirit over that which
" flefh and blood would or could not be
" able to bear." Shortly after, a friend
taking leave of him, afked him if he thought
he fhould recover, " That (faid he) I am
" not worthy to know, however I am con-
" tent; and this I know, that if we abide
" faithful to God to the end, we fhall re-
" ceive a godly portion, fo farewell, and
" the Lord go along with thee." At another time he faid, " He was full of pain,
" yet he could fing of the mercy and good-
" nefs of God to his foul in the midft of
" affliction." Afterwards adding, " Do
" not mourn for me, but be ftill and quiet,
" and let me pafs away quietly, that fo my
" foul may enter into God's everlafting reft;
" for my confcience is clear from guilt in
" the face of all men." Saying, " Come
" Lord Jefus, receive my foul, thy fervant
" is ready, come quickly." This he fpoke
in great frefhnefs and cheerfulnefs of fpirit,
faying, " Now I think I am near my end;"
but reviving again, he fat up, and his children being prefent, he faid to them," " I
" was never covetous to get a great deal of
" this world's riches, but I have endeavour-
" ed to bring you up in the fear of the
" Lord, and educate you in the way of his
" truth to the beft of my underftanding;
" and

" and if you do but wait upon the Lord in
" the fincerity of your hearts, for the drop-
" ping down of the love of God upon your
" fouls in the meetings and gatherings of
" the Lord's people, he will fhed his blef-
" fings amongft you; for he hath been and
" is a father to the fatherlefs, and as a huf-
" band to the widow." This he fpoke juft
before his departure, being frefh in fpirit,
and perfect in fenfe and memory to the laft
hour.

He died the 11th day of the twelfth month
1714, aged fixty-nine years and four months.

---

*A Teſtimony from the Yearly-Meeting of friends
in* Virginia, *concerning* BENJAMIN JOR-
DAN.

HE was born the 18th of the feventh
month 1674, in Nancemond county
in Virginia, of believing parents, who were
careful to educate their children in the bleffed truth for which they fuffered, whofe examples, together with the influence of grace,
were fanctified unto this our friend as well
as feveral others of their numerous offspring.
He was a man who gave up much of his
time in waiting upon God and fervices for
the church, being clerk both to the monthly and yearly meeting; was a good example
of piety and charity, and kept his integrity
to the laft.

The

The day before he died, feveral neighbours coming to fee him, one of them being in a flourifhing ftate as to the world, to
whom the way of truth feemed too low and
defpicable, he faid, " Rejoice O young
" man, in thy youth, and let thy heart
" cheer thee in the days of thy youth, and
" walk in the ways of thy heart, and in
" the fight of thine eyes: But know thou,
" that for all thefe things God will bring
" thee into judgment." He looked upon
another who feemed to be under fome convincement of truth, but did not live in
obedience, and faid, " Bleffed are they that
" hear the word of God and do it." And
to another that appeared to have fought after the honour of this world more than the
Lord's honour, he faid, " He looked too
" big to enter in at the ftrait gate." He
gave particular directions concerning the
place and manner of his burial, defiring
that no more provifion might be made than
was fufficient, having, whilft in health,
borne a teftimony againft making fuch a
time, a time of feafting inftead of mourning. One of his brothers afking him how
it was with him, he replied, " As to my
" eternal ftate, nothing but well." Soon
after, holding up his hands and looking upwards, he faid, " Lord Jefus, into thy
" hands I commit my fpirit, Lord help me
" at this time," And fo departed in quietnefs, the 12*th* of the twelfth month 1716,
aged about forty-two years.

A Teftimony

A Teſtimony from friends in Virginia, *concern-*
ing ELIZABETH SMALL *wife of* Benjamin Small, *of* Nancemond county.

SHE was born the 31ſt of the fixth month
1666. Her parents Edmund and Elizabeth Betfon, were pious friends and zealous
for the truth, whofe care in the education
of their children, had the defired effect on
this our much efteemed friend; for being
obedient to the manifeftation of divine light,
it fo improved a tender, affectionate and affable difpofition, that fhe became qualified
for and endowed with an excellent and acceptable gift in the miniftry, fo as fuitably
to difpenfe doctrine, edification and confolation to the churches. She was very diligent in attending meetings of friends in this
colony, even beyond what could be reafon-
ably expected from fo weakly a conftituti-
on, and was earneft in and much devoted
to the caufe of truth, greatly defiring the
growth and profperity thereof, faying, " She
" could lay down her natural life for it, if
" required." She was a woman of a generous and kind difpofition, as well in helping the poor as entertaining of friends, faying (to fuch as were ready to think fhe would
do more than her circumftances would admit of) that fhe hoped the Lord would fo
provide for her, that fhe fhould never want
what was convenient, having never defired
long life or riches for herfelf or children,
but that they might live in his fear.

She

She was taken ill the 21/l of the feventh month 1717, being the firft day of the yearly-meeting at Chuckatuk, which gave opportunity to divers friends from different parts of the country to vifit her, to whom fhe fignified her peace of mind and fubmiffion to the divine will, faying among other things, " If the Lord has any more work " for me to do, he can raife me up again; " otherwife I am eafy and freely refigned " to his will." To a beloved relation fhe faid, " Dear coufin, thou art bone of my " bone and flefh of my flefh; live in the " fear of the Lord, that every high thought " may be brought down." To two friends belonging to a diftant meeting which fhe had often vifited, fhe faid, " I have not " ceafed to admonifh you heretofore, and " now again defire you would be valiant " for the truth and walk fteadily therein, " and remember my dear love to friends of " the meeting to which you belong." She often fpoke to friends, " To be fteadfaft in " the truth;" And once to a public friend belonging to the fame meeting, earneftly defiring him " To be valiant for the good " caufe." She told her fon William, " She " hoped that that day would be a good one " to her," And faid " She had prayed for " an eafy paffage;" And accordingly fhe quietly departed the 25*th* of the feventh month aforefaid, aged fifty-two, a minifter about 11 years.

An

An account of ELLIS PUGH, *extracted from a testimony from* Gwynedd *Monthly-Meeting concerning him, and also from a short summary of his life, both of which are prefixed to a book he wrote, called* A salutation to the Britains, *&c.*

ELLIS PUGH was born in the parish of Dolgelly, in the county of Merioneth, and dominion of Wales, in the sixth month 1656. His parents were religious people; but his father died before he was born, and his mother a few days after. In the days of his youth, when going with the multitude into folly, it pleased God by his judgment, to stand in his way, and caused him to consider the things that belonged to his soul's everlasting peace. And in the eighteenth year of his age, the Lord visited him more eminently, kindling a zeal in him to serve his Creator more diligently; having been also reached by the testimony of John-ap-John, one of the people called Quakers.

God who promised to be a father to the fatherless, took care of him; and about the year 1680, gave him a part in the ministry of the gospel of Christ, (notwithstanding he was not one of the wife of this world, nor had human learning) yet he was made a profitable instrument to turn divers from vanity, and to exhort and strengthen many

in

in their fpiritual journey, in his native land,
and alfo in this country where he finifhed
his courfe.

In the year 1686, he and his family, with
divers of his acquaintance prepared to come
over to Pennfylvania, and whilft they waited for the fhip to be ready, there came great
trouble and exercife upon him, fo that he
was fick for fome days; in which ftrait the
Lord fhewed him, that they fhould meet
with troubles and exercifes in their way, and
that he had a work for him in that country,
and muft return again to his native land.
After they failed, they met with ftorms,
ftraits and troubles; and having been upon
the tempeftuous fea all winter, they arrived
at Barbados, where they were joyfully and
lovingly received by their friends, and the
fummer following, in the year 1687, they
arrived in Pennfylvania; where this our
friend was a ferviceable inftrument in the
Lord's hand, to cherifh and inftruct us, in
meeknefs and tendernefs, to obey that which
God made known unto us of his will, and
to follow and underftand the operation of
his fpirit, difcovering to us the fnares of the
enemy of our fouls. His pious labours
(among others that were fitted for the fame
fervice) have been profitable in directing
and edifying us in the way of truth; for
by the tendernefs and influence which came
as dew upon our fouls while we fat under
his miniftry, we believed his doctrine was
of God.

E

In

In the year 1706 he was engaged to vifit
the inhabitants of his native country, according to what the Lord revealed unto him
before he came from thence; which fervice
he performed to the benefit and acceptance
of many, and returned to his family in
1708. After he came home, three of his
children, in the flower of their age, who
from their youth walked orderly and were
hopeful, died within one month; in the
time of which trial the Lord was near unto him; he mourned not as one without
hope. Strength was given him to bear his
affliction. He faid in a public meeting " If
he could bear his affliction acceptably in
the fight of God, it would be as marrow
to his bones:" Which teftimony, amongft
feveral other things, was to the edification
and comfort of the hearers. His refidence
was then nearer to us than before, which
render'd his life and converfation more confpicuous, and his fellowfhip more known
unto us. His miniftry was living, profitable and to edification. He was of a meek
and quiet fpirit, confiderate and folid in his
judgment, of few words, honeft and careful in his calling; and feveral were induced
to fpeak of the benefit they received by his
chafte converfation, and his loving and comfortable expreffions while he was amongft
them in their families. He was honourable
among his friends and of good report among
all people generally, therefore his memory
will not foon wear out.

He

He was in a declining ſtate of bodily
health about a year and three months before
his deceaſe, ſo that he was not well able to
follow his calling; but his candle ſhined
brighter, as may be ſeen by peruſing his
treatiſe, called " A ſalutation to the Bri-
" tains;" which he wrote in his own language, in the time of his long ſickneſs, when
his view was towards that which pertains
to eternity, more eſpecially to thoſe, or for
˗ the ſake of thoſe to whom the ſalutation of
his life reached over ſea and land, for the
encouragement and inſtruction of them that
were ſeeking the way to Sion, the New Jeruſalem, the city of the Great King, whoſe
walls and bulwarks are ſalvation.

The laſt meeting he was at among us, he
was weak in body, but fervent in ſpirit, as
one taking his laſt leave in a great deal of
love and tenderneſs, ſaying, that the Lord
granted him his deſire to come and viſit us
once more; putting us in mind to live in
love and unity, and to keep out from amongſt
us as much as we could, all ſtrife and diſ-
cord; and when any thing appeared which
had a tendency thereunto, that hands ſhould
be laid without delay to end it, and that
none ſhould depend upon his own hand,
eye, or balance in judgment.—He was fitted to counſel others, becauſe his life and
converſation was anſwerable to his teſtimony; amongſt his family tender and careful
to counſel them to live in the fear of God.

We

We looked upon him as one who had finiſhed his work, that the time of his diſſolution drew nigh: And that he might ſay in the words of Paul, according to his meaſure, " I have fought a good fight, I have " finiſhed my courſe, I have kept the faith. " Henceforth there is laid up for me a " crown of righteouſneſs, which the Lord " the righteous judge ſhall give me at that " day; and not to me only, but unto all " them alſo that love his appearing."

Being patient in his tedious indiſpoſition, and contented to wait the Lord's time; he ſlept with his fathers on the 3d day of the tenth month 1718, in favour with God.

The following Teſtimony concerning WILLIAM HAIG, *was furniſhed by a committee of the Yearly-Meeting of* North-Carolina.

WILLIAM HAIG ſenior of Paſquotank county, who removed from Antigua with his family and ſettled in this province, was of a loving and ſweet ſpirit. In his laſt ſickneſs, as ſome friends were ſitting by him, he was filled with heavenly joy, and ſaid, " Friends I am glad of your " company, I feel ſo much of the bleſſed " truth, as I hope will carry me into that " joy where I ſhall praiſe the Lord amongſt " the redeemed. I hear that truth proſpers " mightily in England, bleſſed be the Lord " for

" for it." He exhorted all his children with
many heavenly expreſſions, took his ſolemn
leave of them, and in a living ſenſe of truth,
prayed to God for his bleſſing upon them;
charging them " to love and obey their
" mother, learn their books and keep to the
" truth." He ſaid to his wife, " My dear,
" thou haſt been a true wife unto me; when
" my mind was drawn to love thee, I did
" not inquire what thou hadſt, nor thou
" what I had, but we came together in love
" and we have lived in love." And when
his ſpeech was very low, he ſpake to his
wife thus, " The Lord bleſs thee and my
" children, God Almighty protect you."
To a young woman who came to viſit him
he ſaid, " Fear God, keep to the truth,
" never turn thy back upon it, left the days
" come in which thou ſhalt ſay, I have no
" pleaſure in them: As for me, I am going
" to my place, and I hope it will be in ever-
" laſting reſt." To another who had been
viſited with great ſickneſs, he ſaid, " It had
" been better for thee to have died in thy
" ſickneſs, than to live to forget God."
He prayed that God would remember all
his people, and that their dwelling might
be with the Lord, adding, " But what ſhall
" I ſay, there are too many that tread the
" teſtimony of truth under foot; O! gather
" them into thy fold of reſt, I pray thee
" O Lord!" To a friend of the miniſtry
he ſaid, " Thou art of the miniſtry and
" haſt been a great while, and I am but
" young,

" young, but I would advife thee to be
" careful in thy teftimony, not to enlarge
" beyond thy gift or concern; and have a
" care, thou do not ftand in the way of
" others, or fpeak any thing to hurt others
" that may be but fmall or tender; but
" wait until thou art filled and then be
" humble, and not puffed up with pride,
" for pride goeth before a fall." After
praying unto the Lord to fettle him upon
the fure foundation and rock that can never
be removed, he quietly departed this life,
at his own houfe, on the 6th of the eleventh
month 1718, and now refts in joy.

_____

A Teſtimony from the ſame committee concerning
MARY HAIG, *wife of the aforeſaid* William Haig.

SHE was a woman of an exemplary life
and converfation, of a fweet and loving
behaviour, and was favoured with a gift in
the miniftry. In her laft ficknefs, after imparting her mind to a friend about her outward concerns, fhe fpoke as follows, " Ac-
" cording to my fmall gift, I have difcharg-
" ed myfelf, fo that nothing lieth at my door.
" O! that the people would remember the
" words that I have fpoken among them,
" and that this young generation would
" come up in truth. As for me, I had ne-
" ver left the ifland of Antigua, if it were
" not

" not that I might have my poor children
" amongſt faithful friends: I have ſeen the
" wonders of the Lord in the deep ocean,
" and witneſſed his delivering arm in many
" exerciſes, and he hath kept me ſweet and
" clean all along ſince I knew the truth.
" Oh! that my children may remember the
" advice they have received of their father
" and me; I am clear, having done my
" duty." And praiſed God; alſo uttered
many ſweet and comfortable expreſſions.
At another time, ſhe ſaid to ſome friends,
" When I was but nine years old, the Lord
" made himſelf known unto me, but I then
" lived where there were no friends; and
" after ſome time, I went to Pennſylvania,
" and there met with friends, but ſome
" were looſe and light, others were ſolid
" and weighty, and with theſe I joined, and
" received much benefit from the family of
" the Lloyd's. After I was married, we
" went to Antigua, and there in the firſt
" meeting, the power of the Lord was great-
" ly with me, inſomuch that the peoples
" expectations were upon me for words;
" but ſoon after it pleaſed the Lord to ſend
" two of his ſervants, Joſiah Langdale and
" Thomas Thomſon, to viſit the iſland,
" when the power of the Lord did break in
" upon me like thunder:" And ſignified
ſhe had been faithful ever ſince in her meaſure, in giving up to the work of the Lord.
On the day of her deceaſe, ſhe ſaid to ſome
preſent, " Friends, be loving one to another

" ther, that the Lord may bleſs you. The
" love that I feel in my heart is inexpreſ-
" ſible." After a while ſhe deſired a friend
to remember her love to Lydia Lancaſter,
Elizabeth Rawlinſon and friends generally;
adding, " Tell them, I die in unity with all
" faithful friends." Afterwards ſhe ſaid,
" My huſband is gone, but I ſhall not be
" long a ſorrowful widow; yet not my will
" but thine be done; my ſpeech fails apace,
" ſweet Lord Jeſus, thou haſt loved me
" from a child, and I have loved thee ever
" ſince I knew thee, and my caſe is no
" doubtful caſe, I come, 1 come, haſten
" thou my journey."
She died the 13th of the eleventh month
1718, aged about thirty-nine years.

---

*A Teſtimony from the aforeſaid committee, con-
cerning* JOSEPH GLAISTER.

JOSEPH GLAISTER of Paſquotank
county, formerly of Cumberland in
Great-Britain, who removed with his family and ſettled in North-Carolina, was a
valuable miniſter, and very ſerviceable in
diſcipline, being well qualified therefor; a
conſtant attender of meetings with his family, and one who travelled much for the
ſpreading of truth. In his laſt ſickneſs, he
ſaid to ſome friends that viſited him, " I
" am very ill, but am out of all doubt of
" my

" my falvation, being well aſſured of it."
Two other friends coming in, he added,
" Now I think I have moſt of the chief
" friends about me that I deſired; dear
" friends, give me up freely, that I may not
" be kept longer in miſery, for I can ſay
" with one of old, Lord I have long wait-
" ed for thy falvation, and now have an
" aſſurance of it, and altho' the pains are
" great, yet the comfort and pleaſure I ſee
" before me do outbalance them all."—
Again he ſaid, " He hoped that friends
" might keep their places in being faithful,
" and not to ſhrink one from another when
" troubles or differences may ariſe in the
" church, or amongſt neighbours, by any
" evil ſpirit that may get into any unfaith-
" ful one, for want of a due, true and faith-
" ful watch; and then if any ſuch thing
" do happen, pray friends, I hope that ſuch
" as now are, or may then be, do ſtand
" firm together, and give judgment in or by
" a living, freſh and divine ſpirit, and keep
" conſtant in mind, and thereby the tranſ-
" greſſor or tranſgreſſors may be judged .
" down and not able to reſiſt; but if you
" ſee in them any thing tender, then dear
" friends, turn to them with bowels of love
" and perhaps in ſo doing, you may gain
" ſuch as in time paſt may have gone aſtray."
He went on ſpeaking of the great love and
unity, and the many good times he had had
with us; having his ſpirit borne up by the
ancient arm that had been from time to time

his

his great fupport. Near his end, we were fenfible of his being engaged in prayer, but being almoft fpent we could not hear every word fo as to pen it down. Thus this good man ended his life, with a fenfe of the great love of God to his foul, on the 31*ft* of the eleventh month 1718, aged about forty-five years, and a minifter about 24 years.

A Teftimony from Kennet *Monthly-Meeting in* Pennfylvania, *concerning* VINCENT CALD-WELL.

HE was born in Derbyfhire Great-Britain, and was convinced about the 17*th* or 18*th* year of his age, by the miniftry of John Gratton; having received the truth in the love of it and continuing faithful, the Lord was pleafed to commit to him a difpenfation of the gofpel, fo that he had to declare to others of the goodnefs of God to his foul. He came over into Pennfylvania, and after his marriage fettled in Eaft Marlborough in Chefter county. His miniftry was found and edifying, being attended with the power of truth and adorned with an exemplary converfation; in the exercife whereof he twice vifited the meetings of friends in the fouthern provinces, and once in divers of the Weft-India iflands, where he was made inftrumental to the convincing of many; for tho' he had but little fchool-

fchool-learning, yet being as a good Scribe,
well inftructed unto the kingdom, did at
times bring forth out of the treafury things
new and old.

His laft ficknefs continued about fix days,
wherein he was preferved in a fweet, fenfible and tender frame of fpirit, and at times
fpoke in fubftance as follows, viz. The doctor coming to vifit him, he faid with cheerfulnefs, " I would have thee fpeak thy
" mind freely concerning me, for I am not
" afraid to die." The doctor after fome
paufe, fignified the doubt he had of his recovery; which bringing an awful filence
over his mind, he broke forth in earneft fupplication to the Lord for the welfare of Sion,
and exhorted friends prefent to love and
unity, and to beware of that fpirit which
would lead into a feparation. He fpoke
clearly to the ftates of fome, warning them
to fear the Lord and walk humbly before
him, and then they would be made partakers of his divine and heavenly blefling.
He prayed the Lord to profper his work,
and faid, " The Lord will caufe his glorious truth to break forth in the north country, and among the Ethiopians," In a fight
and fenfe whereof he rejoiced. Another
time, his wife fitting by him, he look'd
earneftly at her and faid, " My dear, don't
be furprifed, for in time thou wilt come into that reft that I am going into." She
queried, " Doft thou think fo?" He faid
" I have no doubt of it." Then taking
leave

leave of her, he faid, "Thou haft been a loving wife, a tender mother and a good neighbour." Taking leave of his children one by one, he charg'd them to be loving and obedient to their mother, and not to go out in their marriages. He prayed the Lord to make his paffage eafy, and receive him gracioufly into his arms of reft and peace forever; and defired his love to friends in general at their monthly, quarterly and yearly meetings, and meeting of minifters. After which, being fenfible his end drew near, he faid, "Give me a little water, and "I think I fhall not want any more, till I "drink at that fountain which fprings up "into eternal life."—Thus in a refigned frame of mind, he finifhed his courfe, the 10*th* day of the firft month 1719-20, in the forty-fixth year of his age, and was interr'd in friends burying-ground at Kennet. Concerning whom we believe, he is entered into the manfions of glory, where "The wicked ceafe from troubling and the weary are at reft."

A Teftimony from the Monthly-Meeting of Philadelphia *concerning* ANTHONY MORRIS.

OUR ancient and well efteemed friend Anthony Morris, was a member of this meeting at the early inftitution thereof, and in the year 1701 appeared in the miniftry, miniſtry, and being obedient and faithful, he ſoon became acceptable and edifying, being found in word and doctrine. He was advanced to his forty-ſeventh year when he engaged in this ſervice, and having a proſpect of a great work before him, requiring his cloſe application, he drew his worldly buſineſs into a narrow compaſs, and devoted his time principally to the ſervice of truth; not only viſiting neighbouring meetings, but alſo travelled through New-Jerſey, Long-Iſland, Rhode-Iſland, New-England and Maryland; and about the year 1715 perform'd a viſit to friends in South-Britain. He was early appointed clerk of our monthly-meeting which ſervice he performed many years to ſatisfaction; being zealous and ſerviceable in the diſcipline, a diligent attender of all our religious meetings, careful in obſerving the time appointed and often concern'd to exhort ſuch to amendment as were remiſs herein.

In the eighth month 1721 his ſpeech was much affected by frequent attacks of a paralytick diſorder, but his underſtanding remaining clear, and being favour'd with the enjoyment of divine love, he was enabled to utter ſome ſentences to thoſe that viſited him, ſaying, " That if confiſtent with the di-
" vine will the time of his diſſolution was at
" hand, it would be more joyous to depart
" now, than continue longer in the body."
Yet expreſs'd his free reſignation to the will of God, and in an humble tender frame of
ſpirit

fpirit mention'd the teftimony Chrift gave concerning the woman who poured on his head the precious ointment, fayihg " He " was favoured with the evidence in him- " felf, that he had done what he could, " and felt peace," Exprefling at the fame time, " That his hope for eternal falvation " was alone in the mercy of God through " his fon Chrift Jefus, the only faviour and " mediator." Some friends who were going to attend a neighbouring yearly-meeting coming to vifit him, he took an affectionate leave of them, faying " Remember " my dear love to friends in general; tell " them I am going and all is well."

He departed this life the 23d of the eighth month 1721, aged fixty-feven years; and on the 25th his corpfe was borne to our meeting houfe in High-ftreet, accompanied by many friends and neighbours, as well as friends from the adjacent country meetings, and thence to our burial ground in this city where it was interr'd. Concerning whom we hope, he hath obtained an entrance into the manfions prepared by Chrift Jefus our Lord, for thofe who continue faithful to the end of their time here, as did this our friend.

Two

Two Extracts from Thomas Chalkley's journal *concerning* THOMAS LIGHTFOOT.

IN the eighth month 1725, I went to Derby to vifit our worthy aged friend Thomas Lightfoot, who lay very weak in body, none expecting his recovery; I called as I went from home, and then he was very ill, and told me, " He thought that illnefs " would conclude his time in this world, " but faid that all was well and likewife " that he had a great concern upon his " mind for the growth and profperity of " truth in the earth, and defired with ten- " dernefs of fpirit, that I would give his " dear love to all friends;" And he now faid, " I never thought to fee thee more, " but am glad to fee thee." I ftayed there all night and in the morning we had a com-fortable heart-melting time together, in which was revived the remembrance of the many favourable feafons of God's love we had enjoy'd in our travels in the work of the miniftry of the gofpel of Chrift, and we tenderly prayed if we never met more in this world, we might meet in that which is to come, where we might never part more, but might forever live to fing with all the faints and holy angels, hallelujah to God and the Lamb.

In the *9th* month 1725, I was at the fu-neral of our worthy ancient friend Thomas Lightfoot. He was buried at Derby; the

meeting

meeting was the largeft that I have ever feen at that place. Our dear friend was greatly beloved for his piety and virtue, his fweet difpofition and lively miniftry: The Lord was with him in his life and death and with us at his burial.

This our friend removed from Ireland in an advanced age, and fettled in Chefter county Pennfylvania. In 1724 being then near fourfcore years of age, he with Benjamin Kidd, a young minifter from England, paid a general vifit to friends in New-England.

———————

A Teftimony from Nottingham *Monthly-Meeting in* Pennfylvania, *concerning* A A R O N C O P P O C K.

I T appears he was born in Chefhire in Old England, the 25*th* of the tenth month 1662, was convinced of the truth when a young man, came to America foon after and lived near Chefter; about the year 1714 he, with his family, fettled at Nottingham in faid county; being a man of an exemplary conduct and much efteemed by friends, he was chofen an elder for the particular meeting of Eaft-Nottingham, until he appeared in a public teftimony, and therein was often concerned to exhort friends to a life of felf denial, watchfulnefs and prayer, the which he did in great fincerity,

zeal

zeal and innocency. In the forepart of his laſt illneſs he complained of much poverty, but before he died had a proſpect of happineſs, and a ſure hope of obtaining the ſame. He departed this life on the 10*th* day of the tenth month 1725, and was buried in friends burying ground in Eaſt Nottingham the 12*th* of the ſame month, aged ſixty-three, and a miniſter 7 years.

A Teſtimony from Salem *Monthly-Meeting in* New-Jerſey, *concerning* JAMES DANIEL ſenior.

THE memory of the righteous cannot ſoon be forgotten by thoſe who follow their footſteps, but are as memorials, deeply engraven on their minds, and are worthy to be had in remembrance, of which number was that ſteady friend and exemplary elder James Daniel, whoſe pious life and favoury converſation is freſh in ſome of our memories.

He was born in Ireland about the year 1675; his father Neal Daniel brought him over ſea when about five years of age, and ſettled in Alloway's-Creek townſhip in the county of Salem Weſt-Jerſey; at which time the white people were but few, and the natives a multitude. He learned their language perfectly, and has frequently ſaid, that at that time the natives were a ſober,

F   grave

grave and temperate people, and ufed no
manner of oath in their fpeech. About the
15th year of his age his father died, leaving him in the care of friends to be educated in the way of truth, which he embraced in the love of it; and as he grew in age,
he grew in experience and divine favour,
and had a fhare of the overfight of the flock
and elderfhip conferred upon him, which
he faithfully performed in the fpirit of love
and meeknefs, thereby rendering his fervice
acceptable and obtaining a good report. He
ruled his own houfe well, having his children
in fubjection: Diligent in attending meetings for worfhip and difcipline, altho' for
many years with difficulty, the country being new and roads not made; but afterwards he, with confiderable coft and labour,
got bridges erected over fome creeks and a
public road made near his own houfe. His
houfe and heart were open to entertain
friends according to his ability; was zealoufly concerned for the honour of God and
promotion of truth. He often lamented
that as the country grew older the people
grew worfe, and had corrupted the natives
in their morals, teaching them bad words
and the exceffive ufe of ftrong drink, which
he, during many years in the latter part of
his time, for example's fake took none of,
and frequently admonifhed fuch as were in
the ufe thereof, to obferve great temperance.

In the latter years of his life, he defired
his eldeft fons to take the care of his tempo-

ral concerns upon them, for his mind feemed divefted therefrom as much as tho' he
poffeffed nothing, (a good example for all
elders; for forrowful experience fhews us,
that too many as they grow in years, grow
more clofely attached to the earth; which is
a forrowful profpect and poor example to
the rifing generation) but devoted his mind
and time to truth's fervice, often accompanying friends in their religious engagements, to his great fatisfaction.

Whilft in health, the Lord gave him a
fenfe that his departure drew near; foon afterwards he was taken with the pleurify and
lay about eight days, during which time
he gave much good advice to his family,
friends and neighbours that came to fee him,
to whom he alfo gave evident proofs of a
happy exit. The day before his departure,
many friends and neighbours came and had
a religious meeting, after which, feveral
taking leave, he faid, " I am glad of this
" vifit and of the meeting, but I have a
" great concern on my mind for this gene-
" ration," mentioning many growing evils
then prevalent, and faid, " Many of the
" elders are called away and more muft foon;
" but I hope the Lord will raife up fome
" that fhall be faithful and zealous." The
evening of his deceafe, he took his folemn
leave of all prefent, beginning with his wife,
and afterwards his children in order, giving
each fomething in charge; to one particularly he faid, " Thou doft not know what fer-

" vice

" vice the Lord hath for thee to do in thy
" generation." So remaining fenfible until
about the 10*th* hour, he departed like one
falling into a fweet fleep, at his own houfe
on the 26*th* of the tenth month 1726, in
the fifty-fecond year of his age.

Extract from Thomas Chalkley's journal *concerning* JOHN LEE.

THE 27*th* of the tenth month 1726, I
heard the news of the death of my
dear friend John Lee: It affected me with
forrow, he being an old acquaintance and
inward friend of mine, with whom I had
travelled many miles. He was a living ferviceable minifter of the gofpel of Chrift, and
inftrumental to convince divers of that principle of divine light and truth which we
profefs: Our love and friendfhip was conftant and intire unto the end, having been
acquainted about thirty-five years as near
as I can remember.

A Teftimony from New-Garden *Monthly-Meeting in* Pennfylvania, *concerning* CALEB
PUSEY.

HE was born in Berkfhire Old England,
and educated in the Baptifts profeffion, but after he arrived to years of religious
confideration;

confideration, he was convinced of the principles of truth as profeſſed by the people called Quakers. In the year 1682, he removed to Pennſylvania and ſettled near Cheſter, where he reſided a conſiderable time, then removed to Marlborough in the ſame county, where he dwelt the remainder of his days.

He was a worthy elder in the church, being endowed with a good natural capacity, found in judgment, and zealous in maintaining the cauſe of truth againſt contrary and contending ſpirits. His conſtancy in attending meetings for worſhip and diſcipline was remarkable and worthy of imitation. Much might be ſaid of his zeal and integrity for truth, which he retained to the laſt, but, for brevity's ſake, let it ſuffice, *that he was a juſt man*, therefore let him be had in remembrance.

His laſt illneſs was heavy upon him for ſix days; during which he was preſerved ſenſible; ſignifying *what a brave thing it was to be prepared for death*. The morning before he died, being aſked by his ſon-in-law how he did, anſwered, " The time was near come that he muſt leave the world;" to which his ſon replied, " Father, I hope that is no ſurprize to thee;" he anſwered, " No, No;" after which he ſpoke little that could be underſtood, only deſired " That friends might keep their meetings in uprightneſs."

He

He died the 25*th* of the twelfth month
1726-7, in the feventy-fixth year of his age,
and was interr'd in friends burying ground
at London Grove.

A Teſtimony from the Monthly-Meeting of Philadelphia, *concerning* HANNAH HILL.

OUR worthy and much efteemed friend
Hannah Hill, wife of Richard Hill,
and daughter of Thomas Lloyd (formerly
governor of this province) by Mary the
daughter of Gilbert Jones, of Welchpool,
was born in Montgomeryfhire North Wales,
at the feat of her anceftors called Dolobran,
the 21ſt of the feventh month 1666. She
was a woman highly favoured of the Lord,
poffeffed many excellent chriftian virtues,
as well as natural accomplifhments: Coming over into this country with her parents
when young; foon after their arrival it
pleafed the Lord to remove her pious mother by death, when the care of the younger
children devolved upon her: This clofe trial in the earlier part of her time, was abundantly fanctified to her; for her mind being engaged to feek the Lord for her portion, and her father's God for the lot of her
inheritance, he was gracioufly pleafed, not
only to favour her with the knowledge of
himfelf and the enjoyment of his living
prefence in the days of her youth, but alfo
made

made her a fingular inftrument of good, and
a bleffing to her father's family. As fhe
grew in years, her confpicuous virtues, joined with a 'courteous deportment, juftly gained the efteem and favour of moft if not all
with whom fhe converfed. Being earneftly
folicited in marriage by John Delaval, who
(tho' a worthy man) was not at that time of
the fame religious communion, fhe, by her
prudent conduct and pious refolution to
maintain the principles fhe profeffed without deviating therefrom in a matter of fuch
importance, did not agree thereto; until he
after fome time embraced the truth in fincerity of heart, and bore his crofs like an
humble follower of Chrift; he received a
gift in the miniftry, and continued faithful
therein to his death: Concerning whom fhe
gave this teftimony, viz. " That he never
ufed to her an expreffion of anger, or the
product of a difturbed mind." The deceafe
of her faid hufband proved to her a time of
deep probation, having been heard to fay,
that in eight weeks time fhe loft eight of her
family by death, beginning with the deceafe
of her beloved hufband, and ending with
that of her only child: Under which afflicting circumftances, as well as what attended her the remaining part of her life (of
which fhe had a large fhare) fhe approved
herfelf- a fhining example of patience in
tribulation, and a meek, humble, felf-denying follower of Chrift.

In

In the affluent ſtation wherein divine providence had placed her, her benevolent diſpoſition was conſpicuous in adminiſtring to
the neceſſities of the indigent, her charity
not being limited to thoſe of her own profeſſion. She was a true ſervant of the
church, and in the ſenſe of the apoſtle's expreſſions, " One that waſhed the ſaints feet,"
receiving with joy into her houſe, the miniſters and meſſengers of the goſpel, for
whom her love was great: The low, the
poor and the mean, were objects of her peculiar care.

In her younger years ſhe received a gift
in the miniſtry, which ſhe retained with
faithfulneſs to the end; and tho' not large
in her appearance, yet with great modeſty and
ſoundneſs of expreſſion, " Her doctrine dropped as the dew, and diſtilled as the ſmall rain,"
and was therefore truly acceptable. She
travelled in the ſervice of the goſpel, to New-
England and divers other parts of this continent, and was alſo concern'd for the good
order and diſcipline of the church, having
for a number of years, ſerved in the ſtation
of clerk of the women's monthly, quarterly
and yearly meetings, wherein ſhe gave ſatiſ-
faction.

Although bodily weakneſs frequently attended her in the latter years of her life, it
did not abate her love and zeal for the everlaſting truth, which ſhe experienced to be
her ſupport in every time of trial; and when
her diſſolution drew near, ſhe made divers

ſeaſonable

feafonable remarks and obfervations, alfo fignified her acquiefcence with the divine will, in the difpenfations of his providence towards her; at one time particularly mentioning the expreffions of the apoftle, " That " no chaftening for the prefent feemeth to be " joyous, but grievous, neverthelefs, after- " ward it yieldeth the peaceable fruit of " righteoufnefs unto them which are exer- " cifed thereby." This was her happy experience; and after a well-fpent life, interfperfed with a variety of exercifing viciffitudes, fhe exchanged this ftate of exiftence (no doubt) for a bleffed immortality in the regions of unmixed felicity; after about three weeks illnefs, on the 25th of the twelfth month 1726-7, in the fixty-firft year of her age. Her corpfe was refpectfully attended by a large number of friends and others, to the High-ftreet meeting-houfe in Philadelphia, where divers living teftimonies were borne, after which it was interr'd in friends burial ground.

She was twenty-fix years the wife of Richard Hill, who was a ferviceable member both in church and ftate, and died in good efteem, the 4th of the feventh month 1729.

A Teftimony

A Teftimony from Haddonfield *Monthly-Meeting in* New-Jerfey, *concerning* JAMES LORD.

HE received a lively gift of the gofpel miniftry whilft young in years, was frequently exercifed therein to the edification and encouragement of friends; and was much concerned for the true Sioners, that they might hold on their way, and that the outcafts of Ifrael might be gathered home into the true fold of reft. An exemplary man, by which he greatly adorned the doctrine he preached; was called from works to rewards in the flower of his age, being in his thirty-fourth year and in the year 1727.

Extract from Thomas Chalkley's journal, *concerning the aforefaid* JAMES LORD.

ON fecond-day the 25*th* of the feventh month 1727, I had the forrowful tidings of the death of my beloved friend James Lord; who, on his death-bed, defired that I might be fent for to his burial. In the confideration of that chriftian love which was between us, I think I may truly note, that we were always glad to meet each other; therefore the thoughts of this fo fudden change and final parting, brought, for the prefent, a fadnefs and heavinefs over my mind;

mind; confidering his ftation in that neighbourhood, and fervice in that congregation
to which he did belong; for therein he was
well-beloved and very ferviceable.

And Oh! the lofs that his dear wife and
tender children will have of him, really af-
fects me with forrow in penning thefe notes;
but the forrow, in thefe things, is all on our
fide; for he, without doubt, is at reft with
his great mafter in Heaven. We had a lar-
ger meeting at his funeral than ever was
known to be there before (as an ancient
friend told me) which was folemn and ferviceable to many.

Some account of JOHN BEVAN, *copied from a
manufcript, appearing to be a teftimony from
a meeting in* Wales *concerning him, the conclufion of which is wanting. And tho' he
was born and died in that country, yet having lived many years in* Pennfylvania, *the
following memorial is thought not improper
to be inferted in this Collection.*

OUR deceafed friend John Bevan, the
worthy fubject of our teftimony, having deferved to have his name tranfmitted to
pofterity, for his pious life and converfation, the following account of him, probably, will not only be fatisfactory to his relations, friends and acquaintance, but afford edification and comfort to thofe who
knew him not. He

He was born about 1646, and well de-
ſcended; his parents died when he was very
young, leaving five children, of whom he
was the eldeſt. In 1665 he married a religious woman. His father had left him a
confiderable eſtate, but the reſt of the children were unprovided for; he therefore,
when he came of age, (his ſiſter being dead
before) portioned all his brothers, and gave
them a helpful ſubfiſtence in the world.
Some years after, he was convinced of the
bleſſed truth as it is in Jeſus, the manner
whereof, as he himſelf hath left it in writing, ·was thus,

' My wife was religiouſly inclined in her
' young years, and zealouſly concerned to
' obſerve the ceremonies of the church of
' England, and I believe (as ſhe has often
' told me) ſhe aimed ſincerely therein at
' God's glory and the falvation of her im-
' mortal ſoul. After we were joined in mar-
' riage, ſhe continued very zealous in that
' way; but when a weighty concern came
' upon my mind for the well-being of my
' immortal ſoul, I ſaw it very needful for
' me to make a narrow ſearch after the beſt
' way, and thoſe people who performed
' that worſhip and ſervice that was accept-
' able before God; and being in a weighty
' frame of ſpirit, the people called Quakers
' came before the view of my mind; and
' hearing of a book of George Fox the
' younger's, to be at a relation's houſe, I
' was willing to go thither for it, and in the
' reading

'reading thereof, I was so well satisfied,
'that I can truly say, what I then read,
'answered the witness of God in my own
'bosom, as "Face answereth face in a glass:"
'But soon after I came home, my wife per-
'ceiving me to be more serious and weigh-
'ty in my spirit than formerly, was jealous
'I had an inclination towards that way
'which the people called Quakers made
'profession of; and finding I had the said
'book, came up to the chamber where I
'was, and cautioned me not to be beguil-
'ed: I spoke to her in simplicity and much
'brokenness of heart, of the sense and sa-
'tisfaction I had, that those who were faith-
'ful to that divine principle which the
'people called Quakers bore testimony to,
'were the people God owned, or to that
'import; and it reached to God's witness
'in her, that we parted in much tenderness
'at that time. However she continued some-
'what zealous in her way still, and would
'be often arguing with me in vindication
'thereof, much about twelve months; but
'at one time, when she was at their wor-
'ship, the Priest denounced his excommu-
'nication against me, and she being in a
'seat just under him, it came so near her
'that she was nigh to faint away; when
'their worship was over, she went to the
'Priest and spoke somewhat home to him,
'and that she thought she deserved more
'civility, at least so much as to know afore-
'hand of their excommunication, for he
'might

' might know that she sincerely loved her
' husband tho' he dissented from her in
' judgment. And after that time, she be-
' came more willing to search closely into
' the weighty work of the salvation of her
' immortal soul; and the Lord's love was
' manifested to her, that in a little while af-
' ter, her understanding came to be opened,
' and she came to be convinced of God's
' everlasting truth, that was promised " To
" lead into all truth." And having tasted of
' that living bread that gives life to the soul,
' she came withal to see there was no need of
' the outward bread, which formerly she was
' zealous and conscientious in the observa-
' tion of, to commemorate the death and
' passion of our Lord Jesus Christ; the true
' remembrancer being come and witnessed,
' even he " Who stands at the door of men's
" hearts for an entrance, that he may come
" to sup with them and they with him."
    ' Soon after our convincement, the ene-
' my of souls mustered his forces, and en-
' deavoured to stifle our convictions, and
' we were hard put to it both within and
' without, but as our eyes were to the Lord,
' and in poverty and humility of spirit we
' leaned upon him, he made the hard things
' easy, and in the sense of his divine love
' which was often shed abroad in our hearts,
' we were made willing to deny ourselves,
' to take up the cross, and to despise the
' shame. And tho' we were but a few, we
' thought it convenient to meet together to
                                    ' wait

' wait upon the Lord, being fully satisfied
' it was a duty incumbent upon his people
' in all ages ; and in the performance of our
' duty herein in the year 1675, several
' friends were taken from our house at two
' several times, and brought before two
' justices of the peace, who tendered the
' oath of allegiance and supremacy to them,
' and because, for conscience sake, they
' could not break the command of Christ
' who said " Swear not at all," they were
' committed to prison, where they remain-
' ed about fourteen weeks, and then were
' set at liberty ; ever since which, the meet-
' ing has been kept either at our house or
' at the meeting-house, quietly without any
' more disturbance.

' Sometime before the year 1683, we
' heard that our esteemed friend William
' Penn, had a patent from king Charles the
' second, for that province in America call-
' ed Pennsylvania ; and my wife had a great
' inclination to go thither, and thought it
' might be a good place to train up children
' amongst sober people, and to prevent the
' corruption of them here, by the loose be-
' haviour of the youth and the bad example
' of too many of those of riper years ; she ac-
' quainted me therewith, but I then thought
' it not likely to take effect for several reasons;
' but as I was sensible her aim was upright
' on account of our children, I was willing
' to weigh the matter in a true balance;
' and I can truly say, my way was made
' easy

' eafy and clear to go thither, beyond my
' expectation; and it was the Lord's great
' mercy to preferve us over the great deep
' to our defired port: And what hardfhips
' we met at the beginning of our fettlement,
' the Lord was our helper and fupport to
' go through: And I can in a fweet re-
' membrance fay, many were the bleffed fea-
' fons we had with God's people in that re-
' mote country, and I believe and am well
' fatisfied that the Lord has a remnant there,
' that fincerely aim at his glory and the
' profperity of his truth, bleffed and praif-
' ed be his holy name forever.

' We ftaid there many years, and had
' four of our children married with our
' confent, and they had feveral children,
' and the aim intended by my wife, was in
' a good meafure anfwered.—When a weigh-
' ty concern came upon my mind to return
' to my native country, and that chiefly on
' truth's account. I laid it before my wife,
' and fhe could not be eafy to ftay behind
' me, and we came over in the year 1704;
' and through the Lord's great mercy we were
' preferved in that tedious voyage, north
' about Scotland through many difficulties,
' and from the cruelties alfo of the pri-
' vateers, of which there were many then
' on that coaft, as we were afterward in-
' formed.—This wonderful prefervation de-
' ferves to be remembered with thankfgiv-
' ing; having loft the fleet, we were only
' four fhips coming together from Virginia,
and

' and one of them belonging to Briftol, we
' thought to remove to that fhip, becaufe
' Briftol was nearer to our habitation in
' Wales than London, whither our veffel
' was bound; we agreed with the mafter
' for our paffage, and next morning we were
' to go on board, but that night I was un-
' der a weighty exercife about our removal,
' but in the morning it happened to be fo
' ftormy that he could not take us in, fo he
' parted from us, and bore his courfe to-
' wards Briftol; then the weight I was un-
' der was removed, and I was very eafy in
' my fpirit; and as I was afterward inform-
' ed, that fhip was taken near to Lundy Ifland:
' This deliverance therefore and prefervation
' of us, I afcribe to the Lord's great favour
' and mercy towards us, thanks, honour and
' praifes be rendered and afcribed to him for
' the fame and all other mercies forever.

' In this voyage, our youngeft daughter
' Barbara Bevan accompanied us, and fhe
' was of good fervice on truth's account,
' the fhort time fhe remained in the body;
' her innocency and fweet behaviour preach-
' ed truth wherever fhe came. It is my
' comfort and great fatisfaction, that fhe left
' a good favour, and has finifhed her courfe
' in peace with her maker, and is gone to
' her eternal reft in the manfions of blifs
' and joy, to laud and magnify him forever.†
'We

† A fhort teftimony concerning her, worthy of perufal, is
printed in the 5th part of Piety Promoted.

G

' We landed at laft at Shields in North-
' umberland, and ftaid over the meeting on
' firft-day, where we were comforted with
' friends; next day we fet forward toward
' our habitation in Wales, having near three
' hundred miles to travel. We had feveral
' good meetings in our way, and about the
' beginning of the eighth month 1704, we
' came to our home at Treveyricke; and
' from that time forward my dear wife was
' given up as before, to be ferviceable on
' truth's account, and fo continued during
' her pilgrimage here, being fix years and
' upwards. Her houfe and heart fince her
' convincement, were open to receive the
' Lord's meffengers, both here and in Ameri-
' ca, and fhe was very careful and open
' hearted to help the poor and weak, both
' amongft us and others. In her laft fick-
' nefs, fhe was fenfible fhe was not like to
' recover out of it, and fhe was fatisfied
' and contented therein to fubmit to the
' Lord's will; fpeaking to me, fhe faid, " I
" take it as a great mercy that I am to go
" before thee, we are upwards of forty-five
" years married, and our love is rather more
" now towards one another, than at the be-
" ginning, yet I am willing to part with
" all, for the Lord is better than all." ' She
' quietly departed this life the 26*th* of the
' eleventh month 1710; aged feventy-three
' years and about four months; and tho'
' my lofs thereby is great, yet it is her eter-
' nal gain.'

Our

Our well efteemed friend having left us
this juft account of his convincement, and
of the reafons of his removal to, and return
from Pennfylvania to his native country
again; it remains for us to add, that by
their teftimonials from Pennfylvania, we
find they were all three of good fervice there,
the old friends being examples of meeknefs,
temperance and charity, and having lived
in love and fellowfhip with the brethren and
fifters there, were in good efteem amongft
all. And the young friend being of an
innocent and good life and converfation,
was well beloved amongft them; and further, that the father and daughter had received a gift of the miniftry, which had
been to the comfort and edification of the
churches thereaway.—We heard he vifited
New-England in particular with our friend
Hugh Roberts, about the year 1701.—Soon
after he returned from Pennfylvania, he
and his daughter vifited together feveral
meetings of friends in South and North
Wales, and were eminently favoured therein with the divine prefence.—His fufferings,
confidering his faithfulnefs and the time he
lived in, were not very many; his relations
at times diverting the ftrokes from him;
however after a long profecution by the
Vicar of the parifh for his pretended dues,
he was at laft confined to Cardiff goal in
1721, upon an excommunicatio capiendo,
but there being fome error in it, he was difcharged the following feffions, and ever after left unmolefted.

He

He was endued with a good underſtanding in things ſpiritual and temporal, diſcreet
and prudent in his ways, of an unſpotted
life and converſation, grave and ſolid in his
deportment, and careful to keep concord
and unity among friends, conſtant and un-
moveable againſt that which would divide
and rend, yet labouring to reſtore thoſe that
were beguiled thereby. In his laſt ſickneſs,
he had no ſmall conflict, but he was favoured with much patience and poſſeſſed his ſoul
therein, and bore his indiſpoſition to admiration.—At one time he ſaid, " Ever ſince I
" had the knowledge of the truth, l have en-
" deavoured to be innocent." To a relation aſking him how he did ? he anſwered,
" Weakly, but I find ſome ſtrength to bear
" my weakneſs."

A Teſtimony from the Monthly-Meeting of Philadelphia, *concerning* H A N N A H C A R-
P E N T E R.

SHE was born at Haverford Weſt in South
Wales, where having the opportunity
of ſeeing the patient, innocent and ſteady
ſufferings of friends who were impriſoned
for their religious teſtimony, together with
their good converſation in Chriſt, ſhe was
convinced of the bleſſed truth, and became
very ſerviceable to thoſe who were in bonds
there for Chriſt's ſake. She came over here
in

in the early fettling of this province, and after fome time was married to our well efteemed friend Samuel Carpenter, of this city. She received a fhare of the gofpel miniftry, which was feafoned with a lively favour of divine fweetnefs; and though not frequent in her appearances, was very acceptable. Her heart and houfe ftood open to receive and entertain the true gofpel minifters, to whom fhe was a tender nurfing mother both in ficknefs and in health; being full of warmth and love to faithful friends, a bright example of meeknefs in the church as well as in her own family; and her life and converfation being adorned with the chriftian virtues of benevolence and charity, render'd her beloved, refpected and ufeful in her ftation.

She died the 24*th* of the fifth month 1728, in the eighty-third year of her age.

The following Epiftle to parents concerning the education of children, manifefting her pious regard for the youth, and her anxiety for the increafe and profperity of the church of Chrift, is thought proper to be here annexed, viz.

" UPON the 4*th* day of the fourth month, I was drawn forth to wait on the Lord, and as I was waiting, the confideration of my dear children whom the Lord had taken to himfelf in their innocency came before me, and my foul bleffed his holy name for his

great

great love towards them and me, in that
they are gone to their reft, and fhall never
partake of thofe exercifes and forrows thefe
do that remain in the world; and then my
foul was poured forth before the Lord for
them that remain, that as they grow up in
years, they may grow in grace, and in the
knowledge of our Lord and faviour Jefus
Chrift; or elfe I would rather follow them
to their graves whilft they are young, than
that they fhould live to the difhonour of his
worthy name: And then a more general and
weighty concern came upon me for friends
children that are grown up and do not come
under the yoke nor bear the crofs. Oh! the
cry that ran through my foul, and in the
anguifh and bitternefs of my fpirit, I faid,
*Lord what will thou do with friends children
when we are gone off the ftage of this world;
will thou raife up children, and not thofe of believing parents?* And this was the word that
livingly fprung up in my foul. *They rejeƈt
my counfel and caft my law behind their backs,
and will have none of my reproofs, and tho'
my hand be ftretched forth all the day long, yet
they will not hear, but go after their own
hearts luft.* Then I faid in my heart, *Lord
are they all fo?* The anfwer was, *there are
fome that are innocent, whom I will blefs with
a bleffing from me, and they fhall fhine forth
to my praife.* And now, Oh friends! that
you may dwell and abide in the innocent
life, that fo the bleffing of the Lord you
may

may feel daily to defcend upon you. But as for you that " Reject the counfel of the Lord and caft his law behind your backs, and will have none of his reproofs," which are forrowful fayings concerning you who are the children of believing parents, you who are under the profeffion of the truth, which will do you no good, unlefs you return unto the Lord; therefore I defire you may all return unto him, whilft the day of a long-fuffering merciful God lafteth: But if you ftill reject the counfel of the Lord, the many faithful warnings you have had, how will you anfwer it in the day when he cometh, " To render unto every one according to their deeds?" And now, fomething further is with me to parents of children. Dear friends, you that have been convinced of God's unchangeable truth, and have known the work and operation of it, working out and bringing down that which was of a contrary nature to it. And Oh! that we may all abide faithful in his work, and retain our integrity to the Lord, then let our breathing cries and prayers be offered up to the Lord for our children, that he would be pleafed to look down in mercy upon them, and vifit them as he did our fouls. But as David faid, " If I regard iniquity in my heart, the Lord will not hear me;" fo I defire we may all be clear in our offerings before the Lord, that he may fmell a fweet favour from them.

Dear

Dear friends, what is here written is with
great caution, knowing that I have children
of my own, and that many honeſt parents
have bad children, which is no ſmall exerciſe; but if we keep faithful to the Lord,
and diſcharge our duty to them by precept
and example, we ſhall be clear of them in
the ſight of God: And therefore friends,
faithfulneſs is the word that runs through
me, not only for our own ſouls, but for
our children's alſo; that a generation may
grow up to his praiſe in this part of the
world, when our heads are laid in the duſt.
Great and manifold hath the love and mercy of God been towards us, the conſideration of it, many times hath deeply affected
my mind; and it was he by the ſame arm
of power that reached unto us, and brought
a concern upon us in our own native land;
and I do believe that many had as clear a
call to leave their native country, as ſome
of old had, which cauſed many days and
nights of ſore travel and exerciſe before the
Lord, and no caſe could we have, but in
giving up life and all unto him, ſaying,
" Lord do what thou wilt with us, only
let thy preſence preſerve us." And to his
praiſe we can ſay, he hath been with us ſince
we came to this country, and hath preſerved us through many and various exerciſes,
both inwardly and outwardly. And now
that which lies on our parts I deſire may be
conſidered by us all, that ſo ſuitable returns
may be made unto the Lord, by walking

in

in humility and godly fear before him ; that
fo, good patterns we may be, by keeping
our places " To the praife of him who hath
called us," for he is worthy forever more.
And friends, fomething more is with me
which I thought to omit, but find I can't
well do it, that is, concerning our children,
that we be very careful while they are
young, that we fuffer them not to wear fuch
things that truth allows not; and though it
may be faid, they are but little things and
well enough for children, but we find, that
when they are grown up, it is hard for them
to leave off, which may be, if they had not
been ufed when young, would not have
been expected when grown up: So I defire
we may all be clear in ourfelves, and keep
our children out of the fafhions and cuftoms
of this world. And Oh! that we were all
of one heart and mind in thefe and other
things, then would the work of the Lord
go on eafily, which is the fincere defire of
your friend,

HANNAH CARPENTER.

A Teſtimony from the Yearly-Meeting in Virginia, *concerning* ROBERT JORDAN.

HE was fon of Thomas and Margaret
Jordan, of Nancemond county in Virginia, born the 11th of the feventh month
1668, and carefully educated in the way of
truth

truth by his worthy parents, who lived to
fee the religion of his education become that
of his choice and practice in his mature
years, in which he was preferved to the laft,
without wavering, in great peace with the
Lord and unity of his brethren.

He was an hofpitable man, very ready to
entertain ftrangers, efpecially the Lord's
meffengers, whom he treated with great refpect and affection, honouring them for
their work's fake; being alfo charitable to
the poor, and as a man of trade and commerce, obtained a good reputation, having
declared he had never wronged any man
knowingly in all his life.

In the time of his illnefs, which continued about two weeks, he feemed very patient
and refigned to the will of God, and much
concerned for the everlafting welfare of his
children, which he expreffed in a lively
manner; and often in fervent prayer, defired they might be preferved from the
vanities and corruptions of this world, and
that they might love and fear the Lord in
their youth, faying at one time, " O Lord
preferve my flock, let them never go aftray,
nor forget thee nor one another: O my
God! hold them in thy arms that none of
them be loft, let not the enemy prevail over
them:" Being humbly thankful and bleffed
God, that he had been pleafed to fupport
him through every difpenfation of his providence to that time. He died the 3d of the
eighth

eighth month 1728, and on the 9th of the same month, after a large meeting held on the occafion, was interr'd in the family burying-ground.

A Teftimony from Gwynedd *Monthly-Meeting in* Pennfylvania, *concerning* ROWLAND ELLIS.

OUR ancient and efteemed friend Rowland Ellis, was born in the year 1650, in Merionethfhire North Wales, convinced of the truth about the twenty-fecond year of his age, fuffered feveral years imprifonment with conftancy on account of his teftimony, it being then a time of fore perfecution; the two judges who committed him with many others for refufing to take the oath of allegiance and fupremacy, declared openly at the affizes, " That in cafe they refufed a fecond time to take it, they fhould be proceeded againft as traitors, the men hanged and quartered, and the women burned." In 1686 he came over into Pennfylvania to prepare for a fettlement for his wife and family, with whom he return'd in 1697. He was endued with a gift in the miniftry, and tho' not very frequent in appearance therein, his fervice was acceptable and to edification; being of found judgment, ready and willing to affift his neighbours and friends in all cafes civil or religious when defired.

defired. He was zealous for fupporting our
chriftian difcipline, and exemplary in con-
ducting himfelf agreeable therewith, fometimes faying " If the hedge of difcipline
was not kept up, the labour of the hufband-
man would foon be laid wafte." He was
careful in educating his children religioufly,
by timely endeavouring to inculcate in them
the principles of piety and virtue; a practice
of his tending thereto, was, having meetings frequently in his family, which he long
continued. In the laft monthly-meeting he
attended he was taken unwell, but afterwards faid to divers friends prefent, " I
am glad I was here to day, for I had a lively
meeting, and though I now feel much weaknefs and the infirmities attending my advanced age, yet I can fay, truth is as dear
and as fweet as ever." He alfo faid, " Sa-
" tan fometimes lies in wait like a roaring
" lion to devour me, but I find he is chain-
" ed by a fecret hand which limits his pow-
" er, fo that he cannot harm me." His indifpofition continued a few days, which
he bore with chriftian patience, expreffing
" His fenfe of his near arrival at the haven of reft and quiet, where none could
make him afraid." He expired at the houfe
of his fon-in-law John Evans, in the eighti-
eth year of his age, and was interr'd in
friends burying-ground at Plymouth, (to
which particular meeting he belonged) in the
feventh month 1729. Concerning whom we
truft it may be faid, *he refts, enjoying the re-*
ward of the righteous, and his works do follow.
A Teftimony

A Teſtimony from Newark *Monthly-Meeting in* New Caſtle *county on* Delaware, *concerning* Moses Mendenhall.

HE was born at Concord in Cheſter coun- ty Pennſylvania, about 1693, being the ſon of Benjamin Mendenhall, an early ſettler in that place; in his youth he was religiouſly inclined, loving the converſation of ſuch, and chooſing places of retirement to wait upon God. He married about the year 1719, and ſoon after ſettled at Kennet, where he continued his habitation the re- mainder of his life. As he grew in years he grew in religious experience, and in 1724 appeared in the miniſtry; firſt in a few words, but continuing faithful, he increaſ- ed in his gift, and in time had a ſeaſonable refreſhing teſtimony, which often affected the minds of the hearers. He viſited the meetings in Maryland, New-Jerſey, and ſometimes thoſe near home; being alſo rightly gifted for the diſcipline, and ſervice- able therein. He had a clear diſcerning of a ſpirit of undue liberty that ſeemed at one time to prevail, which afterwards manifeſt- ed itſelf to the exerciſe of the faithful.

Being ſenſible in his laſt ſickneſs that his end was near, he ſignified "He was thank- ful to the Lord, that he was like to be ta- ken from the troubles of this world;" ex- horting friends to faithfulneſs; and died in a
refigned

refigned frame, in the ninth month 1731, aged about thirty-eight, and a minifter about 7 years, and was interr'd in Kennet burying-ground.

***

A Teftimony from Duck-Creek *Monthly-Meeting in* Kent *county on* Delaware, *concerning* JOSEPH BOOTH.

HE was born at or near Scituate in New-England, and educated in the religion of the independants; leaving his native country when a young man, he came and fettled early on Mufpillion in Suffex county upon Delaware, where he filled the ftation of a magiftrate many years, and was alfo chofen a member of the houfe of affembly, difcharging the feveral trufts repofed in him, with reputation.

In the year 1699, he was convinced by the miniftry of Thomas Story, who left this teftimony refpecting him, " That he was the moft fober and knowing perfon in thofe parts." As he gave up faithfully to the manifeftation of truth, it fo operated upon him, as to bring the creaturely part into fubjection, tho' much in the way of the crofs, and the more fo, by reafon of the ftation and character he fupported in the world; but thro' continued obedience, he witneffed love fo to prevail in his heart, as to conftrain him, livingly to declare to others

what

what the Lord had done for him. Being rightly called and anointed for the work, his appearances were folemn and awful, miniftring in the power of truth. He was a nurfing father in the church, conftant in attending religious meetings, and exemplary in humbly waiting therein; having likewife been inftrumental in fettling the meeting at Murtherkiln where he belonged, as alfo that at Cold-Spring; and before any meeting was held at the latter, he frequently vifited the few families of friends adjacent thereto, and was in general good efteem amongft men. He died about the year 1732.

A Teftimony from Wrights-Town *Monthly-Meeting in* Bucks *county* Pennfylvania, *concerning* ANN PARSON.

SHE appeared in the miniftry in her youthful days, and continuing faithful, fhe travelled on that account, feveral times through New-England, the Jerfeys, Pennfylvania, Maryland and Virginia in America, and through England, Ireland, Scotland and Wales in Europe; her miniftry being favoury and to edification. She was a good example, of an inoffenfive life, patient in affliction, and died in good unity with the church,

In

In her laſt illneſs, ſhe ſaid to her brother Abraham Chapman, " I have travelled a " pretty deal in my time, and, according " to my ability, have laboured in the love " of God (in the ſervice of truth, and good- " will to all men) which ſprings in my bo- " ſom now as freſh as ever; bleſſed be his " name. And I deſire thee (if I go) by a " few lines, to remember my kind love to " friends, deſiring they may ſtand in the " counſel of God; for I have often rejoiced " and been glad, to ſee friends ſtand in his " counſel and keep their places in the truth; " and on the contrary, it has often wound- " ed my ſpirit, to ſee thoſe that have made " a profeſſion of the truth, (and ſome of " them children of good parents) take un- " due liberty, taking pleaſure in vanity " and folly, and neglecting that which " would be to their everlaſting peace. It is " my advice to friends, that they ſtand in " the counſel of God, which will be to them " as a mighty rock in a weary land, and " enable them to wade through the various " exerciſes and troubles which may fall to " their ſhare to meet with in this trouble- " ſome world. I have found it by experi- " ence to be a ſure help in every needful " and difficult time, when exerciſes ſeemed " to ſurround me on every hand like the " billows of the main, then I found, to " ſtand in the counſel of God, was the on- " ly place of refuge that I could retire unto, " where I found ſafety, and was often re-

" freſhed,

" frefhed, ftrengthened and comforted by
" the influence of the love of God in me;
" and I would counfel and advife, that all
" friends keep clofe to meetings, and pa-
" tiently wait to feel their ftrength renewed
" in God. And as it has been the defire
" and labour of my fpirit, that friends
" fhould keep up their meetings in good
" order, and in the wifdom of truth; fo I
" recommend it as my advice and counfel
" to friends, to be careful to keep to meet-
" ings, and patiently wait to feel the over-
" fhadowing power of truth, to ftrengthen
" and renew their hope in God, which
" brings down and abafes every thing that
" would exalt itfelf above the peaceable
" government of truth." After having lain
fometime in great ftillnefs, fhe, in fervent
prayer, befought the Lord, " To carry on
" the work he had begun, fo that many
" might flock unto his church, as doves
" unto the windows; and that fin and ini-
" quity might ceafe, and righteoufnefs and
" truth cover the earth, as the waters cover
" the fea;" fervently befeeching the Lord,
" To blefs his people and her near relations,
" and that her companion might be favor-
" ed with the vifitation of divine love, and
" know his laft days to be his beft days;
" and that he might find admittance into
" reft and peace, when time to him in this
" life fhould be no more," with many more
of the like expreflions, at fundry times during her illnefs.

H . She

She died the *9th* of the tenth month 1732, in the fifty-feventh year of her age, having been a minifter 33 years.

A Teftimony from Nottingham *Monthly-Meeting in* Pennfylvania, *concerning* JOSEPH ELGAR.

HE was born (as we are informed) at Folkftone in Kent, Old England, the 30*th* of the fourth month 1690, of believing parents; and came into America about the year 1720, living fome time near Philadelphia, and in 1728, removed within the limits of Eaft Nottingham particular meeting. After his coming to this country, he was called to the work of the miniftry, wherein he was not forward, yet his appearances being lively and edifying, friends had near unity therewith. A good example in attending meetings, a faithful labourer therein, and careful in keeping to the hour appointed. He was induftrious in outward affairs, tho' cheerfully given up to anfwer the requirings of truth; vifiting the meetings of friends in Pennfylvania, as alfo in New-Jerfey and Maryland generally. He was gifted in difcipline, and likewife qualified for the fervice of vifiting families, wherein he was engaged the laft time he was abfent from home, within the limits of Bufh-River and Deer-Creek particular meetings;

ings; in his return from whence, he told a friend, " There was an unufual weight " over his fpirit, and a cloud that he could " not fee beyond, which made him think " his days work was nearly over." The night he return'd home, he was affected with ficknefs and much pain, which continued feveral days, bearing the fame with exemplary patience. Afterwards growing weaker but remaining fenfible, he often expreffed, " He had done with the world, " and was willing to leave it, for he had " been faithful to what was made known to " him, fince he gave up to the requirings " of truth."

Continuing in a fweet compofure of mind, he departed on the 19*th* of the eleventh month 1733-4, in the forty-fourth year of his age, a minifter about 12 years. His remains were interr'd in friends buryingground at Eaft-Nottingham; on which folemn occafion, our friend Mungo Bewley of Ireland, who was then on a religious vifit in America, exercifed his gift to the comfort of many friends.

A Teftimony from the Yearly-Meeting of friends in Virginia, *concerning* JOSEPH JORDAN.

HE was born in Nancemond county in Virginia, in the year 1695, being the third fon of Robert Jordan, as well as one

of

of the third generation who have walked in
the truth. He was of a fprightly genius,
affable difpofition, and even temper, which,
as he grew to manhood, gave him eafy accefs to company, efteemed the better fort.
A vifitation of divine love being extended
to him about the twenty-fecond year of his
age, he like Zaccheus, made hafte, and with
joy embraced, both the meffage and the
meffenger of falvation: And being endued
with a gift in the miniftry, acquitted himfelf " As a workman that need not be
afhamed," and had great place in the minds
of men. Altho' he had not much fchool
literature, yet he might be faid to have had
the tongue of the learned, being both cor-
rect and concife in fpeaking the word in feafon, infomuch that divers have confeffed to
the truth and embraced the doctrine he
preached. Being patient in tribulation, he
was favour'd with that hope which affords
content and folace of mind. After labouring in the gofpel in his own country and
the adjacent provinces, he vifited moft parts
of England, Ireland, and divers parts of
Holland; being abfent on this fervice above
three years, he returned with peace, and
found his prefence neceffary at home; for
his father being deceafed, and his brother
Robert then abfent, the care of the family
devolved upon him, which truft he difcharged with judgment, being a good œcono-
mift, kind neighbour and fteady friend.
He

He often intimated that he should not continue long, and was therefore concern'd to ufe diligence. Not long before his deceafe, he vifited friends in Virginia and North-Carolina, edifying them with his gift; and in the beginning of the month in which he died, (tho' very weak in body) attended their quarterly meeting, fignifying at his return, his great fatisfaction therein, believing it would be the laft meeting of the kind he fhould ever be at, and accordingly he never afterwards went from home, except to a week-day meeting in the neighbourhood.

On the morning of the day of his diffolution, he uttered many favoury expreffions, faying to fome young minifters, " Mind " your gifts and the Lord will blefs you, " and you will be a bleffing to the church. " Be humble and obedient; obedience brings " fweet peace. I have a great defire there " might be a right miniftry continued in " the church, for there are many not ftrict- " ly of this fold, who in due time the Lord " will bring in: And as you come to have " an experience of the work of truth in " your own hearts, you will be able to con- " fute them who perfuade themfelves there " is no living without fin in this world. I " am not in a condition to fpeak much, " neither is it, I hope, very needful ; as you " are thus taught of the Lord, you will " have caufe to rejoice in him on whom you " have believed."

Thus

Thus having happily compleated his day's work, he laid down his head in much refignation and peace with the Lord, the 26th of the ninth month 1735, aged forty years, a minifter about 17.

A Teftimony from the Monthly-Meeting of Philadelphia, concerning RICHARD TOWNSEND.

HE was a meek and humble man, fincerely concerned for the promotion of piety and virtue; his miniftry being found, living, and tending to edification, was well accepted. He vifited friends in the fervice of truth in Great Britain, continued faithful to the end of his days, and departed this life about the 30th of the third month 1737.

A Teftimony from Newark Monthly-Meeting in New Caftle county on Delaware, concerning CHRISTOPHER WILSON.

HE was born in Yorkfhire Old England, of parents who were members of the church of England. In his youth he was inclined to vanity, but his mind being reached thro' the vifitation of divine grace. When he grew up, he joined in fellowfhip with friends; and came to America in 1712, being

being well recommended by certificate, tho'
then a servant. About 1728 he appeared in
the ministry, first in a few words, but growing therein, his appearances were seasonable
and savoury, and attended with a degree of
that life that " Makes glad the heritage of
God;" being likewise serviceable in the discipline of the church according to ability.

He began the world with little, but being
industrious in the creation, and concern'd
for truth's prosperity, the Lord blessed his
labours, so that he lived comfortably and
maintained his family reputably, supporting the character of an honest peaceable
man, and was often instrumental in restor-
ing peace amongst others. In his last sickness, being asked by a friend " How it was
with him?" He answered, " If the messen-
ger of death comes, I see nothing in my
way." Keeping mostly still and quiet, he,
in a resigned, composed frame of mind,
finished his course the 11*th* of the seventh
month 1740, in the fiftieth year of his age,
a minister about 12 years, and was interr'd
in Center burying-ground.

A Testimony from the Monthly-Meeting of Philadelphia, *concerning* THOMAS CHALKLEY.

HE was a member of our monthly-meeting above forty years, so that some of
us had opportunities of being intimately acquainted

quainted with him, and of knowing his
fidelity and diligence in promoting the caufe
of truth, and the edification of the church
of Chrift; this having been the principal
engagement and concern of his mind, and
which he preferred to any other confideration; as will evidently appear to thofe, who,
with an honeft and unprejudiced intention,
perufe his journal of his life and travels.

By which it will appear, that he was, in
the early part of his life, fenfibly affected
with the vifitation of divine life and grace,
and, by adhering thereunto, was preferved
from the vanities and follies, which often
divert and alienate the minds of youth from
the due remembrance and awful regard of
their creator; fo that he was enabled to bear
a teftimony of chriftian patience and felf-
denial in his youthful days, and, by keeping under that exercife, as he advanced in
years, attained to further knowledge and
experience in the work of religion, in which
he had a fight of the neceffity of keeping in
a ftate of humility, and of bearing the crofs
of Chrift, which mortified him to the world;
fo that the lofs many fuftain by the anxious
purfuit of the lawful things thereof appearing to him, he was concerned to avoid it, and
in obedience to the precept of Chrift, to *feek
firft the kingdom of God, and his righteoufnefs,*
having faith in his promife, *that all thefe
things* (neceffary for him) *fhould be added.*

Thus the love of God influencing his
mind, and opening his underftanding, he
became

became concerned for the general good of
mankind, and received a gift of the miniftry of the gofpel of Chrift, before he had
attained the age of twenty-one years; in
the public exercife of which, he foon after
travelled thro' many parts of England, and
into Scotland, and the next year, being 1697,
he came to vifit friends in this and the adjacent provinces of America, where his miniftry and converfation were to the comfort
and edification of the faithful, (as fome of
us can with fatisfaction declare, from our
knowledge and remembrance of him at that
time) and the near fellowfhip and union he
then had with friends here (we believe) contributed to his more fpeedy determination
of fettling among us, which he afterwards
thought it his duty to do, tho' the leaving
his parents and relations (as he afterwards
exprefled) was no fmall crofs to him, being
of a dutiful and affectionate difpofition.

After fixing his refidence among us, he
perfever'd in his concern and labour for the
edification of the churches, and gathering
people to faith and dependance on the inward teachings of Chrift, and for that purpofe only he travelled many long journies
and voyages through the feveral Englifh
colonies on this continent, and moft of the
iflands in the Weft-Indies, and in Europe,
through England, Wales, Scotland, Ireland,
Holland, Frizeland, and feveral parts of
Germany, and the adjacent northern king-
doms; and in many of thefe places his miniftry

niftry and religious labours were bleffed
with the defired fuccefs, of which there are
yet fome witneffes living, and others, who
were convinced of the principles of truth
by his means, became ferviceable members
of the church, and continued therein to the
end of their lives.

But as the wife king Solomon formerly
obferved, that *one event cometh to the righteous, and to the wicked,* fo it happened to this
good man, who met with various loffes and
difappointments in his temporal eftate; after which, the circumftances of his affairs
engaged him to undertake fome bufinefs, in
the management of which he was obliged
to crofs the feas frequently: This, however,
did not abate his zeal and religious care to
make ufe of all opportunities of vifiting the
meetings of friends when among them, and
of calling, at other times, to fuch who
might be accounted as *the outcaft of Ifrael,
and the difperfed of Judah, or as fheep not yet
of the fold of Chrift;* and his fervices of that
kind are worthy to be commemorated,
having been often productive of good effects.

His patience was remarkable in difappointments and afflictions, of which he had
a large fhare; and his meeknefs, humility
and circumfpection, in the general courfe
of his life and converfation, were confpicuous and exemplary; and as he frequently
exhorted and admonifhed others to the obfervation and practice of the many excellent
precepts and rules of Chrift, our Lord and
lawgiver,

lawgiver, and more especially those expressed in his sermon on the mount (which con-
tains the sum of our moral and religious
duties) so he manifested himself to be one
of that number, whom Christ compared to
the wife builder, who laid a sure foundation; so that his building stood unshaken by
the various floods and winds of tribulations
and temptations he met with, both from
within and without.

He was a lover of unity amongst brethren, and careful to promote and maintain
it, shewing the example of a meek, courteous, and loving deportment, not only to
friends, but to all others, with whom he
had conversation or dealings; so that it may
be truly said, that *few have lived so universal-
ly beloved and respected among us*: And it
was manifest this did not proceed from a
desire of being popular, or to be seen of
man: For his love and regard to peace did
not divert him from the discharge of his
duty in a faithful testimony to those that
professed the truth, that they ought to be
careful to maintain good works; and he
was often concern'd zealously to incite and
press friends to the exercise of the good order and discipline established in the wisdom
of truth, by admonishing, warning, and
timely treating with such as fell short of
their duty therein, and by testifying against
those who, after loving and brotherly care
and endeavours, could not be brought to
the

the fenfe and practice of their duty; and thereby he fometimes fhar'd the ill-will and refentment of fuch perfons.

The feveral Effays he wrote on religious fubjects at fea, are further proofs that his mind was principally engaged in the great bufinefs and concern of religion; and as he continued under the fame engagement to the end, we are fully perfuaded the words with which he concluded his laft public teftimony on the ifland of Tortola, may be truly and properly applied to him, *that he had fought a good fight, and had kept the faith, and* we doubt not, *he now enjoys a crown of righteoufnefs.*

Much more might be truly faid of his integrity, faithfulnefs and worth, but we do not think it neceffary; our chief intention being to exprefs our refpectful remembrance of him, and our unity with his labours and fervices; and we are fincerely defirous, that the glory of every good and perfect work may be attributed to that divine power alone, which can qualify others to fupply the places of thofe faithful minifters and fervants of Chrift, who have been of late years removed from among us, and are of that number, of whom it is written, *bleffed are the dead, which die in the Lord, from henceforth, yea, faith the fpirit, that they may reft from their labours, and their works do follow them.*

He departed this life on the ifland of Tortola (where he was engaged on a religious vifit) the 4th day of the ninth month 1741, aged upwards of fixty-fix years.

A Teftimony

A Teſtimony from the Monthly-Meeting of Philadelphia, *concerning* ESTHER CLARE.

SHE was a miniſter well qualified for the publication of the doctrine of the goſpel, and viſited friends in Great-Britain and Ireland in the ſervice of truth. In the latter part of her life, when not prevented by bodily infirmities, we had the benefit of her labours much in this city; her teſtimony being frequently attended with demonſtration of divine help, was well accepted and of good ſervice. She departed this life the 3*d* of the eighth month 1742, in the ſixty-eighth year of her age, in unity and good eſteem among friends.

A Teſtimony from the Monthly-Meeting of Philadelphia, *concerning* ROBERT JORDAN.

IT appears, he was born in the county of Nancemond in Virginia, the 27*th* of the tenth month 1693, of parents in good eſteem among friends, and that about the year 1718 he received a gift in the miniſtry, as did his brother Joſeph about the ſame time; and to their firſt appearance in that weighty work the labours of Lydia Lancaſter and her companion then on a religious viſit from Great-Britain, were, under divine help, made inſtrumental,

Of

Of his firſt travels in the ſervice of truth, the following is an abſtract from an account committed to writing by himſelf.

‘ I early found a concern on my mind
‘ to viſit friends in Maryland, which I did
‘ on both ſides of the bay (Cheaſapeak) in
‘ fear and trembling, being young and
‘ weak, and the work very exerciſing by
‘ reaſon of an obvious declenſion, which
‘ occaſioned me much exerciſe in ſpeaking
‘ and writing againſt the ſpirit of liberty,
‘ ſuperfluity, and conformity to the world,
‘ for a teſtimony againſt which, in many
‘ particulars, ancient friends ſuffered much;
‘ but now, with many is the offence of that
‘ croſs ceaſed, and friend’s ſufferings tram-
‘ pled upon, to the great grief of my ſpirit,
‘ reſpecting tythes, apparel &c. And as the
‘ Lord hath been pleaſed to commit a part of
‘ the miniſtry to me, and of that part which is
‘ more neceſſary than deſirable, in this age
‘ of the church, he hath been gracioufly
‘ pleaſed hitherto to furniſh with a ſuitable
‘ ability for his honour, and my faithful
‘ diſcharge of duty; for, as before my ap-
‘ pearance I was long under the concern,
‘ being fully convinced it was required of
‘ me, but giving way to reaſonings, the
‘ ſuggeſtions and buffetings of Satan, I was
‘ likely to loſe my condition, had not the
‘ Lord been very gracious, who knew that
‘ I did not hold back obſtinately, but thro’
‘ human weakneſs, and contempt of my-
‘ ſelf for ſuch a weighty ſervice; ſo in a
‘ deep

' deep travail of foul once in a meeting,
' breathing for ftrength to bring forth, I
' defired, that the Lord would commit the
' hardeft part of the work to my charge,
' which I think was granted, and a hard
' travail I had in my firft appearance; but
' it fared otherwife with my brother,
' whom I prefer, he was not difobedient to
' the heavenly vifion, fubmitting fpeedily
' to the call, 'and has been very profperous
' hitherto; may the Lord preferve us ftea-
' dy and faithful to the end.

  ' After this, we travelled together in
' Maryland, vifiting friends on each fide of
' the bay, and at the yearly-meeting near
' Choptank, having meetings alfo in the
' way on our return, and were frequently
' employed, and zealoufly concerned in the
' Lord's work; bleffed be his name who
' hath called us out of darknefs, and with
' the day fpring from on high vifited our
' fouls, accounting us worthy of this high
' vocation, even to hold forth the glory of
' this gofpel day, giving encouragement and
' enlargement of heart in the myfteries and
' doctrines of his kingdom, fo that in the
' ability of divine faith, we frequently
' travelled about, both in Virginia and
' Carolina, while young; but as there is a
' diverfity of gifts, fo there is of operation,
' according to the good pleafure of our great
' benefactor, and the emergency of times
' and occafions; fo let not us of the mini-
' ftry, imitate one another in this refpect,
                                    ' but

' but be careful, dear friends, to keep to our
' true guide, the holy fpirit, for youth is
' warm, zealous, and without feafonable
' caution and watchfulnefs, apt to exceed
' ability and experience, and fo may be over-
' ftrained, and fuftain lofs and injury.'

In the year 1722, he performed a religious
vifit as far as New-England, which employed him about ten months, and on his return
home, he was fued in the beginning of the
following year for priefts wages, and for his
refufal to comply with the demand, he offered to the magiftrates in writing, fundry
confiderations, which being taken amifs,
he was, after fome time, indicted by the
grand jury, and fummoned before the governor and council; in this time of trial
(he fays) ' Some forfook me as being afham-
' ed of my teftimony, and of my fufferings
' for it; at my firft appearance the fierce-
' nefs of the dragon was felt, his dark pow-
' er feeming to be great and terrible, as
' though he would have fwallowed me up
' quick, and truth's adverfaries feemed to
' rejoice, for I was made to ftand like a fool
' for them to glory over me; however my
' mind being compofed, and ftayed in ftill-
' nefs on the Lord, with earneft breathings
' for divine aid in this his caufe, for which
' and myfelf, I found it fafeft to fay little
' at that time, being greatly defirous that I
' might not give way one jot from my tef-
' timony, through fear even of death itfelf,
' for I thought I felt the bitternefs of it ftrike
' at my natural life. 'On

‘ On the day when final judgment on the
‘ cafe was to be given, I was brought before
‘ them the third time, and they demanded
‘ what I had further to fay before fentence
‘ was paffed; I then defired liberty to make
‘ my defence, and to give my fenfe on the
‘ contents of my paper, the commiffary or
‘ chief prieft having perverted my meaning,
‘ which requeft the governor feemed dif-
‘ pofed to allow, but it was afterwards de-
‘ nied, as I apprehend, through the influ-
‘ ence of the prieft, howbeit I told them I
‘ remembred to have read a provifo of an
‘ act of parliament, that no man fhould be
‘ punifhed for any offence againft the act,
‘ unlefs he was profecuted within three
‘ months after the fact, but this, faid I,
‘ was about feven months after; but fome
‘ of the court refolving on feverity to in-
‘ duce me to fubmit, they proceeded to give
‘ fentence of a years imprifonment, or bonds
‘ with fecurity for good behaviour &c. when
‘ with a compofed mind and an audible
‘ voice, I faid, *this is an hard fentence and I*
‘ *pray God to forgive mine adverfaries,* which
‘ affected divers of the byftanders with tears,
‘ and one in particular, a judge, and man
‘ of note, was much affected, made him-
‘ felf acquainted, and converfed with me
‘ more than once, appears to be a tender
‘ man, and well convinced, having fince
‘ gladly received meetings into his houfe,
‘ and as he has told me, laid down his
‘ commiffion.——

I   ‘Being

' Being committed to prison, I was first
' placed in the debtors apartment, but in
' a few days was removed into the common
' side, where condemned persons are kept,
' and for sometime had not the privilege of
' seeing any body, except a negro who once
' a day brought water to the prisoners; this
' place was so dark, that I could not see to
' read even at noon, without creeping to
' small holes in the door; being also very
' noisome, the infectious air brought on me
' the flux, that, had not the Lord been
' pleased to have sustained me by his invi-
' sible hand, I had there lost my life; the
' governor was made acquainted with my
' condition, and I believe used his endea-
' vours for my liberty: The commissary vi-
' sited me more than once under a shew of
' friendship, but with a view to ensnare me,
' and I was very weary of him. I wrote
' again to the governor, to acquaint him of
' my situation; so after a confinement of
' three weeks, I was discharged, without
' any acknowledgment or compliance, and
' this brought me into an acquaintance,
' and ready admittance to the governor,
' who said I was a meek man &c.—Thus I
' returned home with praise and thanksgiv-
' ing in my heart to the Lord, who had
' caused his truth to triumph over the strong
' efforts of man and the powers of the earth.'

In the year 1725, accompanied by Thomas Pleasants, he again visited friends in
Maryland, and the yearly-meeting near

Choptank,

Choptank. My concern here (he fays) 'Was
' principally to labour for the reftoration of
' wholefome difcipline, the neglect whereof
' I conceive has been a great caufe of the
' diforder and undue liberty prevailing
' among the profeffors of truth there, and
' when the fervice of this meeting was over,
' we vifited the meetings on the weftern
' fhore, and returned home, having left an
' example of that ufeful and neceffary prac-
' tice of vifiting families, joining friends
' therein for fometime; we are, thanks be
' to God, come and coming into the fame
' in Virginia, which, with fome affiftance,
' I have pretty generally performed through
' our monthly-meeting, and never, I think,
' was more fenfible of the company and
' ability of truth in any fervice, according
' to the dignity of it.'

A malicious perfon getting into his pof-
feffion, the judgment obtained againft him
for the demand of tythes before mentioned,
had feven of his cattle feized and appraifed,
but deferred taking them away until about
two years after, when he procured a new
action againft him, alledging, but not proving, that Robert had converted at leaft a
part of them to his own ufe, and fo managed the matter in his abfence, as to make
the debt amount to twenty-pounds, tho' the
demand was but eight-pounds, and ferving
the execution on his body, he was again
committed to prifon in the twelfth month
1727, where being confined fifteen weeks,

he

he was at length difcharged, without any
perfon paying any thing for him, which he
would not fuffer.

Soon after he was brought under a trial,
with others of his friends, by the operati-
in of a militia-law, whereupon they addreffed governor Gooch on his arrival, reprefent-
ing to him their fufferings by fpoil of goods
and imprifonment, which, with the friends
who attended on the occafion, he received
with kindnefs.

' Having this year (he remarks) fuffered
' perfecution in body and eftate, as a pre-
' parative to a greater affliction, (all which
' doth and will work for good) my dear af-
' fectionate wife was called away.

The next year 1728, he embark'd for
Great-Britain, with our friend Samuel Bow-
nas, who had accomplifhed his journeys on
this continent in the fervice of the gofpel;
and after performing a religious vifit to the
meetings of friends in England, Scotland,
Wales and Ireland, he proceeded to Barbados, and arrived from thence in this city
in 1730, then went to Virginia, and in the
fame year performed a vifit as far eaftward
as Rhode-Ifland, accompanied by his intimate friend Caleb Raper of Burlington.

The following year intermarrying with
Mary the widow of Richard Hill, he became
a member of our monthly-meeting, and
after a vifit to the meetings of friends in
Maryland and Virginia, he embark'd on a
fecond vifit to Great-Britain, from whence
he

he returned in the fummer of 1734, between
which time and the year 1738, he performed another vifit eaftward, and three to the
fouthern provinces, befides one to South-Carolina and Georgia, and from thence proceeded to Rhode-Ifland, and to Bofton, and in
1740 he went on a fecond vifit to Barbados,
and in the fucceeding year, accompanied by
Caleb Raper, he accomplifhed his laft vifit
eaftward as far as Bofton.

Hereby we may obferve his unwearied application and exercife, to fulfill the miniftry
which he had received of the Lord. He was
a member of this meeting above ten years,
and tho' his time was much employed in
his religious duties abroad, he did not omit
the adjacent meetings, being induftrious
and laborious for the general welfare and
profperity of the churches; for the promotion whereof he was, through the divine
anointing, eminently qualified.

His miniftry being convincing and confolatory, his delivery graceful but unaffected; in prayer he was folemn and reverent;
he delighted in meditation, recommending
by example, religious retirement in his
familiar vifits among his friends; in his fentiments he was generous and charitable, yet
a firm oppofer of obftinate libertines in
principles or practice, demonftrating his
love to the caufe of Religion and righteoufnefs above all other confiderations, being
careful to adorn the doctrine of the gofpel,
by a life of piety and benevolence, and we

                                        have

have ground to hope and believe he was prepared for the fudden fummons from his pilgrimage here, which was on the fifth day of the eighth month O. S. 1742, when being at the houfe of one of his moſt intimate friends on the third day of the week in the morning, waiting for the hour of meeting, he was feized with a fit of the apoplexy, which very foon deprived him of fpeech, and he died about midnight following, in the forty-ninth year of his age, being a miniſter about 24 years; his burial on the *7th* of the fame month was attended by a great number of his fellow-citizens, to our meeting-houfe in High-ſtreet, and thence to the grave-yard.

A Teſtimony from Abington *Monthly-Meeting in* Pennfylvania, *concerning* JOHN CADWALADER.

HE was convinced of the principle of truth when young, and underwent many deep baptizing feaſons, by which, it is believed, he was in a good degree made an overcomer. He travelled much in the exercife of his gift in the miniſtry, having vifited his brethren in truth's ſervice, in moſt or all parts of this continent where friends then refided; and croſſed the ſeas twice to Europe on the fame account, and once to the iſland of Barbados. In which concern he was always careful to have the concurrence

concurrence of his brethren, and good accounts and credentials of his acceptable fervice were upon all thofe occafions communicated to this monthly-meeting. He was alfo ferviceable amongft us in meetings of difcipline. His laft vifit was to the ifland of Tortola, in company with our worthy friend John Eftaugh. He was taken unwell on his paffage thither, yet when he landed, proceeded in the fervice he went upon, to the fatisfaction of friends there, as appears from accounts fent hither by a friend of that ifland. But his diftemper increafing upon him, he departed this life in peace on faid ifland, the 26th of the ninth month 1742, aged near fixty-fix years.

A Teftimony from Haddonfield *Monthly-Meeting in* New-Jerfey, *concerning* JOHN ESTAUGH.

THE remembrance of our dear deceafed friend John Eftaugh, remains as a good favour on many of our minds. He was born in Keldevon in Effex in Great-Britain, on the 23d of the fecond month 1676. In the year 1700, he came over to America on a religious vifit, which he performed to the great fatisfaction of friends; after which, he fettled at Haddonfield, in the county of Gloucefter, and weftern divifion of New-Jerfey. He has been heard to fay, that when he firft fettled in our parts, he was nearly

nearly united to a folid remnant of friends
that then belonged to Newtown-meeting,
and that he had been careful to feel the drawings of the father's love in vifiting neighbouring meetings, in many of which, he
was favoured to minifter fuitably to the
ftates and conditions of thofe that heard
him; he being as a fcribe well inftructed,
who brought forth out of the heavenly treafury, things both new and old.—Since his
firft fettlement among us, he vifited friends
in England, Ireland, New-England and
fome of the Weft-India-Iflands, feveral times.
He was an humble minded exemplary friend,
folid and grave in his deportment, well becoming a minifter of Chrift, zealous for preferving good order in the church, and maintaining love and unity, that badge of true
difciplefhip, remarkably careful in his converfation among men, his words being few
and favoury. The laft vifit which he made
was to the ifland of Tortola, where after
his fervice was over, he was taken fick,
and departed this life: And we doubt not but
that he is in the fruition of that glory and
happinefs which will never have an end.

An Abftract

An Abſtract from Elizabeth Eſtaugh's *Teſtimony, concerning her beloved husband* JOHN
ESTAUGH *deceaſed, prefixed to a treatiſe
of his, entitled* " A call to the unfaithful
profeſſors of truth."

SINCE it pleaſed divine providence ſo
highly to favour me, with being the
near companion of this dear worthy, I cannot be altogether ſilent, but muſt give ſome
ſmall account of the early working of truth
in him. He was born of religious parents, but
grew uneaſy with the religious profeſſions
of both father and mother who were of different perſuaſions, and being a ſeeker, fell
in with the baptiſts, and liked them ſo well
he was near joining them. But a neighbour
who was a friend, being dead, he was in-
vited to the burial, where that worthy miniſter of the goſpel, Francis Stamper of
London, being led to ſpeak with life and
power directly to his ſtate, it made ſuch
deep impreſſions on his tender mind, that
put him upon ſearch into the principles of
friends, and being fully ſatisfied, joined with
them in the ſeventeenth year of his age.

About the eighteenth year of his age, he
came forth in the miniſtry, and being faithful he grew in his gift, ſo that in ſome time
he travelled to viſit friends in the north of
England, and Scotland, and in the year 1700
came over on a viſit to friends in America.
We were married on the firſt day of the tenth
month

month 1702, and fettled at Haddonfield in
New-Jerfey. In the fore part of his time he
travelled pretty much; but in the latter part
he was prevented therefrom by an infirmity
of body; and his good mafter, who requires
no impoffibilities of his fervants, favoured
him with being eafy at home; where thro'
mercy, we lived very comfortably; few, if
any, in a married ftate, ever lived in fweet-
er harmony than we did. He was a pattern
of moderation in all things; not lifted up
with any enjoyments, nor caft down at difappointments; a man endowed with many
good gifts, which rendered him very agreeable to his friends, and much more to me,
his wife.

After fome years of indifpofition, (as before is obferved) it pleafed the Lord to reftore him to a ftate of health; and foon after he had a concern to vifit friends at Tortola. This brought on him a deep exercife,
but when he was confirmed it was really required of him, he gave up to it; and was
then weaned from home, and the company
there which ufed to be fo pleafant to him.
He firft wrote to friends on that ifland; but
finding that would not excufe him, he durft
no longer delay; fo, on the 13th of the
eighth month 1742, we parted in the
aboundings of love and affection. And now,
the moft acceptable account I can give of
his fervice in Tortola, is extracted from two
letters which I received from a friend of that
place, directed to me, and to the following
effect, viz.   ‘ On

' On the eighth of the ninth month 1742,
' he arrived at the houfe of John Pickering
' with his companion John Cadwalader,
' where they were received with much love
' and great joy, being made to rejoice together
' in the tender mercies and love of God,
' which was greatly manifefted that day,
' to the honour and praife of his great name,
' and alfo to the comforting of his poor peo-
' ple. The teftimonies of thefe fervants of
' the Lord were with life and power, and
' were as clouds fill'd with rain upon a thir-
' fty land.——

' But to be more particular concerning
' thy dear hufband, whofe memory is dear
' and precious to me, and many more whofe
' hearts were open to receive the glad-ti-
' dings which he brought. His godly life
' and converfation fpoke him to be a true
' follower of the the Lamb, and minifter of
' Jefus Chrift, whom he freely preached,
' and by the effectual power of whofe di-
' vine love, was he called forth to our af-
' fiftance, for which we blefs, praife and
' magnify the God of all our mercies: And
' as a faithful meffenger, with much love,
' in a tender frame of fpirit, would he in-
' vite all to the fountain which had healed
' him. O! the deep humility that appear-
' ed in him in the time of his public tefti-
' mony; and when in private converfation
' with his near and dear friends, as he of-
' ten faid we were to him, how cheerful and
' pleafant would he be, in that bleffed freedom

' dom wherein Chrift had made him free.
' Innocent, harmlefs, of a cheerful coun-
' tenance, yet not without a chriftian gra-
' vity well becoming the doctrine he preach-
' ed. He was valiant for the truth to the
' laft, and tho' he is gone to his grave, his
' memory is fweet and precious.

' He had his health very well until the
' death of his dear companion; but going
' to his burial, we were caught in a fhower
' of rain, which we and he believed was
' the occafion of his illnefs. However, he
' was mightily favoured with the divine
' prefence, which enabled him to anfwer
' the fervice of that day; and the next, be-
' ing the firft day of the week, we had a
' bleffed meeting, the Lord's prefence ac-
' companying us; and tho' thy dear huf-
' band was fo near his end, his candle fhin'd
' as bright as ever, and many that beheld
' it were made to glorify God on his behalf.
' This was the laft opportunity on this ifland,
' fave his farewell upon his dying bed,
' where he both preached and prayed, a lit-
' tle before his departure.

' On the next day, being the fecond day
' of the week, he went to a little ifland call-
' ed Jos Vandicks, accompanied with feve-
' ral friends; but on the 3d day in the
' morning he complained very much, yet
' was enabled to go to meeting, where a
' pretty many people were affembled, and
' a bleffed opportunity we had together, to
' the tendring and melting our hearts into
' a heavenly frame.   ' But

' But he who never fpared his labour
' whilft amongft us, extending his voice as
' a trumpet of the Lord's own founding,
' was fo inwardly fpent he was ready to
' faint. However, he went on board the
' floop that afternoon, and next morning
' came afhore at our houfe; where he had
' not been long before a fhivering fit feized
' him, and a fever foon followed, which
' kept its conftant courfe every day. This
' being the 1ft day of the tenth month, he
' took great notice that it ended forty years
' fince his marriage with thee; that during
' that time you had lived in much love, and
' parted in the fame; and that thou waft
' his greateft concern of all outward enjoy-
' ments. And tho' the laft two days he was
' in much pain, yet he was preferved under
' it in much patience and refignation, and
' had his perfect fenfes to the laft, exhort-
' ing friends to faithfulnefs, &c. And on
' the 6th day of the tenth month, about
' fix-o'clock at night, he went away like a
' lamb, with praifes and thankfgivings in
' his lips but about two minutes before.'
Thus far from the faid letters.

And thus finifhed this dear worthy in the
fixty-feventh year of his age; highly favoured by his great and good mafter in the
very extreme moments; the confideration
whereof, and the account given of his fervice, afford me, at times, fome relief. And
I have a fecret fatisfaction in that I was enabled to give him up (tho' fo dear to me)
unto

unto the fervice into which he was called. This is a hint for thofe who may be under the like exercife and trial, that they may not hold back, but fubmit, and freely give up their all, leaving the confequence to the wife difpofing hand, who knows for what caufe it is, he is pleafed fo nearly to try his people.

A Teſtimony from the Monthly-Meeting of Phi-ladelphia, *concerning* SAMUEL PRESTON.

HE was born in Maryland, but remov-ing to fettle in and near this city, he became and continued a member of this meeting; being an elder circumfpect in his conduct, and carefully concern'd for the good of the church, active and ferviceable in the maintenance of our chriftian difci-pline; and by his attention to the dictates of divine grace, he became well qualified for this fervice. He filled fome ftations in the government, wherein he acquitted him-felf with juftice and uprightnefs; and be-ing endued with a clear judgment and good underftanding, his integrity to what he be-lieved to be his duty, became confpicuous and inftructive; being a lover of truth, and extenfive in his charity to mankind. In his laſt illnefs he difcovered great refignation of mind, and much love and fellowſhip with his brethren, with whom he lived and died in good unity.

He

He departed this life on the 10th of the seventh month 1743, in the seventy-ninth year of his age.

His first wife Rachel, was one of the daughters of our worthy friend Thomas Lloyd, and was said to have been a very serviceable, judicious, and valuable woman.

His second wife, was Margaret the widow of Josiah Langdale (a worthy minister who lived in Yorkshire in Great-Britain, and had formerly visited friends in America, but concluding afterwards to remove with his family to Pennsylvania, he died on his passage in the year 1723.)—Concerning the said Margaret, the aforesaid monthly-meeting of Philadelphia thus testify.

" She was endued with an excellent gift in the ministry, and travelled much in the service of truth through this and the neighbouring provinces; her testimony being lively, sound and edifying, was well received among friends; being likewise well qualified for the maintenance of our discipline, she became an useful instrument for the promotion and support of our christian testimony. She died the 23d of the sixth month 1742, in the fifty-eighth year of her age."

According to John Rutty's account, she went from Yorkshire on a religious visit to Ireland in 1715.

A Testimony

A Teſtimony from friends in Virginia, *concerning*
THOMAS PLEASANTS.

HE was the eldeſt ſon of John and Do-
rothy Pleaſants, and born the 3*d* of
the ninth month 1695; being a youth of
good natural parts, and well inſtructed in
ſchool-learning. His father dying whilſt he
was young, he was deprived of the additional advantage of the admonitions and re-
ſtraints of a worthy parent, ſo beneficial to
the forming the minds of youth: Nevertheleſs he had an eye to the recompence of reward, and about the twenty-ninth year of
his age was called to the work of the miniſtry, in which he laboured both amongſt
friends and other people much to ſatisfaction, having meetings where none had been
held before. Once, in company with his
brother Robert Jordan, he viſited friends on
the weſtern ſhore of Maryland, and alſo attended the yearly-meeting at Choptank, on
the eaſtern ſhore. His ſervices ſeemed much
confined to his own country, where, tho'
the number of friends was ſmall, he was
not diſcouraged thereat, but endeavoured
to diſcharge his duty amongſt them, not
only at the adjacent meetings but thoſe more
at a diſtance, and was made inſtrumental
in convincing ſeveral in the upper parts of
the colony, as well as in ſettling two or
three meetings. A few years before his deceaſe, he wrote an epiſtle, directed to friends
in

in every ftation, but more particularly to
the minifters, thereby further demonftrating that his diligence and labours proceeded from an earneft concern for the promotion of truth and a right gofpel miniftry.
He was indeed a man much devoted to the
fervice of truth, and a confiderable fufferer
for bearing his teftimony againft priefts-
wages, having once been a prifoner on that
account. He married Mary the daughter
of Robert Jordan of Nancemond county,
and left a numerous offspring, fome of them
young, for whofe eternal welfare he was
particularly folicitous; being once on a vifit
to friends at fome diftance from home, he
was taken very ill, and feemed defirous that
he might finifh his courfe among his dear
children, in order that he might have an
opportunity at that awful period, of enfor-
cing his experienced advices to them, and
promoting the caufe of God to which he was
much devoted to the laft. Accordingly he
departed this life at his own houfe the 24*th*
of the eleventh month 1744, and on the
28*th* of the fame month was interr'd in the
family burying-ground at Curles, attended
by a numerous company of friends and
neighbours.

A Teftimony

K

A Testimony from Gwynedd *Monthly-Meeting in* Pennsylvania, *concerning* Cadwalla-der Evans.

HE was a native of the principality of Wales, and arrived in Pennsylvania in the year 1698. And altho' he was not then in profeſſion with friends, yet he ſoon after entered into cloſe fellowſhip with them, and continued ſtedfaſt to his end. He was a diligent and ſeaſonable attender of our religious meetings: On firſt days particularly, he was ready an hour before the time appointed, and then read ſeveral chapters in the bible or ſome religious book: As the time approached, he would frequently obſerve the time of day, and by means of ſuch watchful care, he was ſeated in meetings one of the firſt, and ſcarcely ever after the time appointed. The gravity and compoſure of his countenance as he ſat in ſilence, was no leſs remarkable than his punctual attendance, and beſpoke ſuch inward recollection and divine engagement of mind, as often attracted the eyes and affected the hearts of others.

He received a gift in the miniſtry, in the exerciſe whereof, he was generally led to ſpeak of his own experience in religion and the chriſtian warfare; and his teſtimony, tho' ſhort, was inſtructive, lively, and manifeſtly attended with divine ſweetneſs: Notwithſtanding it was always acceptable,

he

he was very cautious of appearing, left any, as he often faid, fhould be drawn from a right concern of mind, to place their dependance on words.

He was zealoufly concerned for the honour and promotion of truth, and fupport of our chriftian difcipline; and being endued with difcerning, and clear judgment tempered with charity, he was very ufeful in many fervices of the church, efpecially that weighty one of vifiting friends in their families. And altho' he was naturally of a warm difpofition, yet a tender regard to the fervice of truth, and a continual awe of the divine prefence prefided in his heart, infomuch that meeknefs and condefcention were confpicuous in his conduct.

There was a freedom and affability in his behaviour and converfation, which indicated a benevolence of heart, and endeared him, not only to the *houfhold of faith*, but alfo to the profligate and vain; rendering him ferviceable in compofing differences, and in comforting the fick and afflicted; and particularly in that fkilful and tender office of healing difcord in private families, wherein his endeavours were remarkably fuccefsful. In fuch fervices, he fpent much of the latter part of his life, riding about from one houfe to another; and where no caufe of reprehenfion appeared, he interfperfed his difcourfe on common affairs, with ufeful hints, folid remarks, and leffons of inftruction. But where admonition or comfort were ne-

ceffary,

ceffary, the propriety of his advice and the
uprightnefs of his life, added weight to his
labours, and feldom failed of good effects.

In private life, few had a better claim to the
virtues of temperance, juftice, induftry and
frugality, and as he well knew how advan-
tageous it was, " To train up a child in the
way he fhould walk," he took frequent opportunities to drop his experienced advice
among thofe under his care. It was his
practice, in winter evenings efpecially, to
read the holy fcriptures in his family, and
was particularly careful that neither child
nor fervant fhould be from home at unfea-
fonable hours; being highly fenfible how
flippery the paths of youth are, and how
numerous the fnares which attend them.

He was greatly favoured in the ufe of his
natural abilities, and enjoyed an uncommon
fhare of health until his laft illnefs, which
was fhort; during that time, very many
came to fee him, who fhewed great marks
of efteem and affection; and even libertines
whom he had often rebuked and treated
with, were deeply affected with forrow: Indeed it was rare to fee fo many tears fhed at
a fick bed, more efpecially of one of his
years, which gave a proof that he had not
outlived his fervices. His foul overflowed
with love to God and man, and being favoured in his laft moments, with a bleffed
hope and confidence, he was going to that
place which God had prepared for thofe that
love

love him; he had a happy exit from time to eternity, the 30*th* of the third month 1745, aged eighty-one.

A Teftimony from Kennet *Monthly-Meeting in* Pennfylvania, *concerning* W I L L I A M L E V I S.

WILLIAM LEVIS, of Kennet in Chefter county Pennfylvania, fon of Samuel Levis an early fettler in Spring-field in faid county, was born in Spring-field aforefaid, about the year 1688, and removed to Kennet about 1718. By giv-ing heed to the meafure of grace beftowed upon him, he became a ferviceable friend in the fociety in divers refpects ; was a good neighbour, kind and open hearted to his friends, and has left a good report.

His laft ficknefs was the fmall pox, which was heavy upon him, but he bore it with much patience and refignation of mind to the laft; faying, that when the diftemper came into the houfe, it was no furprize to him, for he was freely refigned, and thank-ful he was fo, for he could not of himfelf. The fame evening he was taken fick, he figned his will, and remark'd how good it was to be contented to bear affliction. One night, as thofe that watched with him were preparing fomething for him to take, he faid, ' You fhall fee your endeavours for me will

avail

avail nothing.' He continued in a ſtate of
reſignation and appeared cheerful in the
time of his illneſs. When nearer his end,
he was concern'd that others might do their
duty faithfully according to the beſt of
their underſtanding, ſaying, ' I have often
' thought at other times as at this, of the
' ſhortneſs of our lives and time here, and
' the uncertainty thereof, which ought to
' engage us to circumſpection and faith-
' fulneſs to the Lord, and I charge you here
' that are elders, to diſcharge your truſt
' faithfully in the ſight of the Lord, having
' your eye ſingle to him, and let nothing of
' ſelf rule, and then his work will be car-
' ried on in love and patience. I could be
' glad to have an opportunity once more
' with my friends, but if I ſhould not, I
' would have thoſe preſent, to acquaint
' them with what I have to ſay, and preſs
' it home to the elders, that they may faith-
' fully diſcharge their duty, and acquit
' themſelves of that charge wherewith they
' are entruſted; and alſo that parents of
' children and heads of families, may faith-
' fully diſcharge that great duty which is
' laid upon them, not only in being good
' examples to their children and families,
' but alſo to be concerned that they follow
' their footſteps, adding, it was a noble
' teſtimony that God gave of Abraham, *I*
' *know him, that he will command his chil-*
' *dren and his houſhold after him.* And if
' parents were concerned to teach their chil-
' dren

' dren and bring them up in the way of
' their duty to God, and lefs concern'd to
' deck and fet them off, and provide things
' to make them look great in the world, it
' would be of far more benefit to them.
' And my defire is, that elders may walk
' faithfully as good ftewards, not only in
' their own families, but to the flock which
' they have the overfight of; that fo they
' may leave a good favour to the rifing and
' fucceeding generation. I am fenfible that
' all thofe who are rightly concerned for the
' difcipline and promotion of truth, will
' meet with trials from that libertine fpirit
' which would lay all wafte; thefe will fay,
' that religion confifts not in fuch fmall
' things; but I have obferved, that one
' fmall thing makes way for another, and
' greater things will take place; and if there
' is not a careful watching againft thefe
' fmall things, the eye that fhould be kept
' open to fee the evil of them, will become
' darkened. But keep ye your places, and
' labour in faithfulnefs with fuch, if poffi-
' ble to gain them; but if after friends la-
' bour, they will not be gathered, friends
' will be clear and have peace in themfelves;
' but a blaft will come on fuch troublefome
' fpirits. And as friends faithfully main-
' tain this their difcipline, the Lord will
' preferve them, but if they neglect it they .
' will furely fuffer lofs.' To fome prefent
who had been engaged in the fervice of vifiting families, he faid ' It was a good work
' and

' and defired it might not be forgotten.'
At another time, being in a weighty frame
of mind, he faid, ' There is an enemy bu-
' fy to accufe the innocent, and prompts
' on the wicked in their wickednefs.' Seeing his affectionate wife and fifter with fome
neighbours weeping, he faid, ' Don't weep
' for me, but be you faithful, and we fhall
' meet again, for it is the hardeft of all to
' fee you weep.'

The morning before he died, he defired
to be helped to the chamber where his eldeft
fon lay ill of the fame diforder, and fitting
down by him, he charged his children to
be dutiful to their mother, and have a care
of doing any thing that would be a trouble
to her, but mind to take her advice, and
defired a blefling might attend them; adding, ' My race is almoft run, and I fhall
' lay down my head in peace with the Lord;
' and if you are faithful (meaning his wife
' and children) and live in the fear of God,
' he will blefs you.' After fome time of
filence, he faid, ' Farewell my fon, the Lord
' blefs thee my child, and thine after thee.'
Being then helped down ftairs, he fat in
his chair, and after a time of filence, clafp-
ed his hands together, faying with a compofed countenance, ' I blefs thee O Lord.'
Afterwards laying ftill in a quiet compofed
frame of mind, he grew weaker and weaker, and about the ninth hour in the evening, departed without figh or groan, like
one

one going to fleep, and we believe in peace with God and unity with faithful friends.

He died the 17th of the fecond month 1747, in the fifty-ninth year of his age, and was interr'd in Kennet burying-ground, the 19th of the fame month.

A Teftimony from Gwynedd *Monthly-Meeing in* Pennfylvania, *concerning* EVAN EVANS.

HE was born in Merionethfhire, in the principality of Wales, in the year 1684, and came to Pennfylvania with his parents in 1698; under whom he received a fober religious education; but, being early in life convinced, that a form of godlinefs, without the real enjoyment of the quickening principle of grace and truth, would not afford folid and lafting peace to his foul, he therefore fought earneftly after it, and refigned his heart to the baptizing power of God, which fitted him for eminent fervices in the church.

In his conftant attendance at our religious meetings, he was a remarkable example of unaffected piety; for whilft he fat in filence, the earneftnefs wherewith his foul " wreftled for a bleffing," was obvious in the fteady engaged appearance of his countenance. He was favoured with an excellent gift in the miniftry, which he exercifed in folemn dread and reverence; and as he always

ways retained an awful fenfe of appearing
in public teſtimony, he was particularly
cautious and watchful, not to prefume to
fpeak without aſſurance of a neceſſity being
laid upon him, and equally careful to attend to the continuance of it: And therefore his " Preaching was not with enticing
words of man's wiſdom, but in the demonſtration of the fpirit and of power." His
fervice was rendered more effectual, by the
diſtinguiſhing marks which he bore, of
" An Iſraelite indeed, in whom was no guile,"
a plainneſs and fimplicity of manner in
word and deed, with a zeal feaſoned with
divine love; and as he had large experience
in the work of regeneration and the myſteries of the heavenly kingdom, as well as
the fnares of the world, he was thereby
well qualified to adminiſter to the ſtates of
the people.

He travelled through many of theſe colonies in the fervice of the miniſtry, in company with his relation and dear friend John
Evans. Their friendſhip was pure, fervent, and laſting as their lives, and their
feparation a wound to the latter, the remembrance of which he never wholly furvived. He alfo frequently viſited the feveral counties in this province, and more particularly many of the adjacent meetings in
their infancy; wherein his unwearied labours of love, tended much to their comfort, growth, and eſtabliſhment in the truth.

He

He was religiously concerned for the support of our christian discipline; and as he was always diffident of himself, he laboured faithfully for the discovery of truth and a disposition of mind to embrace it; whereby he was often enabled to lay " Judgment to the line, and righteousness to the plummet," whether in reproof to the obdurate, or instruction and comfort to the penitent. In visiting friends families his service was great; for being endued with a spirit of discerning and the authority of truth, his advice was adapted with great propriety and advantage, to the particular states and conditions of persons and families. His conduct and conversation in common life, adorned the doctrine he preached, being a good example of plainness, moderation, and uprightness of heart.

He was abroad in the service of truth when attacked with his last illness; and as the disorder was slow and tedious, he attended several meetings in the forepart thereof; in some of which, his lively powerful testimonies clearly manifested, that the God of his youth who had raised him up an instrument in his hand, and on whom he had relied all his life, continued to be his shield and support in the evening of his days and period of life; which was on the 24th of the fifth month 1747. He was buried at Gwynedd.

A Testimony

A Teflimony from Buckingham *Monthly-Meeting in* Pennfylvania, *concerning* J A C O B . H o L´ C o M B E.

HE was born at or near Tiverton in Old England, being a defcendant of friends: His father died while he was young, and his mother brought him up to ufeful learning, being naturally of a quick and cheerful difpofition, and his capacity large and extenfive. The prime and ftrength of his days, was, much of it, fpent in folly and vanity, until it pleafed the Lord effectually to touch his heart, and favour him with a clofe vifitation of his bleffed truth, which wrought a willingnefs in him to take up the crofs, and fubmit to the Lord's righteous judgments, whereby he came to witnefs a being redeemed from his former converfation, and was often zealoufly concerned to tell others, what the Lord had done for his foul. He was frequent and diligent in the exercife of his gift in the miniftry, which was acceptable; often fignifying he was as one born out of due time: He was zealous in maintaining the difcipline of the church, wherein he was clear and his labour very helpful and ferviceable; very diligent in attending meetings for worfhip and difcipline, wherein he was exemplary by his fteady waiting and lively labour that life might be witneffed.

In

In his laſt illneſs, which was ſhort, he appeared cheerful, patient and reſigned; ſaying, ' There was no cloud in his way, that
' he was thankful he had known his re-
' deemer to live, and redeem him from all
' iniquity, and that he was well aſſured he
' ſhould ſee a happy eternity.'

He died the 30*th* of the ſixth month 1748,
and was buried at Buckingham. A miniſter upwards of 18 years.

A Teſtimony from Gwynedd *Monthly-Meeting in* Pennſylvania, *concerning* A L I C E
G R I F F I T H.

ALICE GRIFFITH, late wife of Hugh
Griffith, of North Wales in the county
of Philadelphia in Pennſylvania, was one
that feared the Lord from her youth, remarkable for her modeſty and plainneſs.
When ſhe was married and ſettled, ſhe de-
monſtrated a religious concern for the advancement of truth and welfare of the
profeſſors thereof; and being a woman of
great integrity and uprightneſs of heart,
became very ſerviceable in divers reſpects;
zealous for maintaining good order and
chriſtian diſcipline in the church.

She was well qualified for that weighty
ſervice of viſiting families, having, at ſuch
opportunities, to communicate of her own
experience, and tell what God had done for
her

her foul; and under a good degree of divine influence, would often be drawn forth in opening divine myfteries, as if fhe had been in a large affembly, as many witneffes can teftify, that have been fenfibly reached, yea baptized by her religious vifits; at which fhe was moftly full of good matter, well adapted and fuitable to the different circumftances of individuals and families.

She was often concern'd to ftir up her friends, to a clofe attendance of meetings, both on firft and other days, as alfo to obferve the hour appointed, being herfelf a good example therein, until, by old age and infirmity of body fhe was difabled, which was about three years before her removal. And notwithftanding the circumfpect life and watchful ftate fhe was obferved to be in, yet in the time of her weaknefs, fhe was vifited with great difcouragements and dejections, as may appear by her following expreffions.

At a certain time fhe was heard to fay, ' Lord how long wilt thou withdraw thyfelf ' from me, and not fhew for what caufe ' I am thus afflicted; I have been ac- ' quainted with thy righteous judgments, ' which were ever mixed with mercy; but ' now, my trouble is more than I am well ' able to bear, being almoft ready to fink.' Again was heard to fay, ' Lord, where- ' in have I offended thee; what part of my ' duty have I neglected, that thou fhouldft ' thus hide thy face from me? Time was, ' when

' when my hope in full affurance was to
' reft in thee, but now I fear I fhall become
' a caft-away.' At another time fhe faid,
' What have I done that I fhould be thus
' afflicted, Lord fhall there be any end of
' my forrow? Many fweet times and op-
' portunities I have had when alone, but
' now am left as in the dark, fearing to make
' one ftep forward left I ftumble, he that
' once was my guide has now left me.'
Again faid, ' I ftill defire to be willing to
' fuffer whilft in this body, any thing thou
' mayeft pleafe to bring upon me, be the
' exercife of what kind foever, if thou wilt
' favour me with thy living prefence; then
' Lord, fhall not any thing be too near or
' dear to part with, or to fuffer for thy name-
' fake. Yea Lord, if thou fhould fee meet
' to deprive me of my fight or hearing,
' health or fpeech, let me never murmur,
' but Oh! give patience to bear this inex-
' preffible exercife to the end.' One morning, after calling her two daughters, fhe faid,
' Put by your work my children, for I
' have to tell you of a glorious vifitation the
' Lord was pleafed to favour me with. As
' I was making my fupplication to him for
' deliverance and redemption from my fore
' exercife, and to obtain fome refrefhment
' to my poor diftreffed foul, the Lord was
' gracioufly pleafed to anfwer my requeft in
' a fatisfactory manner: He opened the eye
' of my mind, to fee him coming in his
' glory to relieve me from my long diftrefs.
                                        ' May

' May my whole truſt and confidence ever
' abide in him, who has ſo filled my heart
' with joy, that pain and grief vaniſhed
' away. This glorious ſeaſon ſurpaſſed all
' that ever I had known before: At which
' time, the Lord gave me a ſure promiſe,
' that, altho' my afflictions were many,
' and more I had yet to go through, yet I
' ſhould in the end, be rewarded with a
' crown of righteouſneſs in the kingdom of
' reſt and peace ;' with more to the ſame
effect.

It was obſerv'd, that a certain change appeared in her countenance from that time
forward; ſhe being cheerful and pleaſant
and never ſad as before.

Her deceaſe was on the firſt day of the ſecond month 1749, and was buried on the
3d of the ſame.

A Teſtimony from friends in Virginia, *concerning* SARAH PLEASANTS.

SARAH PLEASANTS, fourth daughter
of Thomas and Mary Pleaſants, was
taken ill the 26th of the ſeventh month,
and departed this life the 7th of the eighth
month 1749, in the ſeventeenth year of her
age. In the time of her illneſs, ſhe called
to ſeveral perſons then preſent, to view her
blooming youth, how changed, and likely
in a ſhort time to bid adieu to the world
and

and all its enjoyments; praying that the
moment fhe was prepared fhe might go;
but in a particular manner, fhe defired the
phyfician who attended her, to obferve the
frailty of poor mortals, as well as the uncertainty of time in this life, faying, ' Look
' on me doctor, I am like a bud cropt from
' the vine before it is fully blown, yet young
' as I am, I have fomething to repent of,
' which in health and ftrength we are apt
' to overlook, and flatter ourfelves is no
' crime, which is, I have been too much giv-
' en to laughter and jefting with thofe of my
' companions who fondly embraced and re-
' turned the fame,' naming one in particular,
whom fhe expreffed a great defire to fee before fhe died, that fhe might warn her of
the weight fhe now felt, not only in thefe
two things, but in a third, which was, taking too much delight in drefs. Then directing her difcourfe to the doctor, fhe faid,
' Nothing elfe have I to charge myfelf with,
' yet, dear doctor, I find it enough, there-
' fore let me prevail with thee to take warn-
' ing by me; I am fenfible that fome things
' thou art in the practice of, are full as dan-
' gerous, if not more fo, than thofe which
' now lay fo heavy on me; that of drink-
' ing to excefs to oblige company, as thy
' excufe and many others is, yet thou wilt
' find it of greater weight when thou comes
' to lay in the condition I now am in, than
' now thou may think poffible, thou wilt
' furely wifh it had been left undone, with

L   ' all

' all other unprofitable things.' The doctor replied weeping, ' I take it very kind ' and hope I fhall obferve it.' Many more good expreffions and advice fhe dropt to him and others then about her.—She one day called her brother Thomas to her bed-fide, and faid to him, ' Dear brother, I know ' thy fituation to be very lonefome, and ' deftitute of fuitable company, notwith- ' ftanding, I pray thee, keep as much as pof- ' fible out of low company, not the poor ' do I mean, becaufe they are poor, but ' the loofe and vulgar, whether poor or rich, ' which are of a corrupting fpirit, and ' will tend to the hurt of thofe who affo- ' ciate with them; but keep thy place and ' thou wilt be like a light fet on a hill, as a ' guide to others, who will praife God on ' thy behalf.'

A Teftimony from Gwynedd *Monthly-Meeting in* Pennfylvania, *concerning* W I L L I A M T R O T T E R.

OUR friend William Trotter, late of Plymouth in the county of Philadelphia, fon of William Trotter, was born in the fourth month 1695, of religious parents, and was educated amongft friends; as he grew in years, he was bleffed, in that he grew in grace, and in the fear and knowledge of our bleffed Lord and Saviour Jefus Chrift.

About

About the twenty-firft year of his age, he received a gift in the miniftry, in which he was frequently exercifed during the courfe of his lite. His miniftry was found and favoury, attended with a good degree of that life and power " By which the dead are raifed, and without which all preaching is vain." He was not tedious or burden-fome, but often very reaching and edifying to his hearers. In his life and converfation he was grave, yet innocently cheerful, and ftrictly juft in his dealings, alfo a lover and promoter of peace, unity, and brotherly love amongft friends, of which himfelf was a good pattern. He was generally beloved during his life, and at his death left a good favour. His removal from time to a happy eternity, though certainly his greateft gain, was a confiderable lofs to the meeting where he belonged. He departed this life on the 19*th* of the tenth month 1749, aged about fifty-three years and fix months, and was interr'd on the 21*ft* of the fame month, in friends burying-ground at Plymouth; and we believe is gone from his laborious fervice here, to receive a heavenly reward of peace, " Where the wicked ceafe from troubling, and the weary be at reft."

A Teftimony

A Teſtimony from Salem *Monthly-Meeting in* New-Jerſey, *concerning* E L I Z A B E T H W Y A T T.

ELIZABETH WYATT (wife of Bartholomew Wyatt) a miniſter, removed by marriage, within the limits of our monthly-meeting, in the year 1730, as appears by her certificate from Haddonfield monthly-meeting. Her teſtimony was large and edifying, found in word and doctrine, to the comfort of the humble minded amongſt us; yet ſhe was a ſharp threſhing inſtrument in the hand of the Lord, againſt the backſliders and unfaithful profeſſors of truth.

Her labours were not confined to this meeting, but it pleaſed the great Lord of the harveſt, to ſend her forth in his ſervice into other provinces on this continent, as Pennſylvania, Maryland, Virginia, North-Carolina, New-England, Rhode-Iſland, Long-Iſland, &c. in all which ſhe had good ſervice for truth, as appears by certificates produced to this meeting. She was exemplary in life and converſation, adorning the doctrine ſhe had to deliver; and was in good eſteem amongſt her friends and neighbours. It pleaſed God to take her off the ſtage of this world, on the 20*th* of the eleventh month 1749-50, aged forty-three years. It may be obſerved, that about three years of her time, her reſidence with her huſband

band and family was at Philadelphia, to the fatisfaction of friends there, as appears by certificate from thence.

Her name before marriage was Tomlinfon, fhe firft appeared in public teftimony at Evefham-meeting in New-Jerfey, while fhe lived at the houfe of our friends William and Elizabeth Evans, which was about four years before her marriage. Befides what is truly faid of her above, it may be juftly added, that her capacity, qualifications and improvements were fuperior to moft, and that fhe poffeffed a cheerfulnefs of temper, joined with great difcretion, which rendered her company very defirable and profitable.

A Teftimony from Gwynedd *Monthly-Meeting in* Pennfylvania, *concerning* ANN ROBERTS.

SHE was convinced of the truth in her native country, Wales, when young, which incurred her father's heavy difpleafure, but in time he became reconciled to her. Some years after her convincement, fhe came over into this country, where fhe received a gift in the miniftry, and by a diligent improvement thereof, together with the influence of a pious life, fhe was made

ufeful

useful in her generation and a blessing to many. Her love and compassion for the widow, the fatherless, and others in affliction, appeared by her often visiting them: She was one of the wise in heart, who was favoured to foresee the enemy in his approaches, and would rouse and excite her fellow-soldiers to use their utmost endeavours to repel his attempts, which was often done with desirable success. She was also zealously concern'd for maintaining christian discipline in the church.

She was rightly qualified for the weighty service of visiting friends families, and at those opportunities was frequently favoured with something suitable to every state and condition, which was attended with beneficial effects, especially on the youth. But such indeed was the divine favour which usually accompanied her discourse and conversation, one could rarely be an hour with her without sensible edification.

Her first coming to reside among us was seasonable, for we having but few ministers, the field before her was extensive, in which she laboured fervently, tenderly inviting those afar off to draw nigh, and querying with them, whether they knew what the Lord had for them to do. By the visitations of heaven and a blessing on her labours, many came to have their mouths opened to speak of God's goodness to their souls; whereby was verified, what she had declared at our meeting before she came to dwell

among

among us, though it then feemed improbable, and fome doubted the accomplifhment thereof. To thefe babes in the miniftry, fhe who had a large fhare of experience in the work, was not wanting to adminifter fuitable precaution and advice.

She went pretty much abroad, vifiting friends in this and the adjacent provinces, to wit, the Jerfeys, Maryland, Virginia and Carolina, accompanied to the remoteft parts by her near and dear friend Sufanna Morris. In her more advanced years fhe vifited Great-Britain, accompanied by our efteemed friend Mary Pennel, between whom a near and ftrict union was preferved through-out their travels; and fhe brought home very clear and comfortable accounts of her acceptable fervice in the gofpel miniftry, and her godly converfation in Chrift.

After her return from Great-Britain, fhe met with great difficulties in refpect to her outward circumftances, which fhe fuftained with chriftian fortitude. A near friend of hers afking her how fhe felt under it, fhe replied, ' While I keep my eye fteadily di-
' rected to the object worthy of our chief
' regard, it feems as if a wall was on each
' fide; all is calm, and nothing hurts or
' annoys: But if I fuffer my eye to wander
' to the right hand or the left, the enemy
' breaks in upon me like a torrent, which
' hurries me away, and it is with great
' difficulty I recover myfelf.' After this, fhe met with a very heavy affliction in the

lofs

lofs of her hufband, which fhe likewife bore with becoming refignation and compofure of mind. In a few months afterwards, fhe fell into a lingering diforder; (the dropfy) and as in time of health fhe preferred the profperity of truth to her chief joy, fo in her illnefs fhe rejoiced much to hear of any young people appearing hopeful in the miniftry. On the other hand, fhe would, even in time of great weaknefs, lament with anxiety of mind the low fituation of the feed, and fay, Oh! what will become of us? Will this dark cloud which hangs over our affemblies, terminate in a boifterous ftorm to try the foundations of the children of men?

By the long continuance of her diforder, fhe was reduced to great weaknefs fometime before her end; yet it was evident, that charity, (to wit) Love to God and his people, continued with her to the laft.

She died on the 9*th* day of the fourth month 175c, in the feventy-third year of her age, having been a minifter 50 years, and was buried at Gwynedd aforefaid; on which folemn occafion we had a good meeting, the extendings of divine love being witneffed.

A Teftimony

A Teſtimony from Wilmington *Monthly-Meet-ing in the county of* New-Caſtle *on* Delaware, *concerning* LYDIA DEAN.

SHE was the daughter of Joſeph Gilpin, of Birmingham in Cheſter county Pennſylvania; was born the 11*th* of the eleventh month 1698, and married to William Dean of the aforeſaid place in 1722. In the year 1728 ſhe appeared in the miniſtry, much in the croſs, which was manifeſt by her brokenneſs of heart and contrition of ſpirit under the weight thereof. And as ſhe became willing to give up all for the cauſe of truth, the Lord in his own time made her a living miniſter of the everlaſting goſpel; in the exerciſe whereof, ſhe was drawn to viſit friends in New-England, Jerſey and Maryland. Her miniſtry was plain and powerful, often ſpeaking particularly to the ſtates of meetings where her lot was caſt; her converſation ſolid, weighty and grave, becoming the goſpel of Chriſt; and very helpful to thoſe who ſtood in need. Her place of abode was at Birmingham aforeſaid, until about a year before her deceaſe, when the family removed to Wilmington; where ſhe had the exerciſe of parting with ſeveral of her children, who were taken away by death; which ſhe bore with patience and great reſignation to the will of divine providence, expreſſing a ſenſe ſhe had of her own diſſolution being nigh: And being

ing engaged with friends who were vifiting families belonging to this monthly-meeting, fhe was taken fick, and her illnefs increafing, fhe faid, the day before fhe died, ' It ' was the joyfulleft day fhe ever had.'

Thus having paffed the time of her fojourning here, in a good degree of godly fear, fhe finifhed her courfe, and is gone (we doubt not) into the manfions of undifturbed reft.

She departed this life the 2d of the tenth month 1750, and was interr'd in friends burying-ground at Wilmington, aged fifty-two, a minifter 22 years.

A Teflimony from Richland *Monthly-Meeting in* Pennfylvania, *concerning* T H o m a s L a n c a s t e r.

ABOUT ten years of the latter part of his time, he was a member of this meeting, he was found in the miniftry, and exercifed his gift therein with great fervency and zeal, his life and converfation correfponding therewith. In the fecond month 1750, he laid before our meeting his concern to vifit friends on the iflands of Barbados and Tortola, which the meeting approved of, and gave him a certificate in order thereto: Towards the latter end of the fame year he perform'd faid vifit, and had good fervice there, as appeared by certificates

cates from friends on each of the faid iflands; on his return homewards, it pleafed divine providence to vifit him with ficknefs, of which he died at fea; his removal being deeply felt and lamented by his family and friends at home.

A Teftimony from friends in Virginia, concerning WILLIAM LADD.

WILLIAM LADD, fon of John and Mary Ladd, both from Old-England, was born near Curles in Virginia, in the fixth month 1679, and about the time of his marriage he removed to Wainoak, became a member of that meeting, and refided there the remainder of his days. He had an acceptable gift in the miniftry, and was a great fufferer for bearing a teftimony againft the hireling minifters. In one inftance, a very exorbitant feizure was made upon his effects, yet he lived to fee the officer who made it reduced to fuch low circumftances, that he charitably contributed to fupply his neceffities.—He continued a faithful fufferer to the end of his days, encouraging his children to faithfulnefs, faying, ' The truth is more to me, than my ' all in this world.'—The night of his deceafe, one of the family faying, ' This was ' to be a night of great forrow to them,' he replied, ' It was a night of great joy to him,' which

which was one of the laft of his expreffions.—He died the 27*th* of the ninth month
1751, and was buried in the family burying-ground near his own houfe, aged feventy-two, and a minifter about 25 years.

A Teftimony from the Monthly-Meeting of Philadelphia, *concerning* ISRAEL PEMBER-
TON.

HE was born in the county of Bucks in
Pennfylvania, in the year 1684, being defcended of pious parents, well efteemed among friends in the firft fettlement of
this province. He ferved his apprenticefhip
and fettled in this city. Having chofen the
fear of the Lord in his youth, and being
preferved therein, he eftablifhed and fupported an unblemifhed character, by his
juftice, integrity, and uprightnefs in his
dealings amongft men, and his mild, fteady and prudent conduct through life. He
was a member of this meeting near fifty
years, and being well grounded in the principles of truth, of found judgment and underftanding, he approved himfelf a faithful elder; adorning our holy profeffion by
a life of meeknefs, humility, circumfpection, and a difinterefted regard to the honour
of truth; of great ufe in the exercife of our
difcipline, being a lover of peace and unity
in the church, careful to promote and maintain

tain it; conftant in the attendance of meetings, and his deportment therein, grave,
folid and reverent, and a true fympathizer
with thofe who were honeftly concerned in
the miniftry; a confpicuous example of moderation and plainnefs; extenfive in his charity and of great benevolence. In converfation cheerful, attended with a peculiar fweetnefs of difpofition, which rendered his company both agreeable and inftructive.

A few days before his deceafe, being in
a free converfe with two of his friends whom
he much loved and refpected, he took occafion to recount many occurrences of his
life, and with a great fenfe of gratitude, to
exprefs the lively remembrance he retained
of the merciful extendings of divine love
towards him in his youth, by the continuance whereof he had been enabled to perfevere in a confcientious difcharge of his religious duties to the beft of his knowledge;
and that being ftill favoured with a degree
of the fame love, it was his greateft comfort
in his declining years.

His death was fudden, tho' not altogether
unexpected, having been at intervals, frequently affected with a dizzinefs in his
head; and feveral times fo as to deprive
him of his fpeech.

He was very lively and pleafant the morning before his departure, and in the afternoon went to the burial of an acquaintance,
and accompanied the corps to the grave-
yard, where he was feized with a fit, fup-
poſed

pofed to be of the apoplectick kind, and expired in about an hour; being the 19*th* of the firft month 1754, and was buried on the 22*d* of the fame month, in the fixty-ninth year of his age.

A Teftimony from Haddonfield *Monthly-Meeting in* New-Jerfey, *concerning* HANNAH COOPER.

OUR well efteemed friend Hannah Cooper, was born in Wenfleydale in Yorkfhire Great-Britain, and arrived at Philadelphia in the year 1732, on a religious vifit to friends in America, and performing that fervice, was afterwards married to our friend Jofeph Cooper, a member of this monthly-meeting, where fhe refided the moft of the remaining part of her life, except when fhe was called abroad in truth's fervice, in which fhe travelled much in the fore part of her time; but as fhe grew in years, fhe was under great indifpofition of body, and fo continued the moft of her time, which unfitted her for travelling.

She was indeed a living minifter, an humble tender hearted friend, a true fympathizer with thofe in affliction, and as a nurfing mother to thofe that were young in the miniftry, her fervice was truly very acceptable, and her memory ftill remains as a fweet favour.

Near

Near the conclusion of her time, she defired thofe then prefent, ' Not to mourn for
' her, for that fhe had nothing to do but to
' die.' She departed this life, the 11*th* of
the fecond month 1754, and we hope enjoys
that unmixed felicity which will never have
an end.

Her name before marriage was Dent. She
received a gift in the miniftry when young,
and travelled in that fervice in feveral parts
of England before fhe came to America. In
1739, having our friend Mary Foulke for a
companion, fhe took fhipping for Barbados,
and after vifiting friends and others on that
ifland, went from thence to Rhode-Ifland,
from whence fhe returned home.—The following teftimony concerning her hufband,
whom fhe furvived feveral years, is from
the fame monthly-meeting, of which he
was divers years an elder, viz.

Our well efteemed friend Jofeph Cooper
deceafed, was born in Newtown in the coun-
of Gloucefter New-Jerfey. He was an exemplary friend, and ferviceable amongft us
in many refpects; was generally well refpected, careful to rule well his own houfe.
He departed this life, about the 1*ft* of the
eighth month 1749, having exprefs'd a little before, ' That he had done juftly, lov-
' ed mercy, and hoped he had been careful
' to walk humbly.'

A Teftimony

A Teſtimony from the Monthly-Meeting of Philadelphia, *concerning* MICHAEL LIGHT-
FOOT.

HE came over from Ireland with his family and ſettled in this province, in
the beginning of the year 1712, and was
called to the miniſtry about the year 1725,
and the forty-ſecond year of his age. Being faithful in the exerciſe of his gift, he
became zealouſly concern'd for the honour
of truth and promotion thereof; and in this
ſervice performed a religious viſit to friends
in Great-Britain and Ireland ; from whence
we received very ſatisfactory and comfortable accounts of his labours. He likewiſe
viſited friends in New-England; and in the
year 1753, he travelled on the ſame account
in the ſouthern provinces.

He was a member of this meeting the laſt
eleven years of his life ; being of a grave
and ſolid deportment, and an example of
plainneſs and temperance, was much eſteemed amongſt us. His miniſtry was deep and
penetrating, attended with the demonſtration of the ſpirit and power; under the influence whereof he was frequently led to
unfold the myſteries of the kingdom, and
eminently qualified to ſet forth the excellencies of the goſpel diſpenſation, with the benefit and advantage of inward and ſpiritual
worſhip; recommending diligent attendance on the ſpirit of truth, for inſtruction

and

and affiftance therein. His delivery was clear, diftinct and intelligible, and in fupplication humble and reverent. He was likewife well gifted in difcipline, and often concerned to fpeak in thofe meetings to our edification and comfort.

He departed this life, on the 3*d* day of the twelfth month 1754, after a fhort ficknefs, in the feventy-firft year of his age, and 29*th* of his miniftry. .

A Teftimony from Hopewell *Monthly-Meeting in* Virginia, *concerning* EVAN THOMAS.

HE was born in Wales, and educated in profeffion with the church of England; but in his tender years, joined in fociety with friends; and proving faithful to the gift and meafure of grace beftowed upon him, by the great giver of every good and perfect gift, he came to be early engaged in the work of the miniftry, and was a ferviceable inftrument; being alfo a preacher in life and converfation, remarkably meek, humble and grave in his deportment. He was zealous for the honour of God and promotion of his bleffed truth, and ferviceable among friends, being one of the firft fettlers in thefe parts, and a conftant attender of our meetings whilft in health. He died in a very ferene frame of fpirit, on the 4*th* day of the fecond month 1755, aged about feventy years.

M   *A Teftimony*

A Teftimony from Duck-Creek *Monthly-meeting in* Kent *county on* Delaware, *concerning* WILLIAM HAMMANS.

H E was born in Old-England, in the year 1683, and educated in the profeſ-ſion of the church of England; but as he grew up, he became uneaſy with the ways and cere-monies thereof; and being a diligent feeker after the true way of worſhip, in a ſhort time joined with friends; foon after which, he left his native country, being but a young man altho' married, and coming over to Pennſylvania, fettled in Cheſter county, and after fome time, received a gift in the mini-ſtry; by keeping low and humble, and at-tending thereto, he became an able miniſter, having a particular gift in quoting the fcrip-tures and explaining them clearly to the un-derſtandings of the people. About the year 1738, he removed within the limits of our monthly-meeting, where his ſervice was very conſiderable, being well qualified for the diſcipline of the church, and very ex-emplary in attending meetings both for worſhip and diſcipline, and an humble wait-er therein. Divers within the bounds of our monthly-meeting, were convinced by his miniſtry, and others who had been con-vinced before, were thereby further con-firmed in the truth of the goſpel.

Living in a public place, he had much of friends company, whom he was very hearty

in

in entertaining, and fo continued to the end of his time; and departed this life, the 8*th* day of the fourth month 1755, in the feventy-fecond year of his age. On the 11*th* of the faid month, was interr'd in friends burying-ground at Duck-Creek.

A Teſtimony from Richland *Monthly-Meeting in* Pennſylvania, *concerning* S u s a n n a M o r r i s.

AS the reviving and tranſmitting to poſterity, the memory of the righteous and faithful fervants of God, eſpecially thoſe worthy elders who are to be highly eſteemed and loved for their work's fake, may be conducive to the promotion of truth, the comfort and edification of the living, and to encourage the imitation of their pious examples.

We are concerned to give forth this teſtimony concerning our ancient and worthy deceaſed friend Suſanna Morris, late wife of Morris Morris, who was a member of our monthly-meeting near fifteen years of the latter part of her time: Her memory ſtill lives, and yields a precious favour to thoſe who are meaſurably ſharers of that divine love and life with which ſhe in an eminent degree was endowed, and was frequently made an inſtrument to communicate it to others, by a living and powerful miniſtry,

in

in which she faithfully laboured with unwearied diligence both at home and abroad,
for the space of forty years and upwards,
having travelled much in the service of the
gospel both in America and Europe, made
three voyages over the seas to visit the meetings of friends in Great-Britain, and twice
through Ireland and Holland; in which
voyages and travels, the gracious arm of divine providence was evidently manifested,
in preserving and supporting her through
divers remarkable perils and dangers, which
she ever reverently remembred and grateful-
ly acknowledged.

Her life and conversation was innocent
and agreeable, seasoned with christian gravity; was a bright example of plainness,
temperance, and self-denial; devoted to the
service of truth and the propagating of religion and piety amongst mankind: In which
ardent love and zeal she continued, until it
pleased her great Lord and master in his wisdom to put a period to all her pious labours
and travels, and to take her to himself, as a
shock of corn gathered in due season, after a
short illness of nine days continuance, within
which time, on a first day of the week, friends
at her request, held an evening meeting in her
room, wherein she was wonderfully strength-
ened to bear a lively testimony to the everlasting truth, setting forth, the ground work
of true religion and divine worship, concluding with a fervent prayer to the father
of all our mercies, for the continuance of
his

his love and favours to his children and people. After which, her weaknefs increaf-ing, fhe lay in a calm and quiet frame, without much appearance of pain, until fhe died, which was on the 28*th* day of the fourth month 1755, in the feventy-third year of her age.

The Teftimony of the Quarterly-Meeting of Sandwich *in* New-England, *concerning* NICHOLAS DAVIS.

HE was born at Sandwich, the 28*th* of the eighth month 1690, but lived the greateft part of his days in Dartmouth and Rochefter. He came forth with a living teftimony in the miniftry, before he was twenty years old, in which he grew very faft, and foon became an able fkilful mini-fter of the gofpel, dividing the word of truth aright; zealous againft obftinate of-fenders, but to thofe under affliction, his words were as healing balfam, and his fpeech as dew on the tender grafs. He ftrove to live in peace with all men, and was gene-rally well beloved by his acquaintance and neighbours, more efpecially his brethren of the fame religious denomination. He tra-velled much in vifiting friends in New-En-gland, was very ferviceable in ftrengthen-ing them, and alfo made inftrumental in convincing fome of the bleffed truth. A
diligent

diligent and feafonable attender of meetings, and a lover of the honeft hearted, but
always hated hypocrify in any. He twice
vifited friends in the weftern parts of America,
going once as far as North-Carolina.—Before
he proceeded on his laft journey into thofe
parts, he appeared refigned to the will of God,
and much weaned from the things of this
world; his kinfman Adam Mott accompanied
him, and by teftimonials receiv'd from feveral
meetings, their fervice was well accepted.
On his way homeward, he was taken fick at
Oblong in New-York government, bearing
his pain with great patience to the laft; and
whilft his underftanding was clear, often
mention'd his concern for the profperity of
truth. In the time of his ficknefs he wrote
a letter to his wife, wherein he exprefs'd
his fubmiffion to the will of God whether
in life or death, defiring fhe might experience the fame; and in an efpecial manner
requefted her care in the education of their
children, to bring them up in the nurture
and admonition of the Lord; keep them
from hurtful and unprofitable company,
and endeavour to inftil into their minds the
chriftian principles of patience, temperance,
meeknefs and fobriety, that fo they might
be made fit veffels for the holieft to dwell
in. In another letter wrote to his children,
in the time of his ficknefs, we find thefe
words, ' I hereby let you know, that as I
' am doubtful whether I fhall ever fee you
' more, there refts fomething on my mind
' to

' to write to you by way of advice, which
' I greatly defire may not be forgotten, and
' that is, as you have a tender affectionate
' mother, who is defirous you may do well,
' therefore dear children, be obedient to her
' in all things in the Lord, and fubmit to
' her counfel and advice at all times in love
' to her, and alfo endeavour to live in love
' and peace one with another at all times,
' and let not any contentions or hard
' thoughts arife one againft another by any
' means, but be helpful one to another, and
' be exceeding careful to attend week-day
' meetings, and encourage others alfo, and
' endeavour to let all things be in good or-
' der in the church.' He would fometimes
defire thofe about him to be ftill and quiet,
that they might have a time to wait on the
Lord in filence, and feveral times opened
his mouth in prayer and fupplication in a
living and powerful manner; alfo exhorted
the by-ftanders in the fame life and power.
Thus he finifhed his courfe at Oblong aforefaid, on the *7th* of the tenth month 1755,
in the fixty-fifth year of his age; and we
believe he is admitted " Where the weary
" are at reft." He bore a public teftimony
above forty-fix years, and hath left an unblemifhed character.

A Teftimony

A Testimony from Burlington *Monthly-Meeting in*
New-Jerfey, *concerning* PETER ANDREWS.

IT having pleafed the Lord to beftow on
him a gift in the miniftry, he was faithful thereto, and made helpful to many; being fo devoted to the fervice of God, that
when any religious duty was required of
him, he was fervently engaged to perform
it, as ftrength was afforded.

He was careful to attend meetings for
worfhip and difcipline, and when there, manifefted a real concern to wait upon God
for ftrength and wifdom, that fo our meetings might be truly profitable. Amongft
his neighbours he was ferviceable, his example having a tendency to ftrengthen the
good in them and others, and to difcourage
that which was wrong.

His engagements in the exercife of the
miniftry, occafioned him to be much from
home, yet his regard to his family was becoming his ftation both as a hufband and a
father; it was his frequent practice to fit
down with them to wait upon the Lord,
and we believe his faithfulnefs therein, was
of confiderable fervice.

In the year 1755, he, in a weighty manner laid before us, a concern that had fometime refted on him to vifit friends in England. And having obtained the concurrence of friends here, and fettled his temporal affairs, he embark'd about the 29*th*
of the fourth month the fame year.

For

For an account of his fervices in that nation, we refer to the following teftimony of the
monthly-meeting of friends in Norwich, at
which place he departed this life, aged about
forty-nine, and a minifter about 14 years.

A Teftimony from Norwich *Monthly-Meeting*
concerning PETER ANDREWS.

OUR dear friend Peter Andrews, from
Weft-Jerfey in North-America, being
on a religious vifit to friends in this nation,
deceafed in this city; and the lively fenfe of
his fervices, and the regard we bear to his
memory, engages us to trafmit the following
teftimony concerning him.

His firft vifit to us was in the eleventh
month 1755, and his fervice and exemplary
deportment will remain as a lafting teftimony for him, and to the truth he preached,
in the minds of many; and we have good
reafon to believe he was made inftrumental,
in a very particular manner, to the help and
furtherance of fome amongft us, whom it had
pleafed the Lord to vifit with a frefh vifitation of his love. And by the information
of other friends, who well knew him, and
particularly our friend Edmund Peckover,
who frequently accompanied him, as well
as from our own knowledge, we are enabled
to give the following brief account of his
labours and travels, from the time of his
arrival to his death.

He

He landed in the fouth part of England, in or about the fixth month 1755, and came directly up to London, where he was kindly received by friends, and had very good fervice during a fhort ftay there; but being defirous of being at the quarterly-meeting to be held at York, in company with feveral friends of London, he went as directly to the faid city as he could well do, being near two hundred miles, and reached there by the 24th of the fixth month, at which time began the quarterly-meeting; and this our dear friend had a very memorable and weighty opportunity in miniftry, in the meeting of minifters and elders at the opening thereof; but, in the fucceeding meetings for worfhip, was moftly filent; yet in thofe for difcipline, was divinely led to fet forth the nature, good end and tendency of the fame, and very zealoufly preffed to the keeping them up, in the fame wifdom and power in which they were firft eftablifhed; evidently fetting forth, ' that they proceeded from that which ' gathered our fore-fathers to be as a pecu- ' liar people unto God;' to the no fmall edification and comfort of many fincere hearts, who rejoiced greatly in having his company, which remains frefh in their remembrance; his fervices being as bread caft upon the waters, which, according to the wife man's obfervation, *fhall be found after many days.*

After the quarterly-meeting was ended he went to Pickering. where a very large meeting is kept annually for worfhip, and had

feafonable and profitable fervice. He travelled to many other places in that county,
and friends were greatly refreſhed and edified by his chriſtian viſit, though not always
attended by public declarations in their religious meetings appointed on his account,
which were moſtly very large, and expectations high, yet his eye was to his great maſter's putting forth. He often was led to
famiſh that too eager defire after words; and
in feveral public meetings he had nothing to
fay amongſt them; which tho' a great diſ-
appointment to many for the prefent, yet
there afterwards appeared a fignal fervice
in it.

He was at Yarm, Stockton, Bainbrig, and
feveral other meetings in and about the Dales;
then came to Leeds, Bradford, Wakefield,
Doncaſter, and fo into Lincolnſhire; which
county he vifited pretty generally, alfo the
iſle of Ely, and came into Norfolk, and to
this place in the eleventh month 1755, as
afore-mentioned; was at moſt, if not all, of
friends meetings in our county; then went
into Suffolk and Eſſex, and returned to London the latter end of the firſt month 1756,
where he remained a few weeks, being exceeding ill; yet was at moſt of the meetings in that city, and was very ferviceable,
with many other friends, in affairs particularly relating to the fociety in Pennfylvania
at that time.

He went back again into Eſſex, and fo for
Hertfordſhire, fome parts of Buckinghamſhire,

fhire, Oxfordfhire, Gloucefterfhire, and to the yearly-meeting at Briftol in the fifth month 1756; and had good fervice both in meetings for worfhip and difcipline, which was well received, and, it is hoped, made lafting impreffions on the minds of many who had the opportunity of being prefent.

His indifpofition ftill continued, but did not hinder him from travelling: From Briftol he paffed through fome part of Gloucefterfhire, Wiltfhire, and Oxfordfhire, and got to the yearly-meeting at London in the fixth month, and altho' his illnefs continued upon him, was enabled to bear feveral living teftimonies, in the demonftration of the fpirit and of power.

After the faid yearly-meeting was ended, he came down to the yearly-meetings at Colchefter and Woodbridge, where he was eminently fupported to be ferviceable in the churches. At Woodbridge he was ftrengthened to bear a large, powerful and affecting teftimony in the laft meeting of worfhip, to the tendering of many hearts, whofe ftates were fo effectually fpoken to, as that it may be fitly compared to the excellency, and glorious fituation which the Pfalmift defcribed, when he fays, " How " good, and how pleafant a thing it is, for " brethren to dwell together in unity! It is " like the precious ointment upon the head, " that ran down upon the beard, even Aa- " ron's beard, that went down to the fkirts " of his garments: As the dew of Hermon, " and

" and as the dew that defcended upon the
" mountains of Zion; for there the Lord
" commanded the blefling, even life for
" evermore," Pfalm cxxxiii. 1, 2, 3. It
was indeed a moft heavenly, precious, baptizing feafon, (this being the laft public opportunity our dear friend had) in which he
was wonderfully led to fet forth the progref-
five fteps the Almighty was pleafed to make
ufe of, in appearing to Gideon, confirming
him in the certainty of his requirings, condefcending to grant his requefts in a very
peculiar manner, and fealing them with his
prefence, and giving him victory over his
enemies, as he was faithful to follow the
blefled author that pointed forth the beginning as well as finifhing that great work, to
which that extraordinary fervant of God,
Gideon, in his day was called; which memorable fervice of our dear friend, there is
great reafon to believe the great Lord, who
prepared him for the fame, was gracioufly
pleafed to fix as a nail in a fure place; and
may it fo continue in the remembrance of
thofe then prefent, who are left for a fmall
fpace yet in mutability.

He continued very weak in body all his
ftay in Woodbridge, being above five days,
and no perfuafions could prevail with him
to hinder his fetting forward for his journey, having ftrong defires in his mind to
fee friends in this place again; and to a particular friend he exprefled his love fo great
to us, ' That he thought he could willingly
' die

' die with us.' He was favoured to accomplifh it in two days after he left Woodbridge,
though with great difficulty, and lodged at
the houfe of our friend John Oxley, as he
had done before, but took to his bed foon
after he got in, to which, the remaining
part of his time, he was moftly confined.

It being the time of our yearly-meeting,
many friends went often to vifit him, and
he expreffed to fome, ' That he was fatisfied
' he was in his place, in giving up to follow
' the requirings of the Lord, in leaving his
' outward habitation, and thofe near blef-
' fings of a moft tender affectionate wife
' and dutiful children.'

The feverity of his illnefs kept him moftly delirious, yet he was favour'd with fome
clear intervals; in one of which, being in
a fweet heavenly frame of mind, he broke
forth in the following fervent fupplication,
viz. ' Oh! this poor foul hath been for many
' days on the brink of the pit of diftrefs;
' but thou, dear father, doft not afflict thy
' children willingly, but for fome great and
' good caufe known only to thyfelf: Dear
' father! fuffer not thy children ever to de-
' fpair of thy mercies, but that we may be
' helpful, as much as may be in our pow-
' er, to one another in all fuch times of
' trouble. Deareft father! thou haft been
' pleafed to open, and to favour with thy
' goodnefs; my foul is thankful, and can
' fay, thou art worthy of glory and praife
' for evermore.'

He

He continued to the 13*th* of the feventh month 1756, and then departed this life, and was interr'd in friends burying-ground the 18*th* of the fame, after an awful meeting, (his corps being attended by a very large number of friends and others) and no doubt he refts, with the fpirits of the juft made perfect, in thofe glorious manfions prepared for all thofe that hold out in faithfunefs to the end. His memory is very precious and dear to many who are yet furviving, and we believe it may truly be faid, that few friends who have travelled in this nation, have been more approved, or had more general fervice in fo fhort a fpace of time.

A Teftimony from Gwynedd *Monthly-Meeting in* Pennfylvania, *concerning* JOHN EVANS.

HE was born in Denbighfhire, in the principality of Wales, in the year 1689, and arrived in Pennfylvania with his parents in 1698, under whom he received a pious education.—He was a man of good natural underftanding and favoured early in life to fee the neceffity of a diligent attention to the voice of divine wifdom, to eftablifh and preferve him in peace with God; and by a fteady adherence to it, he became honourable in fociety and eminently ferviceable in the church of Chrift.—In the twenty-third year of his age he appeared in the miniftry

of

of the gofpel, his deportment therein was
reverent as became a mind fenfible of the
awful importance of the fervice. He had a
clear engaging manner of delivery, was
deep in heavenly myfteries, and plain in declaring them ; being well acquainted with
the holy fcriptures, he was made fkilful in
opening the doctrines therein contain'd, and
was often led to draw lively and inftructive
fimilitudes from the vifible creation. He
travelled through moft of the northern colonies in the fervice of truth, and feveral
times thro' this province.—He was often
drawn to attend general meetings, funerals
and other public occafions, particularly the
adjacent meetings after their firft eftablifh-
ment, over which he had a tender fatherly
care, as a good fhepherd taking heed to the
flock ;—and the great fhepherd of Ifrael
bleffed his labours, and afforded him at
times great fatisfaction and comfort.—The
latter part of his time, the vifible declenfi-
on of many from the life and power of
truth, frequently made forrow and deep
lamentation his portion.—His labours were
fervent with the youth, in much love and
zeal, that they might come to know God
for themfelves, bow their necks to the yoke,
and lay their fhoulders to the work, faying,
" That their remembering their creator in
" the days of their youth, would be as mar-
" row to his bones." It was indeed his
great joy to behold the peaceable fruits of
righteoufnefs, and his labours for the promotion

motion thereof made him honourable a-
mongft men of various ranks and profeffions, and his teftimony generally acceptable
to them.

In the fupport of our chriftian difcipline,
he was zealous, active and unwearied, and
favoured with qualification to advife in difficult cafes, which feldom failed of fucceeding. His teftimony was clofe againft hypocrify and an outfide fhew of religion only,
but full of parternal tendernefs to the afflicted, weak, or diffident in fpirit; of
found judgment, and deep in divine experience, yet modeft and condefcending, and
being favoured with the defcendings of the
father's love, that at times appeared to clothe
him as with a mantle; he had an open-door
in the hearts of his friends, and an afcend-
ency over the fpirits of gainfayers.—He was
a zealous promoter of vifiting friends in
their families, was many times engaged
therein, and his labours were awakening
and ufeful; often employ'd in vifiting the
fick, the widow, and the fatherlefs and others
in affliction; on thefe occafions he was feldom large in expreffion, but his filent fympathy and fecret breathing for their relief,
were more confolatory than many words; a
confiderable part of his time was fpent in
affifting widows, and the guardianfhip of
orphans, which, though laborious to him,
was of much advantage to them.

The importance of love and peace to civil and religious fociety he was deeply fen-

N   fible

fible of, diligent in promoting them both by precept and example, and fuccefsful in re-ftoring harmony where any violation of it appear'd.—His conduct and converfation in private life was exemplary, and fuch as implied an inward clofe infpection into the fecret operations of his own heart.

He was apprehenfive of his approaching end for fometime before his laft illnefs, and told a friend, ' He fhould not furvive one ' year,' who admir'd he was fo pofitive; but he made no further reply than, ' See what ' will follow.' In his public teftimony alfo, he frequently faid, ' He had but an inch of ' time to treat with us.' In the firft part of his illnefs, he went to fome meetings, one whereof was large, and he was favour'd with ftrength to fpeak in a powerful and in-ftructive manner to the youth, for whofe welfare his defires were ardent.—His difor-der was flow and lingering, wherein he was favour'd with his underftanding almoft to the laft; and altho', at fome feafons, he was much concern'd on account of the gloomi-nefs of the times in religious and civil re-fpects, yet in general he poffefs'd a very great degree of calmnefs and ferenity of mind, with a perfect refignation to the will of God, whether life or death fhould be his portion. On the day of his departure, ob-ferving his wife troubled, he faid with a cheerful-countenance, ' I am eafy, I am ea-' fy, and defir'd her to be eafy alfo;' indeed it appear'd that the Lord had ftrengthened

him

him on the bed of languishing, and made
all his bed in his sickness. And thus having served God in his generation, he departed the 23d day of the ninth month 1756,
aged sixty-seven years; having, we hope,
shaken himself from the dust, put on his
beautiful garments, and enter'd the wed-
ding chamber of the bridegroom of his soul,
and enjoys the reward of his faithful labours; was buried on the 25th day of the
same month, in friends burying-ground at
Gwynedd.

A Testimony from the Monthly-Meeting of Philadelphia, *concerning* THOMAS BROWN.

HE was born in Barking, in the county
of Essex, Great-Britain, on the 1st of
the ninth month 1696, came whilst young
with his parents into this province, and
lived some time in this city, from whence
he removed with them to Plumstead in Bucks
county, where he first appeared in the ministry; some years after which, he settled in
this city. His gift in the ministry was living, deep, and very edifying; and in the
exercise thereof, he was remarkable for an
awful care, not to appear without clear and
renewed evidence of the motion of life for
that service: And though not a man of literature, was often led into sublime matter,
which was convincing and persuasive, in set-

ting

ting forth the dignity and excellence of the
chriftian religion, yet was very attentive
that thofe heighths fhould not detain him
beyond his proper gift, but to clofe in and
with the life, which made his miniftry always acceptable to the living and judicious.
Although he was not led to vifit the churches in diftant parts, yet was fometimes concern'd to attend fome of the neighbouring
meetings, of two of which he has preferv'd
fome minutes, which being a lively de-
fcription of his concern of mind for the
promotion of the caufe of truth, it is thought
well to fubjoin them here in his own words.

' 1756, eighth month 9th, I went to Con-
' cord quarterly-meeting, but found no
' caufe to efpoufe the caufe of God in a
' public manner that day. The next day
' went to the youth's meeting at Kennet,
' which was to great fatisfaction; my foul
' was fo bended towards the people, that I
' could fcarcely leave them, being engaged
' in a ftream of the miniftry, to extol the
' divinity of that religion that is breathed
' from heaven, and which arrays the foul
' of its poffeffor with degrees of the divini-
' ty of Chrift, and entitles them to an eter-
' nal inheritance; alfo introduces a lan-
' guage, intelligible only to the converted
' fouls which have accefs to a celeftial foun-
' tain, which is no lefs than a foretafte of
' eternal joy, to fupport them in their jour-
' ney towards the regions above, where re-
' ligion has room to breathe in its divine
' excellencies

' excellencies in the foul; here it is inftruct-
' ed in the melody of that harmonious fong
' of the redeemed, where the morning ftars
' fing together, and the fons of God fhout
' for joy.—

' 1756, the 29th of the eighth month, I
' vifited Gwynedd-meeting, where in wait-
' ing in nothingnefs before God, without
' feeking or ftriving to awake my beloved
' before the time, by degrees my foul be-
' came invefted with that concern that the
' gofpel introduces, with an opening in
" thefe words; I think it may conduce to
" my peace, to ftand up, and engage in a
" caufe dignified with immortality and
" crowned with eternal life." The fubject
' raifed higher and brighter until my foul
' was tranfported on the mount of God
' in degree, and beheld his glory; where I
' was favoured to treat on the exalted ftati-
' on of the redeemed church, which ftands
' in the election of grace, where my foul
' rejoiced with tranfcendent joy and adored
' God. Returned home in peace.'

His conduct and converfation was innocent and edifying, being much weaned from
the world and the fpirit of it. He was careful not to engage in worldly concerns fo as
to encumber his mind, and draw it off from
that religious contemplation, in which was
his chief delight; which happy ftate of
mind he maintained to the laft, as evidently appeared to thofe friends who were with
him

him towards his conclusion; to some of whom he expressed himself in the following manner, viz.

   ' I am fine and easy, and don't know but
' what I may recover; but if I should, I
' expect to see many a gloomy day, but
' nevertheless I am willing to live longer, if
' I might be a means of exalting religion,
' that the gift bestowed on me, might shine
' brighter than it hath ever yet done, or else
' I had abundance better go now; for I
' think I have shone but glimmeringly to
' what I might have done, had I been still
' more faithful; tho' I cannot charge my-
' self with a presumptuous temper, nor wil-
' ful disobedience; but I can say, it has of-
' ten happened with me, as with the poor
' man at the pool of Bethesda, whilst I was
' making ready another has stepped in. I
' am sensible that my gift has been different
' from some of my brethren, I have not
' been led so much into little things, but I
' am far from judging them.

   ' I have often to pass through the valley
' of the shadow of death, and have experi-
' enced the possibility of a soul's subsisting
' the full space of forty days without re-
' ceiving any thing, only living by faith
' and not by sight, provided they keep up-
' on the foundation of convincement and
' conviction, and not turn aside to take a
' prospect of the world, and desire to draw
' their comfort from visibles; they will be
' supported by an invisible yet invincible
               ' power;

' power; for he will be fure to appear, and
' when he doth appear at times, doth rend
' the vail from the top to the bottom, with
' an invitation, as Samuel ufed to fay (mean-
' ing Samuel Fothergill) " Come up hither,
" and behold the bride the lamb's wife;"
' then the foul will have to enjoy, and fee
' things beyond expreffing; my tongue can
' do little or nothing at fetting it forth.
' The foul will be filled with holy admirati-
' on, and fay, " Who is fhe that looketh
" forth as the morning, fair as the moon,
" clear as the fun, and terrible as an army
" with banners."

 ' Although the foul has at times to be-
' hold the glory, fplendor and magnitude of
' the true church or fpoufe of Chrift, yet
' thofe extraordinary fights are but feldom,
' not often: Though I have had at times,
' caufe to efpoufe the caufe of God, yet
' there are times that the foul is fo veiled,
' and furrounded with temptations and fiery
' trials, and all out of fight, that I have
' wondered that I was made choice of; but
' I have experienced, that they that would
' reign with Chrift muft fuffer with him; I
' never expect to get beyond it, while I am
' cloathed with this clog of mortality.

 ' People may have a regular outfide, and
' be diligent in attending meetings, and yet
' know little or nothing of it; for formality
' and externals are nothing; religion is an in-
' ternal fubject, fubfifting between Chrift and
' the foul: I don't confine it to our name,

' but

‘ but amongſt the different names there are,
‘ that my ſoul is nearly united to, who are
‘ in a good degree, I do believe, in poſſeſſion
‘ of that religion which is revealed from
‘ heaven: And I am in the faith, that there
‘ will be them raiſed up, that will ſhine as
‘ bright ſtars, and religion will grow and
‘ proſper, and the holy flame riſe to a great-
‘ er height than it hath ever yet done. I can
‘ ſay with the holy apoſtle, “I have nothing
“ to boaſt of, ſave my infirmities,” yet thus
‘ much I venture to ſay, that if I die now,
‘ I die a lover of God and religion.’ And after expreſſing a compaſſionate ſympathy with
the poor afflicted churches up and down, concluded with this ſaying, “ Be of good cheer
“ little flock, for greater is he that is in you,
“ than he that is in the world.”

In the ſixty-firſt year of his age, he was
ſeized with an apoplectick diſorder, which
gradually increaſing, deprived him of life,
on the 21ſt of the ſixth month 1757, and
was interr’d in this city the next day.

————————

A Teſtimony from Newark *Monthly-Meeting
in* New-Caſtle *county on* Delaware, *concerning* BETTY CALDWELL.

SHE was the daughter of George Pierce,
of Thornbury in Cheſter county, was
born in Glouceſterſhire in Old-England, and
came into Pennſylvania with her parents,

about

about the year 1683, who fettled in Thornbury aforefaid. She was married to Vincent Caldwell in 1703, and foon after they
fettled in Marlborough, Chefter county, where
fhe continued, and belonged to Kennet meeting, till a few years before her death, when
fhe removed to Wilmington. She was from
her youth, remarkably exemplary for plainnefs and fobriety, much concern'd for peace
in the church and amongft neighbours, labouring to reftore it according to ability as
occafions required, often with the defired
fuccefs. She was very ferviceable in that
weighty work of vifiting friends families, in
which fhe had at times to impart to others, of
her own experience in the work of religion,
and to exhort to faithfulnefs and obedience to
what the Lord requires; was a conftant attender of meetings, and exemplary for folid
and humble waiting therein, and much concern'd that her children might walk in the
truth. After the death of her hufband in
1720, fhe had the care of the family upon
herfelf, remaining in a ftate of widowhood
upwards of 37 years, in which ftation fhe
behaved with fuch prudence and circumfpection, that her conduct, in bringing up
her children without much correction, is
worthy of imitation; which together with
her pious concern for the welfare of the
church, entitled her to be accounted of the
number of the " Widows indeed." She had
many years been in the ftation of an elder
for Kennet meeting, and feveral years before

fore her death, had a few words in testimony in meetings, which was generally
well received, being seasonable and weighty.

Her last sickness was a fever, which
brought her very low, often ' Praying the
' Lord to be near her, and by his support-
' ing hand to bear up her spirits now in this
' pinching time;' and finished her course
here, we believe in peace with the Lord and
in unity with friends, the 27*th* of the tenth
month 1757, and was interr'd in Kennet
burying-ground the 29th of the same month,
in the seventy-seventh year of her age.

A *Testimony from* Burlington *Monthly-Meeting
in* New-Jersey, *concerning* ABRAHAM
FARRINGTON.

HE was born in Bucks county, Pennsylvania, of parents professing the truth
as held by us the people called Quakers.
About nine months after his birth his father
dying, and his mother sometime after mar-
rying from among friends, exposed him to
a loose irregular education; about ten years
of age being put apprentice, where through
eleven years servitude, he suffered great
bodily hardship, and much greater danger
as to the better part; yet (says he in a manu-
script left for the use of his children) ' I
' took delight in my bible, and believe the
' good hand was with me, that inclined my
' mind

' mind thereto.—Tho' I followed lying va-
' nities, and fo forfook my own mercies,
' yet I could fay my prayers every night,
' till I grew afraid to fay them any more,
' and feemed like one abandoned from good
' for feveral years.' Having ferved his time
out, he providentially became a refident in
Benjamin Clark's family at Stony-brook, who
were exemplary and kind to him ; ' I thought
' (fays he) they were the beft people in the
' world, careful in their words, yet cheer-
' ful and pleafant, fo that I thought I muft
' be a Quaker.' And Edward Andrews,
from Eggharbour, being at a quarterly meeting at Croffwicks, ' He came (adds he) with
' power to give me my awakening call ; I
' was much reached, but after the manner
' of the world, looking at the man, gave
' him the praife, viz. he is a brave man,
' he preaches well, I wifh I lived near him,
' I would go to hear him every firft day ;
' at fame time not minding what he direct-
' ed to, Chrift in ourfelves, the true teach-
' er, that will not be removed till we re-
' move from him ; in us is the place he has
' ordained to reveal himfelf.—I afterwards
' went more to friends meetings than I had
' done before, and read much in friends
' books, but was yet in the dark, the time
' of my deliverance was not come, the fins
' of the Amorites were not full ; I was un-
' der Mofes in the wildernefs, come out of
' Egypt, but Jofhua's time was not come,
' the Saviour, the warrior that brings
                                   ' through

' through judgment, and makes war with
' the old inhabitants; yet I fometimes long-
' ed for fomething which I could not find,
' a lot in the good land. I think this year
' Thomas Willfon and James Dickenfon,
' came into the country, and fometime af-
' terwards to vifit the meeting of friends at
' Croffwicks, I happened to be at the meeting
' before they came in; the fight of them
' ftruck me, the heavenly frame of mind
' which their countenances manifefted, and
' the awe they feemed to fit under, brought
' a ftillnefs over my mind, and I was as
' ground prepared to receive the feed: James
' ftood up in the authority of the gofpel,
' and in it he was led to unravel me and all
' my works from top to bottom, fo that
' I looked on myfelf like a man diffected
' or pulled to pieces, all my religion as
' well as all my fins were fet forth in fuch a
' light that I thought myfelf undone: Af-
' ter he fat down, Thomas ftood up and
' brought me together again, I mean what
' was to be raifed, bone to his bone, with
' the finews and ftrength that would con-
' ftitute a chriftian; I almoft thought
' myfelf new born, the old man deftroyed
' and the new man made up, concluding I
' fhould never be bad again, that my fins
' were forgiven, and I fhould have nothing
' to do but to do good; I thought I had got-
' ten my lot in the good land, and might
' fit now under my own vine and fig tree,
' and nothing more fhould make me afraid.

' Poor

'Poor creature! I had only a fight, I did
'not yet think what powerful adverfaries I
'had to war with; this has been the mife-
'rable cafe of many, they have fat down
'under a convincement, and in a form of
'religion, fome depending on former expe-
'rience or former openings, fome on their
'education, fome a bare belief, and know-
'ledge hiftorical of the fcriptures and prin-
'ciple of truth.—Thus tho' I received the
'truth, yet I was like the ftony ground;
'I received it with joy, but had not root in
'myfelf, my heart grew hard again, for
'when tribulations, perfecutions, tempta-
'tions and trials came upon me, I fell. Oh!
'how I moped at times and wandered about
'as a prifoner at large, I would have run,
'but I could not, my offended judge, my
'accufer was in me, I could not fly from
'him; yet, great goodnefs was near, and
'his power kept me from grofs evils in a
'great degree.—I kept pretty much to meet-
'ings, but there was fuch a mixture of un-
'digefted matter in me, it was not to be
'foon feparated. Oh! the neceffity there
'was, and ftill is of a continual watch
'againft our foul's enemies both within
'and without.'

Having paffed thro' various probations,
he had confiderable openings of the divine
fenfe of the fcriptures, and alfo faw that
the Lord had a work for him to do, to which
he at length gave up, and being faithful
therein, was made helpful to many, being
enlarged

enlarged and found in teftimony, and at times very particularly led to explain paffages in the fcriptures, to the comfort and information of hearers.

He was an affectionate hufband and parent, diligent in attending meetings for worfhip and difcipline, and manifefted therein a zealous concern for the promotion and honour of truth, waiting for wifdom to fee his duty, and ftrength to perform it.—He divers times travelled abroad on this continent in the fervice of truth, and frequently to the neighbouring meetings to fatisfaction; his outward circumftances being at times difficult, gave him an opportunity to fhew an example of chriftian refignation, and to fee its effects in divers providential affiftances.

In 1756 he laid before this meeting a religious concern to vifit friends in Great-Britain, which had been on his mind upwards of ten years, wherewith the meeting concurring, he had our certificate, and embarking, landed in Ireland; and after vifiting the meetings in that country, arrived in England and performed his religious vifit in feveral counties, but was taken ill, and died in London the 26*th* of the firft month 1758; finifhing his days work with a firm affurance that the gates of Heaven were opened to him; very acceptable accounts of his fervices both in England and Ireland have been received, as are more fully fet forth in the annexed teftimony of Devonfhire-houfe monthly-meeting concerning him.

He

He died aged about fixty-feven, was in the profeffion of the truth near 44, and an acceptable minifter upwards of 30 years.

A Teftimony from Devonfhire-houfe *Monthly-Meeting in* London, *concerning* ABRAHAM FARRINGTON.

THIS worthy minifter and elder, having had drawings in fpirit for feveral years, as we are informed, to vifit the churches of Chrift in this nation and Ireland, in the fervice of the gofpel; when he apprehended the time approached wherein he was to enter upon this weighty engagement, he fettled his outward affairs; and having the concurrence and unity of the brethren, embark'd in a veffel bound from Philadelphia to Dublin, in company with three friends from Europe, who had performed a religious vifit to the churches in America.—After a favoured voyage of about four weeks, landing at Dublin, he vifited the meetings of friends in Ireland, and by the accounts from thence, had very weighty and acceptable fervice there: Having laboured faithfully in that nation to ftrengthen the brethren and affift in building up the wafte places in Zion, he embark'd for England, vifited the churches in fome of the northern counties, attended the yearly-meeting at Penrith, and afterwards that

in

in this city, his labour of love in the work
of the miniſtry, being to edification and
comfort, was truly acceptable.—After attending the yearly-meetings of Colcheſter,
Woodbridge, Norwich and the quarterly-
meeting of York, he viſited many meetings in
the northern and midland counties, from
whence good accounts have been received of
his weighty and affecting labours. He return
ed to London the lattter end of the twelfth
month 1757. Having travelled with great
diligence and laboured fervently, his health
was impaired; nevertheleſs he attended meetings till his diſorder increaſed ſo as to render
him incapable of further ſervice.

As this our dear friend ſpent but little
time in this city, we cannot from knowledge
and experience give ſuch a teſtimony concerning him as might be thought requiſite;
yet, as ſome of us partook of the benefit
of his religious labours, we find ourſelves
engaged to give forth this teſtimony concerning him.

His converſation was innocently cheerful,
yet grave and inſtructive; he was a man of
a weighty ſpirit, a valiant in Iſrael; a ſharp
reprover of libertine and looſe profeſſors; but
tender to the contrite and humble; and a
lover of good order in the church.

He was ſtrong in judgment, found in
doctrine, deep in divine things; often explaining, in a clear and lively manner, the
hidden miſteries wrapt up in the ſayings of
Chriſt, the prophets and apoſtles; and it
may

may truly be faid, he was well inftructed in the kingdom, bringing forth, out of his treafure, things new and old.

His miniftry was in plainnefs of fpeech, and attended with divine authority, reaching the witnefs of God in man, and to the habitation of the mourners in Zion; frequently pointing out, in a lively manner, the paths of the exercifed travellers, and the fteps of heavenly pilgrims; by which he was made helpful to fuch as are feeking the true reft, which the Lord hath prepared for his people. It may truly be faid, he was eminently gifted for the work of the prefent day, remarkably qualified to expofe the myftery of iniquity, and to point out wherein true godlinefs confifted.

His diftemper increafing, he was confined to his bed, at the houfe of our friend Thomas Jackfon, in Devonfhire-fquare, where all neceffary care was taken of him. During his illnefs, he was very fweet and tender in his fpirit, and remarkably patient. He uttered many comfortable and heavenly expreffions, and feveral times faid, ' He ' apprehended his time in this world would ' be but fhort;' and feemed fully refignе l to quit mortality, having an evidence, ' That ' he fhould be clothed upon with immorta- ' lity, and be united to the heavenly hoft.'

He had frequently been heard to fay, in time of health, ' That he thought he fhould ' lay down his body in this nation, and not ' fee his friends in America more;' to which

O   he

he appeared freely given up. He often expreſſed his deſire, 'That he might be fa-
' voured with an eaſy paſſage,' which was
gracioully granted.

He departed this life, the 26th of the firſt
month 1758, like a lamb, without either ſigh
or groan, as one falling into a ſweet ſleep,
aged about ſixty-ſix years; and on the 30th
of the ſame, his body was carried to Devon-
ſhire-houſe, where a large and ſolemn meeting was held, which was owned by him
whoſe preſence is the life of our meetings;
and from thence his body was carried, by
friends, to their burying-ground in Bunhill-
fields, a large concourſe accompanying it,
and was there decently interr'd among the
remains of many of our primitive worthies,
and valiant ſoldiers in the lamb's war, who
loved not their lives unto death, for the word
of God and teſtimony of Jeſus.

A Teſtimony from Kennet *Monthly-Meeting in*
Pennſylvania, *concerning* H A N N A H
C A R L E T O N.

HANNAH CARLETON, late wife of
Thomas Carleton, of Kennet, in Cheſter county Pennſylvania, was born at Haverford in the ſaid county, about the 5th month
1689; ſhe was ſenſible of the Lord's viſitation of love to her in her young years, and
as ſhe gave heed thereto, was preſerved in a
good

good degree from the vanities and evil converfation of the world; as fhe grew in years
fhe grew in the truth, was a ferviceable
friend in the fociety and her neighbourhood
in divers refpects; and of latter years was
helpful in that weighty work of vifiting
friends families, having at times to impart
(not only in fuch opportunities, but in our
more public meetings) of her experience of
the work of truth in her young years, and
urging to others the neceffity of the fame
work in them; which was well receiv'd by
friends. Being taken with an excefs of
bleeding at the nofe, fhe was thereby fo
weakened that for fome months before her
deceafe, fhe did not go from home nor much
out of doors; fhe apprehended her end was
near, and when it was propofed to fend to
a doctor for help, fhe faid, ' It feemed needlefs, for I am in the hands of the great phyfician who knows what is beft for me.' A
neighbour fignifying fhe hoped to fee her
better, fhe anfwered, ' Better I fhall be in
' a little time.' The friend replied, ' In a
' better ftate of health I mean;' fhe anfwered, ' I neither expect nor defire it,' admiring
the kindnefs of the almighty in favouring
her fo, that fhe felt neither ficknefs nor pain.
Another time fhe faid, ' As I have laboured
' for peace and love, fo now I fee nothing but
' peace before me,' with feveral other fentences which manifefted, that the peace and quietnefs fhe was favoured with, came from the
father of mercies to her in her laft moments.

She

She departed this life, the 6*th* of the fifth month 1758, about the 3*d* hour in the afternoon, and was buried in friends buryingground in Kennet, the 8*th* of the fame month, in the fixty-ninth year of her age.

A Teftimony from Gwynedd *Monthly-Meeting in* Pennfylvania, *concerning* JANE JONES.

JANE JONES, wife of John Jones of Montgomery townfhip, was educated amongft friends, and as fhe grew in years, fhe increafed in divine knowledge, and became a ferviceable member of the church. The affability and fweetnefs of her difpofition, and her love to all, render'd her very near, not only to the faithful, but many others alfo. As a parent, fhe was much more concern'd for her children's eternal welfare, than for their acquiring of wealth or preferments in this world. And as fhe poffeffed affluence and plenty herfelf, the fenfibility of her heart towards the needy, would not permit her to eat her morfel alone. She fought for the poor, and diftributed bountifully to their wants. As fhe advanced to old age, fhe became frail, and fubject to pain and diforders, which difabled her from attending meetings as duly as fhe defired; neverthelefs her love to truth and the profperity of Zion brightened and increafed, and fhe bore her weaknefs with patience, as a difpenfation permitted for her probation.

She

She departed this life, the 11*th* of the fifth month 1758, and was interr'd the 14*th* of the fame month in friends buryingground at Gwynedd, in the feventieth year of her age.

A Teſtimony from Haddonfield *Monthly-Meeting in* New-Jerſey, *concerning* J O S E P H T O M L I N S O N.

O U R well eſteemed friend Joſeph Tom-linſon deceaſed, was convinced of the truth in the early part of his life. His zeal for attending religious meetings when but young, was ſuch, that he frequently travelled many miles on foot to them, and continued remarkably diligent in attending all our religious meetings. As he grew in years, he became more and more ſerviceable amongſt friends, being ſeveral years an overſeer of Haddonfield meeting, and likewiſe an elder; careful to maintain the diſcipline. His life ſeemed to be unblameable. He was nearly united unto his friends, and their love to him was very great.

He died the 3*d* of the ninth month 1758, and we believe he was prepared to receive the anſwer of " Well done, &c."

A Teſtimony

A Teſtimony from Wrights Town *Monthly-Meeting in* Bucks *county* Pennſylvania, *concerning our ancient friend and ſiſter* AGNES PENQUITE, *who departed this life, the 20th day of the eleventh month* 1758, *being upwards of one hundred years old.*

SHE brought a certificate with her from Europe, dated the 6*th* day of the ſecond month 1686. She was of an innocent pious life and converſation, a good example in attending meetings both on firſt and week-days, until a few years before her death. She was a miniſter above ſeventy years; her teſtimony, tho' generally ſhort, was moſtly to ſatisfaction and edification; and in her declining age, when nature ſeemed almoſt ſpent, ſhe appeared more divinely favoured than common, to the admiration of ſome. When ſhe could no longer attend meetings, ſhe would often, at meal times, appear in prayer, with praiſes to the Lord, to the comfort and ſatisfaction of thoſe preſent; and frequently ſignified, ' She had ' the evidence of divine peace.' Not long before her departure ſhe ſaid, ' That her ' ſweet Lord had not forſaken her, but was ' ſtill with her to comfort and refreſh her in ' her old age.' Thus ſhe was removed from time to eternity, like a ſhock of corn fully ripe.

A Teſtimony

A Teſtimony from Goſhen *Monthly-Meeting in* Cheſter *county*, Pennſylvania, *concerning* CADWALLADER JONES.

HE was born the *27th* of the firſt month 1687, near Bala, in Merionethſhire, in the principality of Wales, and removed with his parents into Pennſylvania about the year 1697; ſoon after their arrival, he was placed with a friend until he came of age, in this time of his youth, he was naturally very wild and airy, and delighted much in vain company, until by convictions he broke off from his companions. In the year 1710 he married, and ſoon after ſettled at Uwchlan in Cheſter county, where he remained until his deceaſe. A meeting being eſtabliſhed at that place ſhortly after his removal thither, he duly attended the ſame both on the firſt and other days of the week; ſometimes remarking, ' That he knew the bene-' fit of leaving the hurry of the world to ' attend meeting,' where he was a good example, both in keeping to the time appointed, and his ſolid ſitting in ſilence. He was zealous for the ſupport of our chriſtian diſcipline and active therein, as well as in overſeeing the flock and other ſervices in the church.

He ſerved in the ſtation of an elder about 28 years, diligently attending thoſe meetings even until old age and under bodily weakneſſes. In his ſickneſs, he often exprefs'd

prefs'd much concern and forrow for fome
of the profeffors of truth, faying, ' They
' are on the decline, what will become of
' them?' And further faid, ' This thing had
' often been a burden to him, and he thought
' he had difcharged his part, and it would now
' foon become the burden of others;' expreffing a concern for the right management
of the difcipline, and remarking the remiff-
nefs of fome herein. He frequently expreffed his refignation to the will of God; and
on the 21/t of the eleventh month 1758,
quietly departed this life, and was buried
the 23d in friends burying-ground at Uwchlan aforefaid.

A Teftimony from Woodbridge *Monthly-Meeting in* New-Jerfey, *concerning* S A R A H
S H O T W E L L.

SARAH SHOTWELL departed this life,
in the eighth month 1759, in the forty-
fourth year of her age. She was educated
amongft friends on Long-Ifland, and was
early engaged in a public teftimony. In the
twenty-feventh year of her age, fhe was
married to Jofeph Shotwell of Rahway; was
a woman much beloved, of a fweet, free
and hofpitable fpirit, guarded in her expreffions, careful to give no juft occafion of
offence, a prudent loving wife, a tender exemplary parent, an affectionate and kind
neighbour;

neighbour; often fympathizing with thofe in affliction, efpecially fuch as were religious and virtuous; the rich and poor of thofe were equally near to her, and nearer than natural kindred where truth had not united in fpirit: She gladly received ftrangers; and her carriage and behaviour to young minifters and burden-bearers, manifefted her concern for and fympathy with them, often dropping feafonable hints for their encouragement. Although fhe did not travel much abroad, yet fhe was diligent in attending meetings at and about home, being endued with a found and living miniftry, clear and diftinct in her teftimony, whereby many were alarmed, fome convinced, ftrengthened and confirmed in the faith through a blefling on her labours. She was much engaged in filent humble waiting on the Lord, who was pleafed to own her, and often raife in her memorials and fongs of thankfgiving to the God of all mercies, who never forfook his people in the deep, nor left them to perifh in the wildernefs, but was faithful and true, and failed not to bring to the promifed land. The gofpel truths fhe was enabled to open, were fo affecting to many, that fome who were prejudiced againft women's preaching, have been heard to fay, ' If fuch a thing could be, fhe was a true ' gofpel minifter.'

She was a pattern of humility, not feeking applaufe, nor forward in her public appearances, and tho' fometimes large, was

generally

generally careful not to ſtand long; fervent and living in prayer, wherein, we believe, ſhe had accefs to the father. She frequently exhorted all to come up in faithfulneſs, fignifying, ' That God would have a people ' that would ferve him in uprightneſs and ' integrity of heart.'

Having had a fight fometime before her laſt ſickneſs, that her time here was nearly accompliſhed, ſhe departed this life, after about four days illneſs, in a reſigned frame of mind.

A Teſtimony from Hopewell *Monthly-Meeting in* Virginia, *concerning* ISAAC HOLLINGS-WORTH.

IN his youthful days he was deeply affect-ed with the viſitation of the love of God, and by adhering and carefully waiting in his counfel, he was preſerved from the deluding vanities of the world, which are too apt to draw and divert the minds of young people, from an awful regard to him who created them. He received a gift in the miniſtry when about twenty-one years of age, and was, we believe, a faithful labourer in his maſter's work, being much con-cern'd for the promotion of truth and the eternal well-being of mankind: Of a fober and grave deportment, diligent in attending religious meetings, and exemplary in hum-ble

ble waiting therein. He vifited the churches in divers parts of the neighbouring colonies; and we find by accounts from thence,
that his ferviccs and labours of love were
well accepted among them. In the year
1757 he removed with his family within the
limits of Fairfax monthly-meeting, fo that
we cannot give a very particular account
of him, towards the latter part of his time,
which we refer to that meeting.

A Supplement to the foregoing Teftimony, from
Fairfax Monthly-Meeting in Virginia.

THE foregoing teftimony concerning
our worthy friend Ifaac Hollingfworth,
was read in this meeting, to which we are
free to add, that the few years he refided
among us, he was a diligent attender of our
religious meetings, and alfo a promoter of
opportunities for retirement in families.
He greatly defired, ' That truth might prof-
' per in the hearts of the youth,' being frequently concern'd in meetings, to fpeak to
and encourage them, ' To come up in their
' duty,' and alfo to warn the difobedient,
' To forfake the evil of their ways;' A
degree of the holy anointing accompanying
his miniftry, it tended to the encouragement and edification of the fincere in heart.

His laft illnefs was a nervous diforder,
which continued on him nineteen days;
within which time he attended our meeting
on a firft day, and bore a living teftimony
much

much to the fatisfaction of friends, whereby he feemed much fpent; and on going
home he immediately took his bed, uttering
but few words, and departed this life, eafy
and quiet, on the 10th of the ninth month
1759, and on the 12th of the fame month,
was interr'd in friends burying-ground at
Fairfax, aged about thirty-feven years; and
we doubt not he is a partaker of that joy
which crowns the labours of the faithful.

A Teſtimony from Buckingham *Monthly-meeting, Bucks county* Pennſylvania, *concern-
in* EDMUND KINSEY.

HE was born in Philadelphia, in the
year 1683, and it pleaſed the Lord to
make him acquainted with truth, which he
embraced in a good degree, and became fober, grave and ſteady in his deportment.
In his early days he received a gift in the
miniſtry, wherewith friends had unity; being alſo ſerviceable and exemplary to the
particular meeting of Buckingham when it
was ſmall, by his diligence in attending it,
his humble waiting therein, and lively miniſtry to the refreſhing and encouraging of
the little flock. Though his underſtanding
as a man was not very extenſive, yet that
was abundantly ſupplied by his meek, innocent, loving and inoffenſive deportment
to all people. He was very diligent and in-
duſtrious

duftrious in his outward affairs, a good example in his family, and affectionate to
friends. His latter days were attended with
great affliction of body, which he bore with
patience and refignation, frequently fignifying his ' Dependance on the Lord, the great
' phyfician of value;' faying, " He was
" travelling towards the city of reft, whofe
" builder and maker God is." Having attained to the age of feventy-fix years, he
departed this life, the 24th of the twelfth
month 1759, in great peace and good will
to all men. A minifter upwards of 40 years.

A Teftimony from Salem *Monthly-Meeting in*
New-Jerfey, *concerning* ELIZABETH DA-
NIEL, *wife of* James Daniel.

SHE was born in the year 1709, was a
woman endowed with a lively gift in
the miniftry, and by yielding in obedience
to the heavenly call and following the paths
of true wifdom, it became as a crown and
royal diadem on her head; for the truth
was her chief adorning, and by it fhe was
advanced from a poor, low, defpifed girl, to
be as a mother in our Ifrael; and by wifdom was enabled to ftand in the midft of
the congregation, with reputation and honour for the caufe of our God, and to plead
with gainfayers and the lukewarm, to join in
with the glorious truth that had made her
free,

free, in the demonſtration of the power of
pure love; and in the ſtream thereof ſhe
was often led forth, to comfort the mourn-
ful travellers in Zion, and in the line of experience could tell what great things the
Lord had done for her ſoul, thro' her obedience and truſt in him, to whom ſhe freely
attributed all ſhe received as from his boun-
tiful hand, and thereby gave the glory to
God, and adminiſtred comfort to weary
travelling ſouls. But being of a backward
ſpirit, from a ſenſe of her own weakneſs,
was loath to give up to travel in truth's ſervice, which often brought her very low under ſuch exerciſes. She ſometimes travelled
in Pennſylvania and Maryland, of which
ſervice we had comfortable accounts, and
was alſo uſeful in building up the church
within the limits of our monthly-meeting.

She was very lively to the laſt, and her
teſtimonies were accompanied with power
that made them truly ſeaſonable to the au-
ditory, the divine preſence being ſenſibly
with her, under a ſenſe whereof ſhe was
very much reſigned, and rather deſirous to
depart and be at reſt with the Lord. On
being aſked how ſhe was, ſhe anſwered with
much calmneſs, ' I am in great pain of bo-
' dy, but quite eaſy in mind, free to depart
' and be releaſed from my various exerciſes;
' and feel as if my day's work was done,
' and that I might lay down this tabernacle
' in peace. But Oh! the pain at times is ſo
' great, nature is ready to ſhrink, and am
' afraid

' afraid I fhall not be able to bear it with
' that patience I ought, tho' I ftrive for it,
' for my mind is quite eafy and refigned.'

Her pain was great under the extremity
of a fharp pleurify, and after feven days,
this fervant of the Lord quietly departed in
peace, on the 30*th* of the tenth month 1760,
in the fifty-firft year of her age, and the 26*th*
of her public miniftry.

A Teftimony from Haddonfield *Monthly-Meeting in* New-Jerfey, *concerning* J O S H U A
L O R D.

HE was born the firft day of the eleventh
month 1698, near Woodberry, in the
county of Gloucefter Weft-New-Jerfey, of parents profeffing with friends, and appeared in
the miniftry about the year 1727, being early
favoured to experience a growth therein,
becoming a ufeful member in fociety. The
forepart of his time he travelled pretty much,
having twice vifited friends in New-England
and Long-Ifland, as alfo Maryland, Virginia and North-Carolina; of which fervices
we had fatisfactory accounts by certificates;
he alfo frequently vifited the neighbouring
meetings in Pennfylvania and the Jerfeys;
the latter part of his time he fpent moftly at
home.

His

His laſt illneſs was of ſhort continuance, in which he was favoured with a quiet and reſigned mind; expreſſing, ' That he had ' gone through a ſeries of trouble, but had ' been ſupported by the beſt of ſupport;' and we believe he is gone to enjoy that un-mixed felicity that will never have an end.

He departed this life, the 19th of the eleventh month 1760, aged about ſixty-two years, and on the 22d of the ſame month was interr'd in friends burying-ground at Woodberry Creek.

———————

A Teſtimony from Cheſterfield *Monthly-Meeting in* New-Jerſey, *concerning* ISAAC HORNOR.

HE was ſon of John and Mary Hornor, born the 17th of the ſecond month 1678, in the town of Tadcaſter, in York-ſhire Old-England. In 1683, he came with his parents to America, and ſettled within the limits of this meeting. After his fa-ther's deceaſe, it pleaſed the Lord to viſit him with his bleſſed truth in his young years, which he received in the love of it, and being obedient thereto, as he grew in years he grew in grace, and in the ſaving knowledge thereof, whereby he became a ſerviceable member amongſt friends, both as an overſeer and elder. Although he did not appear in public teſtimony, he had a ſenſe of the true miniſtry, and was particu-

larly

larly qualified to adminifter counfel and admonition; often advifing to a fteady courfe of life, and fetting forth the way and leadings of truth in a very informing and encouraging manner, to the edification and comfort of many, which render'd his converfation agreeable, not only amongft thofe of our fociety, but others alfo; being likewife ufeful in fettling differences. His fitting and waiting in meetings was grave and folid becoming a true worfhipper; was a nurfing father and a faithful elder, ferving in that ftation divers years. He departed this life, after a fhort illnefs, on the 24th of the eleventh month 1760, and was interr'd in a burying-ground on his own plantation, aged eighty-two years and fix months.

A Teftimony from Evefham *Monthly-Meeting in* New-Jerfey, *concerning* OBADIAH BORTON.

HE was born in the townfhip of Evef-ham, in New-Jerfey, in the year 1708, and the influence of divine grace made early impreffions on his mind whilft young in years, which led him to love folitude and fobriety, and to fhun thofe vices incident to youth. About the twenty-fecond year of his age, a difpenfation of gofpel mini-ftry was committed to him. He was very awful at times in his public approach before

P. the

the divine majefty in prayer, and often engaged to exhort friends to humility, and to fhun arrogancy and pride, being a good example herein himfelf; fo that his upright innocent deportment, gained him the good efteem of his friends and others. He departed this life, the 7th of the feventh month 1761, aged fifty-three, a minifter 31 years, and was buried at Evefham.

A Teftimony from Haddonfield *Monthly-Meeting in* New-Jerfey, *concerning* E L I Z A B E T H E S T A U G H.

SHE was daughter of John and Elizabeth Haddon, friends of London; born in the year 1682, her parents gave her a liberal education; who having an eftate in lands in this province, propofed coming over to fettle; and in order thereto, fent perfons over to make fuitable preparation for their reception; but they being prevented from coming, this our friend with her father's confent, came over, and fixed her habitation where he propofed if he had come; fhe being then about twenty years of age, in a fingle ftate of life, and exemplary therein.

In the year 1702, fhe was married to our worthy friend John Eftaugh, who fettled with her where fhe then dwelt, the place being called Haddonfield, in allufion to her maiden name; there they lived together,

near

near forty years (except in that space, her
several times crossing the sea to Europe, to
visit her aged parents, and when he was
called abroad on truth's service, to which
she freely gave him up.) She was endowed
with great natural abilities, which being
sanctified by the spirit of Christ were much
improved, whereby she became qualified to
act in the affairs of the church, and was a
serviceable member, having been clerk to
the women's meeting near 50 years, greatly
to satisfaction. She was a sincere sympathi-
zer with the afflicted, of a benevolent dif-
position, and in distributing to the poor,
was desirous to do it in a way most profitable and durable to them, and if possible,
not to let the " Right hand know what the
" left did;" and tho' in a state of affluence as to this world's wealth, was an example of plainness and moderation; zealously concern'd for maintaining good order
in the church, diligent in attending meetings at home, where her service seemed
principally to be, and from her awful sitting, we have good cause to believe she was
an humble waiter therein, which admini-
stered edification to the solid beholder. Her
heart and house was open to her friends,
whom to entertain, seemed one of her greatest
pleasures; was prudently cheerful, and well
knowing the value of friendship, was careful not to wound it herself, nor encourage
others in whispering and publishing their
failings or supposed weaknesses.

Her

Her laft illnefs confined her about three months, being often in great bodily pain, but favoured with much calmnefs of mind and fweetnefs of fpirit, which render'd her confinement more eafy to herfelf and thofe with her, which affords matter of encouragement to furvivors, to prefs after the mark of the high calling in Chrift Jefus. She departed this life, the 30*th* of the third month 1762, as one falling afleep, full of days, like unto a fhock of corn fully ripe. Her body was interr'd on the 1*ft* of the fourth month following, in friends burying-ground at Haddonfield, being accompanied by many friends and others, where a folid meeting was held; aged about eighty-two years.

A Teftimony from Woodbridge *Monthly-Meeting in* New-Jerfey, *concerning* ANNA WEBSTER.

ANNA WEBSTER, an elder, wife of John Webfter of Plainfield, departed this life, the 20*th* day of the fifth month 1762, in the thirty-fixth year of her age. She was favoured when young, to have her mind turned to him who is able to preferve all that put their truft in him; and by her obedience to the manifeftations of divine light, fhe was enabled to conduct herfelf in a fteady and upright manner; and in the time of her laft ficknefs, gave much ufeful and

and inſtructive advice, to her huſband, children and friends. She divers times entreat-
ed her huſband, ' To give up to the Lord's
' diſpoſings, and not to be over troubled
' about her,' expreſſing, ' Her dependance
' on the Lord and reſignation to his will,'
with deſires, ' That the Lord would be with
' and comfort him, and that he might ſeek
' for heavenly wiſdom, and thereby be di-
' rected how to walk before the Lord, and
' bring up their children in his fear, that
' they may have a portion in heaven;' charging her children, ' To conſider the poor and
' adminiſter to their neceſſities.'

At a time, ſpeaking to her eldeſt ſon, ſhe
ſaid, ' My dear child, let it never be ſaid
' of thee, " The foxes have holes, and the
" birds of the air have neſts, but the ſon
" of man hath not whereon to lay his head."
She earneſtly importuned friends, ' To keep,
' not only themſelves, but their offspring,
' to week-day meetings, and teach them to
' wait on the Lord, that he might merci-
' fully bleſs them.' Alſo recommended,
' Unity amongſt friends,' expreſſing, ' Her
' ſorrow in the breach thereof,' and urged
cloſely, ' The neceſſity of living in love;'
entreating friends, ' To notice her huſband
' and children in their diſtreſs, and watch
' over and adviſe her children, not ſparing
' to tell them their faults.'

She adviſed her children, ' In all their
' undertakings to ſeek the Lord for counſel,
' eſpecially in that of chooſing companions,'

and

and exprefs'd her experience of favours received thereby, faying, ' She had often
' magnified that gracious hand which was
' with her when a poor orphan child; and
' preffed them to ferve the Lord in their
' youth, which would draw divine bleffings
' on them;' adding, ' There are excellent
' accounts of God's love to fuch as give up
' all in their youth;' and charged them,
' To avoid bad company, and keep to plain-
' nefs;' ftrongly advifing, ' Againft difobe-
' dience to parents.'

At a time when feveral young people were
prefent, one of whom was light and airy,
fhe teftified againft her vain practices in very
moving expreffions, and informed her, ' That
' the enemy would incline the mind in
' meetings, to fuch vanities as were prac-
' tifed out of meetings.'

She was divers times concern'd in fervent
prayer and fupplication to the almighty,
' That fhe might have fure hope before her
' change, and bear patiently her diftrefs;
' and for the poor afflicted feed, that the
' Lord's work might be carried on in the
' earth, and that he would deftroy all the
' inventions of the enemy, which lead peo-
' ple to fin againft him.' Many more deep
and weighty expreffions fhe uttered, which
for brevity fake are omitted.

May the dying penetrating language of
one whofe general conduct was virtuous,
have a proper impreffion on our minds,
and ftir us up to prepare for our great and
final change, is our fincere defire.

A Teftimony

A Teſtimony from Cheſterfield *Monthly-Meeting in* New-Jerſey, *concerning* Sarah Murfin.

THIS worthy woman was one whom it pleaſed the Lord, to call out of the broad way and vanities of the world, and make acquainted with his bleſſed truth ; and as ſhe abode under the crofs, it pleaſed the almighty to manifeſt unto her, that ſhe was a choſen veſſel or inſtrument for his ſervice, to preach the goſpel. She was fervent in prayer, ſerviceable in viſiting families, and her godly example in life and converſation, great humility and ſelf-denial, much adorned her miniſtry ; careful to bring up her family in the fear of the Lord, and in plainneſs of ſpeech and apparel ; being indeed a mother in Iſrael.

We fervently deſire that the great Lord of the harveſt, may be pleaſed to continue to his church and people, a living miniſtry ; and that many may be made willing to run his errands and be ſerviceable in his hand, as was this our worthy friend, who departed this life, the 26*th* of the ſeventh month 1762, aged about ſeventy-ſix years.

A Teſtimony

A Testimony from Rahway *Monthly-Meeting in*
New-Jersey, *concerning* ELEANOR SHOT-
WELL.

ELEANOR SHOTWELL, late wife of
Jacob Shotwell of Rahway, was a tender hearted friend, and encouraged such as
sought the Lord. She was an elder of sound
judgment, concern'd for the church's welfare, and that Zion might be restored to her
primitive beauty, and was a pattern of plainnefs and felf-denial. In the ninth month
1762, being on her journey to attend the yearly-meeting at Philadelphia, a friend mentioned the danger of going to said city, on account
of an infectious diftemper then prevalent
there; to which she replied, ' She had no
' fear on that account, and that it was no
' matter where we departed the world, fo
' that we were in our duty.' She accordingly went to the meeting and attended the fittings of it, until she was suddenly seized
with a violent diforder, attended with extreme pain near three days, which she bore
with a calm and even mind. To a friend
who vifited her, she faid, ' She was almoft
' gone, and in great pain of body, but ex-
' ceeding peace of mind.' At another time
faid, ' It was fatisfactory that her peace was
' made with the Lord, and that it would be
' terrible to have a wounded confcience at
' fuch a time to ftruggle with.' Concerning
her hufband and children whom she dearly
loved,

loved, fhe faid, ' Though fhe was not like to
' fee them more, fhe was glad in the Lord,
' that fhe had given up to attend the yearly-
' meeting;' exprefling her defire, ' That her
' offspring fhould be brought up in plain-
' nefs, and that friends watchful care might
' be over them; and that her hufband might
' be preferved in felf-denial, and humble re-
' fignation to the Lord's will in all his trials.'

She departed this life, on the 2*d* day of
the tenth month 1762, in the forty-fixth
year of her age, and was interr'd in friends
burying-ground at Philadelphia.

A Teftimony from Burlington *Monthly-Meeting*
in New-Jerfey, *concerning* PETER FEARON.

HE was the fon of John and Elizabeth
Fearon, of Great-Broughton, in Cumberland, and born in or about the year
1683. He came amongft friends on a principle of convincement, during his apprenticefhip with his uncle Peter Fearon, and
appeared in a few words in meetings before
he was twenty years of age. In the latter
end of 1703, with the concurrence of friends,
he left England, and landed in Virginia,
where he ftaid about three months, then
came to Burlington in the fecond month
1704, and from that time until his deceafe,
he was a ufeful member of this meeting.

Between

Between the years 1704 and 1730, he travelled in the fervice of the gofpel, through moſt parts of this continent where meetings were then fettled, and to fome provinces feveral times; and employed above two years in vifiting friends in England, Scotland and Ireland; returning with fatisfactory certificates of the approbation and unity of friends with his religious labours.

After thofe travels, his worldly circumſtances being attended with difficulties, and his defires earneſt that he might get through them with credit, he went many voyages to fea as a factor, chiefly to Boſton and the iſland of Barbados; and thro' many difficulties, he was enabled to pay his debts, and to fave fufficient, with induſtry and care, to yield a comfortable fubfiſtance in old age, and to be helpful to fome others. In thofe undertakings he took certificates, and returned fuch as were very fatisfactory, both of his diligence in his outward bufinefs, and of his care to edify the churches with the gift of miniſtry which had been committed to him. Whilſt in Barbados in the beginning of 1746, a concern came upon him to vifit friends on Tortola, which by their large and full certificate, appears to have been very feafonable; and was the firſt after our worthy friends Thomas Chalkley, John Cadwallader and John Eſtaugh, had laid down their heads in peace among them. They fay, ' He came in a needful time, as
' a cloud

‟ a cloud full of rain upon a thirfty land,
‘ greatly to our mutual comfort and joy in
‘ the Lord, and in one another.'

·One of his laſt voyages by fea, was in
1750, and on purpofe to perform a religious
vifit to friends in Barbados and Tortola,
having our friend Thomas Lancaſter for his
companion; and when they had performed
their fervice, the faid friend was, after a
fharp ficknefs, removed by death at fea.
Befides this, he met with other fore trials
in his pilgrimage through life, particularly
in the long confinement of his wife, who
was feized with the palfy five years before
her death, and lay moſt of that time entirely
helplefs. His behaviour towards her, was
as an affectionate hufband, with much tendernefs and care; and indeed his frequent
practice of vifiting the fick and afflicted,
evidenced a fympathizing heart, and was
very becoming his ſtation.

He was preferved in the exercife of his
miniſtry, in much love and gofpel fimplicity. And his fenfe of the nature and fpirit
in which the difcipline fhould be managed,
is thus exprefs'd in an epiſtle which he wrote
to friends on Tortola, viz. ‘ That you may
‘ grow up together a fpiritual houfe that
‘ holinefs becomes, and a care according to
‘ gofpel order may be kept to amongſt you,
‘ and that no harfhnefs be ufed one towards
‘ another, but tender and helpful, and not
‘ apt to judge or cenfure one another, that
‘ you may be kept in that univerfal fpirit
‘ of

' of love, that feeks the good of all and
' hurt of none, and yet gives all their due,
' and what is right and juft.'

His diligence in attending religious meetings was remarkable, for though he lived three miles from the particular meeting of Burlington to which he belonged, it was very uncommon for bodily infirmities, or any extremities of weather to keep him at home on meeting days; and the year before his deceafe, he vifited feveral general meetings both in this and the neighbouring provinces.

A life fo fpent in fervent endeavours to promote truth and righteoufnefs among mankind, was, we have caufe to hope, in a fuitable preparation to be clofed at a fhort warning. He was feized with a fit by his own fire fide, which quickly deprived him of underftanding, and about three days after he breathed his laft, on the 21ft of the twelfth month 1762, in the feventy-ninth year of his age, having been a minifter about 60 years. He was interr'd on the 23d in friends burying-ground at Burlington, after a folid meeting held on the occafion.

Having obferved ftrict temperance and moderation, he finifhed his courfe in a good old age; being an example of prudence and fteadinefs, which we defire may be often remembred, and ufefully improved to the advantage of fuch as are left behind.

A Teftimony

A Testimony from Shrewsbury *Monthly-Meeting in* New-Jersey, *concerning* Thomas Tilton.

ON the 4*th* day of the first month 1763, died our friend Thomas Tilton, in the seventy-ninth year of his age. Some of whose last expressions were as follows, viz.

' That his passage was very long and
' hard, and many times prayed God to car-
' ry him through, that his poor wife's trou-
' ble was greater for him than she could
' well endure, and that he was not insensi-
' ble, she laboured for him both in body
' and mind.' Some time after he said, ' It
' was a comfort to him to see his children
' concerned for themselves,' and desired
them, ' To keep to their duties, for there
' was a falling away of some, but that they
' might not neglect theirs; that they would
' live in love and in the fear of the Lord,
' which would be to their advantage, but
' to live loose and wanton would make hard
' work on a dying bed;' observing, ' That
' people thought too little of their latter end,
' although they think of it sometimes, it
' soon goes out of their minds.' Then prayed, ' That the Lord would carry him
' through,' saying, ' His passage was very
' hard, and his pain and affliction great;
' yet his peace was steady, for the Lord did
' not charge him with any thing.'

A Testimony

A Testimony from Rahway *Monthly-Meeting in* New-Jersey, *concerning* ELIZABETH HAY-DOCK.

OUR friend Elizabeth Haydock, late wife of James Haydock, of Rahway, was religiously inclined from her youth, and an early pattern of self-denial and plainness to those of her age and sex. Being called to the work of the ministry, it became a trial to her, and such a cross to her own will to give up to the Lord's work, that she was ready to give way to consultations, and on account of her own incapacity and frailties, to question its being his call; so that (as she expressed) could she have found peace, she would rather have chosen death than obedience; but finding the love of God, as it is abode in, to be stronger than the world, she yielded thereto; and confiding in the Lord alone, came forth an instrument of his own preparing; and continuing to walk in the way of self-denial, she grew in her gift, increasing both in understanding and utterance to the close of her days.

In her last illness, she signified, ' She had ' near done with time, and was fully resign- ' ed;' and departed this life, in the seventh month 1763, in the twenty-seventh year of her age, and the 4*th* of her ministry.

A Testimony

A Teflimony from Exeter *Monthly-Meeting in*
Pennfylvania, *concerning* ELLIS HUGH.

THOUGH few of us were perfonally acquainted with this our dear ancient
friend in the early part of his life, yet as
we have information by good authorities, of
fome things remarkable therein, we think
it not amifs to tranfmit fome hints of them,
with what hath fallen out within the compafs of our knowledge concerning him.

He was born in Merionethfhire, in the
principality of Wales, and came over with
his parents into Pennfylvania, when about
twelve years of age.

He was naturally of a very cheerful difpofition, and for fome time indulged himfelf
in keeping company with fuch, whofe converfation and conduct were unprofitable and
vain, for which, though we do not underftand he was guilty of immoral practices, he
was clofely reproved by the witnefs of God
in fecret, and his condition being thereby
plainly manifefted to him, as likewife the
danger of purfuing fuch courfes, he did not
dare to go any longer in vanity; but fubmitting to the reproofs of inftruction, was
brought under great exercife and godly forrow; in which ftate, the converfation of his
former companions, once his delight, became a burden and increafed his diftrefs;
but avoiding to feed their light airy difpofi-
tions, keeping his mind retired, and reading

ing the holy fcriptures, when they fought to
entice him, had fuch an effect, that they
forfook him, which was a great eafe to his
mind, in that it afforded him opportunity for
a further fearch after the will of him, who
in mercy had called him to glory and virtue.
As he was thus engaged, after many deep
baptifms and trials, it pleafed the Lord,
about the thirty-fourth year of his age, to
call him to the work of the miniftry; which
was an exceeding humbling exercife to him,
and many fore conflicts he had therein,
through the buffetings of Satan; but by endeavouring to follow the Lord in the way of
his requirings, help was adminiftred, fo
that he at times, had to experience, that he
gives " The oil of joy for mourning, and
" the garment of praife for the fpirit of
" heavinefs."

His chief inducement to come and fettle in thefe parts, was a ftrong draught of
love attending his mind, which however he
did not haftily give way to, having felt
drawings hither near eight years before he
came; of fo great moment did the removing
himfelf and family appear to him.

He was a diligent attender of firft and
week day meetings for worfhip, as alfo of
our monthly, quarterly and yearly meetings, even when age and infirmity of body
rendered travelling very difficult to him.
He likewife vifited fome of the neighbouring provinces on truth's fervice, with the
unity of friends; and by accounts which

we

we have had from the places he vifited, his labours of love were well received and ferviceable.

From the time of his coming amongft us, he was always one of the number, who went on the vifit to friends families; which weighty work he undertook in much diffidence of himfelf, and fear of a forward fpirit, often faying, ' That former appoint-
' ments and engagements thereto, were of
' no account for future fervices; but that
' fuch as went, muft wait for renewed
' qualifications to enter upon that work,'
which he ufed to fay, ' He thought muft
' be a good one, fince it occafioned greater
' nearnefs, and was a renewal of love, both
' among vifitors and vifited:' And by accounts received, it was fo in a good degree.

In meetings for worfhip he was a good example in filent patient waiting upon the Lord, and when raifed to bear a public teftimony, it was with that power and authority, which accompanies a true gofpel minifter, and hath made lafting impreffions upon fome minds. Though he was of an exceeding tender difpofition, yet being a lover of good order in the church, and well knowing the dangerous tendency of undue liberty, he both by precept and example, endeavoured to promote the former and difcourage the latter; in which he gave repeated proofs, that the near connections of natural kindred did not bias his judgment.

Q His

His deportment being meek and loving, and his converſation familiar and inſtructively cheerful, gained him the eſteem of moſt who knew him, of different ranks and religious perſuaſions. He was a nurſing father in the church, and particularly ſo to divers whom the Lord had viſited that were under affliction, whether of body or mind; nor was his charity in this reſpect confined to the members of our ſociety.

He was an affectionate huſband, a tender parent, a kind maſter; and having, by the bleſſing of divine providence on his honeſt induſtry, obtained a competency of the neceſſaries of life, was very hoſpitable, entertaining both friends and others freely and kindly, not with oſtentation or for applauſe, but for the promotion of piety and virtue, and the good of mankind.

As his natural ſtrength abated in the laſt years of his life, he appeared more bright and lively in his public miniſtry, both at home and abroad; and the day he was taken ill of his laſt ſickneſs, at the funeral of one of his ſons, which was the laſt meeting he was at, he was remarkably favoured in his public teſtimony to a large gathering of people; and in ſupplication at the ſame meeting, his great Lord and maſter was pleaſed to favour him with a tranſcendent view into the beauty of holineſs, crowning a life, a great part of which had been, according to the meaſure received, devoted to his honour, with evident tokens of his being near

to

to the kingdom of reſt and peace everlaſting.
And the ſame evening he was taken ill at
his own houſe in Exeter aforeſaid, and continued for about eleven days, moſtly in extreme pain, yet bore it with patience and
reſignation to the divine will; and though
he inclined much to be ſtill and quiet, uttered many comfortable expreſſions, ſome of
which were taken down in writing. At one
time he ſaid, ' It is a fine thing to have a
' clear conſcience.' And one morning,
' Here is another day, Lord ſo preſerve me
' through it, that I may do nothing to of-
' fend thee.' In the evening he ſaid, ' Lord
' bleſs this night to me.' And taking ſomething to give him eaſe, he ſaid. ' He that
' turned water into wine is able to give a
' bleſſing.' After laying ſtill ſome time, ſaid,
' Sorrow at night, but joy cometh in the
' morning.' And in the morning he ſaid,
' I remember a dream I had about fifty
' years ago, I thought I was in a room alone,
' juſt going to die, and as I was much con-
' cerned and troubled becauſe there was no
' one preſent to ſee me die, I thought the
' great phyſician of value ſtood by me and
' ſaid, *I will be with thee;* and I have a lit-
' tle faith, that he will be with me, and if
' I am favoured with my ſenſes, hope I ſhall
' not give over wreſtling for a bleſſing.' A
little before noon he ſaid, ' Lord, this is
' the way of mortal men, when they come
' to lie on a ſick bed, they crave thy favour,
' though at other times many are forgetful

Q 2   of

‘ of thee.’ At another time he faid, ‘Though
‘ affliction may not feem pleafant during
‘ its continuance, yet it worketh an exceed-
‘ ing great joy to them that love and fear
‘ God.’ And in the evening, being in great
bodily pain, faid, ‘ Lord give me eafe if
‘ it be thy bleffed will.’ The next day being the firft day of the week, feveral friends
came to fee him before meeting, to whom
he faid, ‘ Fear God and ferve him, and his
‘ regard will be unto you, but if you neglect
‘ to worfhip him, he will caft you off for-
‘ ever,’ or words nearly to that import. And
being fearful they would over ftay the time
for meeting, inquired what hour, faying to
them, ‘ Don’t neglect the bufinefs of the
‘ Lord:’ And when they were going, defired, ‘ They would remember him when
‘ it was well with them.’ In the evening
inquiring what fort of a meeting they had
that day, and being anfwered, a good meeting; he faid with feeming joy, ‘ The Lord
‘ is not limited to perfons, but all that wor-
‘ fhip him aright fhall be accepted of him,’
or words to that effect. A little after midnight, being in great bodily pain, and from
the fymptoms, it was thought for about an
hour he was departing, during which he
appeared to have his mind retired to the
Lord, and then reviving a little faid, ‘ This
‘ has been a bleffed meeting.’ The next
morning taking leave of a neighbour, he
faid, ‘ Farewell, and if we never meet again
‘ in this world, I hope we fhall meet in a
‘ more

' more glorious place among the righteous.'
The day before his departure his fpeech failed much, tho' he remained very fenfible; and
the láft words he was heard to fay, were,
' Lord in heaven receive my foul.' Then
growing weaker until the third hour next
morning, being the 11*th* of the firft month
1764, he departed this life, in a quiet frame
of mind, aged feventy-fix years and fome
months. His corps was interr'd in friends
burying-ground at Exeter aforefaid, accompanied by a large number of his friends and
neighbours.

A Teftimony from Bradford *Monthly-Meeting in*
Pennfylvania, *concerning* MARY PENNEL.

SHE was born in Radnorfhire, in Wales,
and educated by her parents in the profeffion of the church of England. About
the thirteenth year of her age, going with
her elder fifter to a meeting of friends, who
were fitting in awful filence, with tears dropping down the cheeks of divers, it made
fuch religious impreffion on her tender
mind, that fhe thereby became in fome degree, convinced of the truth. About the
fixteenth year of her age, fhe arrived in
Pennfylvania, where living in a friend's
family, and experiencing the renewed vifits
of truth, fhe became willing to come more
clofely under the difcipline of the crofs, and
joined

joined with friends; was married to John Pennel, and refided within the compafs of Concord meeting many years. Being divers years under a weighty exercife to appear in public miniftry, about the year 1722, fhe gave up thereto, and increafing in her gift, had in time, a refrefhing edifying teftimony; being well approved by her friends at home, and frequently led into the ftates of meetings where her lot was caft; in the exercife of the miniftry fhe travelled into the eaftern provinces, alfo into Great-Britain and Ireland, where in divers places, fhe had acceptable fervice, to the ftrengthening fome tender minds in the way and work of truth. Afterwards removing with her hufband to Eaft Caln, they refided there the remainder of their time; and feveral years before her deceafe, her underftanding by reafon of age, became weak, yet fhe was preferv'd in much innocency, having a love and regard to friends, and was always pleafed with their vifits.

She died the 10*th* day of the fifth month 1764, and was interr'd in friends buryingground at Eaft Caln aforefaid, aged eightyfix years.

An additional Teftimony concerning MARY PENNEL, *by a friend from* Great-Britain.

HAVING read the preceeding memorial, concerning our worthy deceafed friend Mary Pennel, it is in my heart to make a
fmall

fmall addition thereto. In the courfe of her travels in England, fhe vifited friends at Ipfwich in Suffolk, and had good and acceptable fervice there, among a number of young perfons who were newly convinced of the truth. Her converfation was folid and inftruꞔive, accompanied with fweetnefs of fpirit, and having obtained to a confiderable growth in experimental religion, fhe fpoke in a feeling effeꞔual manner to our inward ftates. At a certain time giving fome account of her own convincement, fhe faid, ' In her very young days, fhe was a watch- ' ful obferver of the conduꞔ of friends at ' markets and public places, that fhe might ' fee whether in their dealings they kept to ' the principle of truth, of which fhe was ' convinced; and feeing their words were ' few and favoury, their countenances and ' behaviour weighty, and that they were ' juft and upright in their commerce a- ' mongft men, it had a great tendency to ' confirm and eftablifh her mind in the truth ' fhe had embraced.'

I. H.

A *Teftimony from the Monthly-Meeting of* Philadelphia, *concerning* RACHEL PEMBERTON.

S H E was born at Burlington, in Weft-New-Jerfey, in the year 1691, being the daughter of Charles Read, who was one of the early fettlers of Pennfylvania under the

the grant to William Penn. It pleafed the Lord to extend his gracious vifitation to her in her tender age, which as fhe fubmitted to and abode under, fhe happily experienced to lead her into a life of righteoufnefs and great circumfpection. About the eighteenth year of her age, fhe was married to our worthy friend Ifrael Pemberton, who united with her in a pious concern for the profperity and prevalence of the caufe of truth, her fincere love to which and the friends thereof, fhe uniformly manifefted by her kind fympathetic care as a " Mother in Ifrael." She ufefully filled the ftation of an overfeer and elder, being carefully concerned to rule her own family well, and that her offspring might have a portion in that treafure which faileth not. She was a true fympathizer with thofe under affliction of body or mind, demonftrating her fenfibility herein, by her frequent vifits to fuch, which were weighty and comforting, her converfation being folid and inftructive.

In the firft month 1754, it pleafed divine providence to deprive her of her beloved hufband, in whom was removed, a father, a friend, and counfellor to her and the church; which clofe trial (after 40 years living together in much harmony) fhe was enabled to bear with chriftian calmnefs and refignation; having often to experience the reality of that truth left upon record, " A father " to the fatherlefs, and a judge for the wi" dow, is God in his holy habitation."

She

She continued her houfe open for the reception of friends near and from remote parts, as it had been in her hufband's time, particularly for the entertainment of thofe who came from Europe on religious vifits to America, with whom fhe was often dipt into much feeling fympathy under their weighty travel and exercife.

Few have been more zealoufly concerned, and diligent in the attendance of religious meetings, feldom allowing the inclemency of weather to prevent her; and continued to manifeft the like concern when very feeble; which diligence, was, in the time of her confinement and languifhing ftate, a fatisfactory reflection to her, as her attendance had been from a real fenfe and perfuafion of duty.

On the 22*d* day of the tenth month 1764, fhe attended the fecond day's meeting of minifters and elders, which was the laft meeting fhe was at, her feeble ftate requiring her confinement to her chamber the 25*th*, and gradually weakened; yet love to the caufe of truth continued, and her concern was great, that the profeffors thereof might live under its preferving influence.

She uttered many lively expreffions at different times in the courfe of her illnefs, in acknowledgement of the goodnefs and mercy of the Lord, ' In preferving her in ' patience under great bodily pain, and ' with an evidence of her future well-being.
She

She departed this life, on the 24*th* day of the second month 1765, and was interr'd in our burial ground in this city, on the 27*th* of the same month.

A Testimony from Gwynedd *Monthly-Meeting in* Pennsylvania, *concerning* ELLEN EVANS, *an elder of said meeting.*

SHE was the daughter of Rowland and Margaret Ellis, born near Dollegelle, in the principality of Wales, in the year 1685. She was favoured with a good understanding, which being improved by a religious education and strict attention to the dictates of divine grace, soon distinguished her as one seeking after heavenly treasure, which made her in riper years, an honourable member of society.

She married our worthy and much esteemed friend John Evans, of this place, to whom she was truly a help-meet, more especially in public religious services; for whenever she discovered the least inclination in him, to visit the meetings of friends whether far or near, she did all in her power to cherish and encourage the motion; she was also a great support and comfort to him under his spiritual conflicts about the time of his appearing first in a public testimony.

In her family, she was an example of piety and industry, rising early in the morning, and

and encouraging others fo to do, often obferving that thofe who lay late, loft the youthful
beauty of the day, and wafted the moft
precious part of their time; that the fun
was the candle of the world, which called
upon us to arife and apply to our feveral
duties. When the affairs of the morning
were tranfacted it was almoft her invaria-
ble practice, except on meeting days, to
retire about noon, with the bible or fome
religious book; where a portion of her time
was fpent alone; from which retirement
fhe often returned with evident tokens, that
her eyes had been bathed in tears.

She was remarkably well acquainted with
the holy fcriptures, as alfo the writings and
characters of our ancient worthy friends,
together with thofe of her own time; frequently exprefling, ' The many advantages
' fhe reaped from often converfing with the
' dead and abfent; endeavouring to cultivate
' the fame difpofition in her family, by often
' calling them together in the winter even-
' ings, and requiring one of her children to
' read audibly in the bible or fome other reli-
' gious book;' repeatedly obferving to them,
' The benefit which attended preferving the
' characters of thofe faithful minifters and
' elders in the church, whofe pious lives and
' happy diffolution, if held up to the view
' of pofterity, might be a likely means of
' kindling the fame holy zeal, and refoluti-
' on to tread in their footfteps.' And as
miniftring friends (whom fhe truly loved
from

from her infancy as brethren and fifters in gofpel fellowfhip) in the courfe of their vifits came this way, generally lodged at their houfe, at which times fhe feldom miff-ed to prepare her family, and inform the neighbourhood of an intention to fit a while together in the evening ; which felect opportunities, many can yet remember, were often fingularly bleffed with divine comfort and edification.

Her diligence in attending meetings for religious worfhip, was no lefs manifeft than her fteady zeal for fupporting our chriftian difcipline, and that we might adorn the doctrine of God our Saviour in all things : Yet was her zeal mixed with charity, for having long experienced how few were qualified to lay juftice precifely to the line and righteoufnefs to the plumbline, fhe thought it fafeft rather to incline to the merciful fide ; firmly believing that the grace of God which bringeth falvation, had appeared unto all men ; delighting to converfe with our uninftructed Indians about their fentiments of the fupreme being ; and often faid, ' She difcovered evident traces of divine ' goodnefs in their uncultivated minds.'

In her friendfhips fhe was warm and fteady, and on her death bed earneftly preffed her children, ' Not to forget the friends of ' their father and mother ;' and the fenfibility of her heart, made her very attentive to the wants of the poor in her neighbourhood.

Some

Some years before her deceafe fhe loft in
the hufband of her youth, a bofom friend,
and the great fupport of her age, which
proved fo great a trial, fhe faid, ' That if
' God whom fhe loved all her life long, had
' not enabled her to fuftain it, fhe muft
' have funk under it.' This difpenfation
of providence weaned her from all temporal enjoyments. She continued attending
meetings, and frequently vifiting the fick
and afflicted while her ftrength permitted,
and when that failed, much of her time was
fpent in reading the holy fcriptures and in
meditation.

The early ftate of religion in this province was a grateful fubject of converfation to her in the evening of her day, but
upon turning her eye to the prefent time,
fhe would fay with a deep figh, ' Oh! what
' is become of the morning dew and celefti-
' al rain, that ufed to fall and reft upon our
' affemblies.' For herfelf, fhe often prayed,
' That fhe might poffefs a lively relifh of
' truth to the laft, and retain the greennefs
' of youth in old age, which God was gra-
' cioufly pleafed to favour her with.

Her laft illnefs began about a year before
her deceafe, in the forepart thereof fhe felt
a lownefs and depreffion of mind, that caufed her to cry, ' Tell me, Oh! thou whom
' my foul loveth, where thou feedeft, where
' thou makeft thy flocks to reft at noon.'
But after fome time, this cloud was removed,

ed, and she was enabled to say, 'He brought
' me to the banqueting house, and his ban-
' ner over me was love.'

And thus, by remembring her creator in
the days of her youth, and a steady perse-
verance therein, she was enabled to meet
the king of terrors with a serene countenance, and resigned her breath without a
sigh or groan, the 29*th* day of the fourth
month, and was buried at Gwynedd, the
2*d* of the fifth month 1765; being, we trust,
admitted to the general assembly and church
of the first born, which are written in
heaven.

A Testimony from Kingwood *Monthly-Meeting
in* New-Jersey, *concerning* S A M U E L
L A R G E.

OUR ancient friend Samuel Large, departed this life, the 9*th* of the sixth
month 1765, and was buried the 11*th* of said
month, in friends burying-ground at Kingwood, aged about seventy-seven years, having been a minister upwards of 40 years.
He was religiously inclined when young,
insomuch (as he related) that at times
he thought he could freely declare to
others of the goodness and merciful dealings of God to his soul; but for want of
giving diligent heed to the inshinings of
that divine light which had measurably
redeemed

redeemed him, he fuffered a lofs of that
fweet and heavenly communion which he
had been made a fharer of, and began to
join with folly and vanity, which youth
are apt to do; but in procefs of time, being
revifited by an all-merciful God, he gave
up to bear the crofs; and about the thirtieth
year of his age, was made willing to bear
a public teftimony, and declare to others
what God had done for him; which teftimony was living and powerful, and tended
to the refrefhing and watering the. Lord's
heritage and people; being often concern'd
where his lot was caft, to invite and perfuade people to feek the Lord for themfelves, that they might know the work of
regeneration wrought and compleated in
and for themfelves. He freely gave up to
fpend both time and fubftance on truth's
account when called thereto, having vifited
feveral provinces on this continent, and
fome of them divers times. He was a generous kind friend, ready to do good to all,
efpecially the houfehold of faith, very ready
in affifting the fervants and meffengers of
Chrift when travelling on that account;
bringing up his children in the principles
of the chriftian religion, and in plainnefs
of fpeech and apparel, a great encourager
of his family and others in attending meetings, that they might difcharge their duties which they owed to their maker. In
the latter part of his days, when old and
infirm, he met with exercifes and difficulties,

ties, yet we have good reafon to believe, he was carried through them all, and died in peace with the Lord and goodwill to all mankind, and is enter'd into reft, and reaps the reward of the faithful, where trouble and exercife are at an end. He had a fight of his approaching exit, and gave orders that his burial fhould be plain. Some of the laft words he utter'd, were to his wife, a few hours before he expired, when he faid, ' All is done that is needful, now I muft ' leave thee.'

A Teftimony from New-Garden *Monthly-Meeting in* Pennfylvania, *concerning* WILLIAM MOTT.

OUR worthy friend William Mott, of Mamaroneck in New-York government, being on a religious vifit to friends in this province; after attending our yearly-meeting at Philadelphia, intended proceeding to Nottingham, and on his way thither, was at our monthly-meeting in the tenth month 1765; where, after a time of filence, he appeared in a fhort yet fatisfactory teftimony; but being much indifpofed, left the meeting in a few minutes afterwards, and went to a friend's houfe, where his diforder, which proved to be the fmall pox, increafed and lay heavy upon him. Two days afterwards, fome friends going to vifit him, he mention'd mention'd his defire of having a time of retirement together, in which opportunity he exprefs'd in a lively and fenfible manner, his refignation to the will of God refpecting his indifpofition, and fpoke of the great advantage it would be to the members of our fociety, if they were more drawn from the fpirit and friendfhip of the world, and the eager purfuit after the riches and grandeur thereof; faying, that the profeffors of truth fuffered great lofs in a fpiritual fenfe, for want of being often deeply inward, when about their lawful callings, labouring to have their minds retired, where true comfort and inftruction is to be witneffed; and that friends who are heads of families, ought to wait for the movings of truth, to make way for them to call their children and fervants together; and if this was but the engagement of their minds, way would be made for fuch opportunities beyond their expectation. On which and fome other fubjects, he, at that time, fpoke in a fenfible humble manner.

At other times he frequently mention'd his uneafinefs in beholding, that many of the profeffors of truth did not keep within the bounds of true moderation refpecting cloathing and furniture, but rather pleafed the natural difpofition, to no real advantage, and confumed much precious time that might be profitably fpent in doing good among mankind; faying, that if friends lived near enough to the inward teacher

R that

that difcovers things to be as they really are; there are many things amongft us termed fmall or trifling, which would appear inconfiflent with the pure truth.

Notwithftanding his affliction was great, yet he bore it with remarkable patience, appearing more concern'd for the glory of God and the good of his church and people, than any temporal confiderations: And frequently exprefs'd his refignation to the divine will, being freely given up either for life or death. The retired frame of mind he generally appeared in, was inftructive; often faying he felt eafy in mind, having witnefled a comfortable refrefhing feafon, and exprefs'd his thankfulnefs for fuch peculiar favour in fo trying a difpenfation: Yet he had no other profpect but that he fhould recover, until a few hours before his deceafe, when he fignified, ' He had almoft ' done with time.' And changing faft, he quietly departed, the 15*th* of the tenth month 1765, in a fenfible compofed frame of fpirit. On the 17*th* his corpfe, accompanied by many friends, was interr'd in friends burying-ground in New-Garden, after a folid meeting.

A Teftimony

A Teſtimony from the Quarterly-Meeting of Philadelphia, *concerning our eſteemed friend*
MARGARET ELLIS, *late of* Radnor *meeting, deceaſed.*

SHE was born in the principality of
Wales, of parents profeſſing epiſcopacy,
and religious in that way. By a ſhort memorial ſhe hath left, of ſome occurrences
in her life, we find, ſhe was early viſited by
the almighty, which ſhe expreſſes in this
manner. ' At fourteen years of age, the
' call of the Lord was to me, when ſeeing
' ſome of my companions carried to the
' grave, a concern came over my mind,
' with a conſideration, whither their ſouls
' were gone, and where mine would be, if
' I ſhould then be taken away; and that
' followed and remained with me for many
' days:' But being young and not willing
to bear the croſs, the witneſs for God was
ſo far ſuppreſſed, that ſhe gave way to follow the vanities and diverſions of the world;
yet the Lord did not forget her; but ſome
years after, the viſitation was renewed,
and then, ſhe ſays, ' I returned in earneſt
' to look within, to my own ſtate and con-
' dition, and to the anointing mentioned
' by the apoſtle John, which opened clearly
' in my mind.' This brought her to a cloſe
exerciſe, and often in ſecret prayer, that
the Lord would be pleaſed to manifeſt her
duty. Soon after this, ſhe went to viſit a

brother

brother at Dolobran, who had a fhort time
before joined in communion with friends;
and being at a meeting, fhe was further
reached unto, and the thoughts of her heart
declared by a worthy minifter then prefent.
Her father took pains to diffuade her from
joining friends, and got feveral priefts to
affift him with their endeavours, but being
enlightened to fee the formality and dead-
nefs of the profeffion of religion in which
fhe had been educated, and the blindnefs
and emptinefs of their priefts, fhe aquaint-
ed her father, ' She would never come more
' to their church, unlefs it was to his and her
' mother's burial.'

In a few years after this, fhe found a concern to appear in public teftimony in friends
meetings, and foon afterwards removed to
this province; in which fhe apprehended a
divine direction, believing the Lord would
go along with her, which fhe experienced
to her comfort, and was cordially received
by friends; increafing in the gift beftowed
on her.

She paffed through various baptifms and
trials in her young years in her native land,
and many conflicts and exercifes afterwards,
yet experienced the arm of the Lord revealed
for her help and fupport.

She was a fincere hearted woman, diligent
in the exercife of her gift, which was in
much plainnefs and fimplicity. She vifited
the meetings frequently in fome parts of
this province and New-Jerfey; and in the
year

year 1752, with the concurrence of friends, embarked in order to vifit friends in fome parts of Great-Britain, which fhe performed, and was in feveral places engaged to vifit many of the families of friends; which as we have underftood, were acceptable and ferviceable. She was favoured to return, and continued lively in the exercife of her gift.

Being taken ill in Philadelphia, in the eleventh month 1765, immediately after our quarterly-meeting which fhe attended, after a few days illnefs, fhe departed this life. She had divers times, to her particular friends, expreffed her defire, if it was the Lord's will, to finifh her days in this city; and in her ficknefs expreffed her willingnefs to depart, but requefted fhe might be favoured with fome interval of eafe from extreme pain, that fhe might take her leave of her friends, which was granted her. She uttered many lively and favoury expreffions in her ficknefs, was favoured with an evidence of her future well-being, and as fhe lived in the fear of God, we doubt not fhe was accepted of him, and enjoys the reward of her faithfulnefs.

She died the 13*th* of the eleventh month 1765, in a good old age; her body was carried to our meeting-houfe in High-Street, and after a folid meeting, buried the 15*th* in friends grave-yard.

A Teftimony

A Teſtimony from Nottingham *Monthly-Meeting in* Pennſylvania, *concerning* D I N A H J A M E S.

S H E was born the 7*th* of the ſixth month 1699, near Cheſter, in the county of Cheſter in Pennſylvania. When ſhe was about five years old, her parents John and Hannah Churchman, removed and ſettled at Nottingham, in the county aforeſaid; and ſhe being religiouſly educated by them, ſoon became inwardly ſenſible of the bleſſed truth; and taking heed to its teaching, was early a- dorned thereby with a meek and quiet ſpirit; was a great lover of meetings for the wor- ſhip of God, and a humble exemplary wait- er therein. About the thirty-fourth year of her age ſhe appeared in the miniſtry, and being faithful in her gift, though ſhe did not increaſe in many words, and but ſeldom appeared therein, being rather a pattern of awful ſilence, yet her teſtimony when ſhe did appear, was remarkably ſeaſoned with the baptiſing power of the ſpirit, which made it truly acceptable to friends. She was often heard to expreſs her apprehenſion of the danger of words increaſing in the church, without ſufficient weight and aw- fulneſs; and at different times, eſpecially in the latter years of her life, both in pub- lic teſtimony and in private, ſhe ſpoke of a winnowing time at hand, wherein ſhe ap- prehended the chaff was to be blown away,

and

and the church reftored to as great, if not
a greater degree of purity than heretofore;
which is now frefh in the memory of divers
perfons.

She was an example of plainnefs herfelf,
and careful prudently to fupprefs the contrary in her children, as long as they remained under her immediate care, meekly
diffuading in a moving manner, againft any
appearance of corruption in converfation,
as well as the world's vain fafhions and fuperfluity in drefs; firmly maintaining parental authority in this fteady refolution
which fhe never departed from, viz. that
while her children were clothed at her expence, they fhould fubmit to have their clothes
fafhioned agreeable to her mind. She was no
lefs remarkable for humility and charity, a
promoter of good order in the church, and of
true peace upon the right foundation; for
which virtues fhe gained the general efteem
of her friends and others.

Between the years 1742 and 1754, fhe
vifited moft of the meetings of friends in
Pennfylvania, New-Jerfey, Long-Ifland and
the Eaftern-fhore of Maryland. Her care to
attend meetings was memorable and worthy
of imitation, even when under great bodily
weaknefs and infirmity, as fhe was for many years in the latter part of her life, feveral of her joints being greatly affected
with the violence of rheumatic pains; all
which fhe bore with fuch patience and humble refignation of mind, as truly becomes a
chriftian

chriftian, and befpoke a well grounded hope of a lafting habitation at the end of a weary pilgrimage in this world.

She was at meeting a few weeks before her deceafe, but feeling much bodily weaknefs, fhe expreffed her doubt of ever coming again; having at divers times before manifefted a fenfe of her end being near. About five days before her deceafe fhe was feized with a fever and inward pains, which weakened her very faft. The night before fhe died fhe had feveral refrefhing naps of fleep, and on awaking was often heard quietly to repeat thefe words, ' A happy change, a ' happy change;' and about the 8*th* hour on the 1*ft* of the firft month 1766, fhe quietly departed, as one falling afleep, being cheerful and fenfible almoft to the laft moments of life; in the fixty-feventh year of her age, a minifter about 33 years; and on the 3*d* of the fame month, was interr'd in the burying-ground of friends at Eaft-Nottingham.

***

A Teftimony from Sadfbury *Monthly-Meeting in* Pennfylvania, *concerning* MARY MOORE.

OUR well efteemed friend Mary Moore, late wife of James Moore, and daughter of Jofeph and Sarah Wildman, of Bucks county, was born the 8*th* day of the eighth month 1720, fhe was adorn'd with a meek and

and quiet fpirit, favour'd with a gift in the
miniftry, whofe teftimony was generally well
received, her words being few and favoury,
and her awful deportment and exemplary
conduct both at home and abroad, worthy
of imitation. About a year before her deceafe fhe was taken with a lingering diforder, in which time of weaknefs fhe was
often tenderly affected, advifing her children
and others, ' To prepare for their latter end,
' and not leave their work behind hand;'
obferving, in an humble manner, what an
awful bowed people we ought to be.

About four hours before her departure
many friends came to fee her, whom fhe
earneftly beholding, defired they would fit
down, that they might truly wait in God's
fear, and that thofe who knew how to wait
would get deep in true filence: At which
time, notwithftanding her great weaknefs,
fhe was divinely favoured, and her tongue
loofed to leave her laft teftimony, faying,
' Friends, if you love God, he will love you,
' and if you do not love God, how can you
' expect to be beloved of him?' Adding,
' If you would gather your families more
' often together, and fit down in his fear,
' and wait in true filence, to have your
' minds drawn from this world, you would
' grow in the truth,' with more to the fame
effect, defiring they might remember her
words. After which fhe defired her hufband would freely give her up and not
mourn after her, at the fame time encouraged

raged him to faithfulnefs, and defired friends would be ftill and quiet until her departure. Being fenfible to the laft, fhe quietly expired the 13*th* of the feventh month 1766, and was interr'd in friends burying-ground at Sadfbury, aged forty-five years.

A Teftimony from Haddonfield *Monthly-Meeting in* New-Jerfey, *concerning* T H O M A S R E D M A N.

H E was born in the city of Philadelphia, the 31*ft* of the third month 1714, and being ftripped of his parents when young, was placed apprentice in faid city, after which he removed and fettled at Haddonfield aforefaid. About the twenty-fecond year of his age, he appeared in the miniftry, and we believe laboured faithfully until the conclufion of his days. He travelled into New-England on a religious vifit, in company with Edmund Peckover, of Great-Britain, who was here on a vifit to the churches in America, from whence, at his return, we received a good account of his fervices, which, with his company, was very acceptable to us. He was often deeply exercifed for the growth and profperity of truth, which we believe he truly loved. In family vifits he was much favoured with divine ability, and had to deliver fuitable advice to the benefit and refrefhment of many:

His

His teſtimony was plain, found and edifying; a lowly minded ſeeker of divine help,
which made him very uſeful in the carrying
on the affairs of the church. He ruled well
in his own family, bringing them up in moderation and plainneſs, and was a good example therein himſelf. Although he did not
travel much in diſtant parts, yet he viſited
moſt of the meetings in New-Jerſey and
Pennſylvania. He was ſometimes fervently
engaged to call to the youth, for whom he
was much concerned; he was prudent,
charitable and benevolent, whoſe houſe was
open freely to receive his friends. And altho'
we ſenſibly feel the loſs of ſo worthy a friend
and member, we deſire to ſubmit. believing
our loſs is his great gain, and that he now
inherits a place prepared for the righteous.

He departed this life, at his own houſe in
Haddonfield, the 23d day of the ninth month
1766, in the fifty-third year of his age,
and was interr'd the 25th in friends burying-ground at Haddonfield, after a large
and ſolid meeting on the occaſion.

A Teſtimony from Uwchlan *Monthly-Meeting in*
Pennſylvania, *concerning* SAMUEL JOHN.

HE was born in Pembrokeſhire, in the
principality of Wales, in the year
1680, and educated in profeſſion with the
church of England, being (as we have been
inform'd

inform'd by thofe who then knew him) a fober youth, religioufly inclincd, and concern'd for an inward acquaintance with the Lord, who had touched his heart with a fenfe of his own ftate and condition, whence defires being raifed after that which is fubftantial, he continued feeking for many years, and among divers profeffions.

He came over to Pennfylvania, in the year 1709, and fome time after fettled at Uwchlan aforefaid, and foon joined in fociety with friends, having for divers years before been under fome convincement of the principle of truth as held by us; and being meafurably faithful to the manifeftation of grace received, the Lord was pleafed to beftow upon him a difpenfation of the gofpel to preach, in which we believe he laboured faithfully, and became a found and able minifter: His fitting in meetings for divine worfhip was folid and exemplary, often in filence, tho' at times when moved thereto, doctrine hath dropped from him as the dew, and his fpeech diftilled as the fmall rain, to the refrefhing the hungry and thirfty foul.

He was an example of plainnefs and moderation, his converfation weighty and inftructive, alfo very encouraging to fuch as were well minded; and divers fmall pieces found among his papers, which appear as the produce of his private meditations, manifeft that his converfation was often in heaven, and his meditation on heavenly things.

It

It was his lot to pafs through divers bap-
tifing and afflicting circumftances (occafioned by the conduct of fome who ought to
have been a comfort to him in his declining
years) which he bore with becoming patience, and retained his greennefs to the laft,
appearing in a fweet comfortable frame of
mind; he often exprefs'd himfelf in a deep,
fenfible and affecting manner, to fome who
vifited him during his laft weaknefs which
continued a confiderable time, being confined at home thro' bodily infirmity and
old age, for near two years before his deceafe.

He quietly departed this life, on the 16th
of the tenth month 1766, in the eighty-
feventh year of his age, having been a minifter about 54 years, and was buried the
18th of the faid month; when a folemn
meeting was held, wherein the overfhadowing
of truth was meafurably felt, under the influence whereof the unruly were warned, and
the feeble minded comforted and encouraged
to perfevere in the way which leads to peace.

A Teftimony from New-Garden *Monthly-Meeting
in* Pennfylvania, *concerning* JOHN SMITH.

HE was born at Dartmouth, in New-
England, the 3d of the fourth month
1681; his parents were Prefbyterians, but
joined with friends in their latter years. As
he

he grew to years of underſtanding, the Lord was pleaſed to favour him with the know-ledge of his bleſſed truth, through the divine light ſhining in his heart, whereby he became acquainted with the diſcipline of the croſs, and was, whilſt young, in a good degree weaned from the vanities and periſhing enjoyments of this world.

About the twenty-ſecond year of his age, he bore a teſtimony againſt wars and fightings, for which he was fined and ſuffered ſeven months impriſonment. In the twenty-fourth year of his age, he embark'd for England, and on his arrival there, was preſſed on board a veſſel of war, where he was kept about ſix weeks; and for refuſing to fight or be an aſſiſtant therein, he underwent ſufferings, trials and many exerciſes, but thro' the Lord's mercy and goodneſs, he was preſerved ſteady in his teſtimony, and found peace and the preſence of the Lord to be with him in a large degree, rejoicing that he was accounted worthy to ſuffer for the teſtimony of truth. He came over to Pennſylvania ſoon after, and when married, reſided ſeveral years at or near Cheſter, and about the year 1713, he removed with his family into Eaſt-Marlborough in Cheſter county, where he dwelt upwards of 40 years. About the year 1714, a meeting for worſhip was ſettled at his houſe, which continued until a meeting-houſe was built in London-Grove townſhip not far diſtant.

He

He was one whom we think dwelt near the truth, having received the fame in the love of it. His miniftry was favoury tho' not very eloquent, zealous for good order and ferviceable in the difcipline of the church. He often fpoke of the degeneracy from the primitive plainnefs confpicuous amongft friends, both in drefs and addrefs, and the great need of a reformation; expreffing his fervent defires for the reftoration of ancient purity; and being himfelf an example of plainnefs, and in converfation cheerful, inftructive and edifying; was often concern'd to ftir up the negligent to their duty, both in refpect to attendance of meetings and humble waiting therein.

He cheerfully entertained his friends, whofe company and converfation he greatly defired; and tho' in the decline of life, he met with fome afflicting occurrences, yet he bore them with a good degree of chriftian fortitude, looking over them to that which is invifible, having an eye to the recompence of reward.

The laft place of his refidence, was within the limits of New-Garden particular meeting, which he carefully attended when able; the Lord being pleafed to preferve him as a fruitful branch, frefh and green, which was manifefted by his converfation, folid deportment in meetings, and particularly in his miniftry; a fweetnefs of fpirit and lively fenfe of truth apparently attending him to the laft.

His

His bodily infirmities gradually increafing, he departed this life, the 24*th* of the
tenth month 1766, and was buried at London-Grove aforefaid, in the eighty-fixth
year of his age; and we truft he is at reft,
receiving the reward of the faithful.

A Teſtimony from Warrington *Monthly-Meeting
in* Pennfylvania, *concerning* ALEXANDER
UNDERWOOD.

H E was born in Maryland in the year
1688, and being convinced of the
truth fome time after he arrived to man's
eftate, was chofen an elder of the meeting
where he then refided; afterwards removing to this then remote part of the country,
in the fifty-feventh year of his age he appeared in the miniftry, and travelled twice
on that fervice to North-Carolina, of which
vifits we receiv'd comfortable accounts
from friends there; and when at home was
enabled to minifter fuitably to the ftate of
the church, to the comfort of the true
mourners in Zion, and encouragement of
the faithful travellers. Towards the latter
part of his time, his bodily ftrength much
failed, yet he vifited fome of the neighbouring meetings, and families of friends, to
the comfort of the faithful, his miniftry
continuing to be found and lively.

In

In his laft ficknefs he feemed much refigned, and at one time faid, ' He had the
' company of his good mafter to comfort
' him in his affliction.' At another faid,
' That he could fay with the Pfalmift, that
' the good hand that was with him in his
' young years, had not forfook him now in
' his old age.' And divers times fignified,
' He ftill felt the comforter with him;' faying, ' His day's work was done.' A little
before his departure, he fang praifes and
hallelujahs, to his great Lord and mafter.
Then prayed for the little handful; and
taking leave of all prefent, continued in a
fweet frame of mind, finging praifes until
he could not be underftood, and quietly departed this life, the 31*ft* of the tenth month
1767, and was interr'd the 2*d* of the eleventh
month, in the feventy-ninth year of his age.
May we who are left behind, be engaged to
follow his example, that fo our end may be
like unto his.

A Teftimony from Bradford *Monthly- Meeting in*
Pennfylvania, *concerning* ABRAHAM MAR-
SHALL.

WE underftand he was born at Gratton, in Derbyfhire Old England,
and educated in the profeffion of the church
of England; in his youth he was favour'd
with a vifitation of divine love, but not
keeping

keeping clofe thereunto, when amongft his companions he fuffered lofs. When about fifteen or fixteen years of age, our worthy friend John Gratton being abroad in truth's fervice, was concern'd to have a meeting at a town called Alnwick, where this our friend then refided, who fo powerfully declared the truth, that he amongft divers others was convinced; and carefully abiding under the difcipline of the crofs, he in time received a part in the miniftry. About the year 1697, he came over to Pennfylvania, and for fome time refided near Derby, where he enter'd into a married ftate, and in a few years afterwards removed to the forks of Brandywine, then a new fettled part of the country, the neareft meeting being about eleven miles, which he feldom miffed attending when of ability of body; he was alfo inftrumental in fettling this called Bradford meeting, within the compafs of which he refided the remainder of his days. He was an example of plainnefs and felf denial, and concern'd for the fupport of the difcipline. He travelled into New-Jerfey and the fouthern provinces where his fervice in the miniftry was acceptable, his doctrine being found, and his life, converfation and deportment adorning the fame. When far advanced in age, his hearing and memory failing, render'd his ufefulnefs not fo extenfive as in his younger years. For fome time before his deceafe, he feemed very defirous of his change, often expreffing,

' That

' That people fhould fo live in this world
' as to fit them for another.' About twenty-
four hours before he died, he faid to thofe
with him, ' Let me go, let me go. People
' fhould live in love:' Then faid, ' Farewell,
' farewell;' after three or four weeks illnefs
or rather growing weaker with age, he departed in a compofed frame of mind, on
the 17*th* of the twelfth month 1767, and
on the 20*th* was interr'd in friends burying-
ground at Bradford. By the general account, in the ninety-feventh year of his age,
but we have fome reafon to believe he was
one hundred and three.

Mary Marfhall, his widow was born in
Kent in Old England, and came to America
with her father when about two years and
an half old. She furvived her hufband about
fifteen months, and departed this life, after
about four days illnefs, quiet and eafy, in
the eighty-feventh year of her age, leaving
a good favour in our remembrance.

———————

*A Teftimony from the Monthly-Meeting of
Friends in* Philadelphia, *concerning* BEN-
JAMIN TROTTER, *who was born in this
city, in the ninth month of the year* 1699.

HE was early vifited, and reached unto
by the reproofs of divine light and
grace, for thofe youthful vanities and corrupt converfation, which by nature he was

prone

prone to and purfued, to the grief of his
pious mother, who was religioufly concerned to reftrain him; but as he became obedient to the renewed vifitations of the heavenly call, denying himfelf of thofe things he
was reproved for, he not only learned to
ceafe from doing evil, but to live in the
practice of doing well; and continuing faithful, became an example of plainnefs and
felf-denial, for which he fuffered much
fcoffing and mocking of thofe who had been
his companions in folly; yet he neither
fainted nor was turned afide by the reproaches of the ungodly, which thus fell to his lot,
for his plain teftimony againft their evil
conduct.

In the twenty-fixth year of his age, he
appeared in the work of the miniftry, and
laboured therein in much plainnefs and
godly fincerity, adorning the doctrine he
preached, by a humble circumfpect life and
converfation, being exemplary in his diligence and induftry to labour honeftly for a
livelihood, though often in much bodily
infirmity and weaknefs, defiring, as he fometimes expreffed, that he might owe no man
any thing but love. His inoffenfive opennefs and affability, drawing many of different denominations to converfe with him,
he had fome feafonable opportunities of ad-
monifhing and rebuking the evil doer and
evil fpeaker, which he did, in the plainnefs
of an upright zeal for the promotion of piety and virtue, tempered with true brotherly
kindnefs

kindnefs and charity; refpecting not the perfon of the proud nor of the rich, be- caufe of his riches, but with chriftian free- dom, declaring the truth to his neighbour, and was thus in private as well as public, a preacher of righteoufnefs.

In his public miniftry he was zealous againft errors both in principle and practice, and conftantly concerned to prefs the ne- ceffity of obedience to the principle of divine grace; a manifeftation of which is given to every man ; knowing, from his own ex- perience, that it bringeth falvation to all them that obey and follow its teachings, and was frequently enabled with energy and power to bear teftimony to the outward coming of our Lord Jefus Chrift, his mira- culous birth, his holy example in his life and precepts, and his death and fufferings at Jerufalem, by which he hath obtained e- ternal redemption for us.

In his public teftimony a little before his laft ficknefs, he expreffed his apprehen- fions, that his time among us would be fhort, and fervently exhorted to watchfulnefs and care, to keep our lamps trimmed, and our lights burning, and urged the neceffity of being prepared to meet the bridegroom, as not knowing at what hour he will come.

He travelled feveral times, and vifited moft of the meetings of friends in this pro- vince and New-Jerfey, and fome in the ad- jacent provinces, but was not much from home; being upwards of forty years a dili-

gent

gent attender of our religious meetings in this city, zealoufly concerned for the maintaining our chriftian difcipline in meeknefs and true charity, careful in the exercife of that part of pure religion, vifiting the widow and fatherlefs in their afflictions, and often qualified to adminifter relief and confolation to their dejected minds.

Afflictions of divers kinds, and fome very deep and exercifing, fell to his lot through the courfe of his life, which he was enabled to bear with exemplary patience and refignation, and particularly through his laft illnefs, in which, for upwards of fix weeks, he underwent great difficulty and pain, being afflicted with the afthma and dropfy, fo that he fuffered much, yet was never heard to utter a murmur or complaint, but frequently expreffed his thankfulnefs, that he had not more pain, and often engaged in prayer, that he might be preferved in patience to the end, which was gracioufly granted him; fo that he was capable of fpeaking to the comfort and edification of thofe who vifited him; and from the fervent love of the brethren, which evidently appeared thro' his life, and moft confpicuoufly during his laft illnefs, and even in the hour of his death, we have a well-grounded affurance that he is paffed unto life, and hath received the reward of the righteous.

His body was attended by a great number of friends and others, his fellow-citizens of divers religious denominations, to our meeting-houfe

ing-houſe in High-Street, on the 24*th* of the
third month, 1768, and after a ſolemn
meeting, was interr'd in our burial-ground
in this city.

———————

A Teſtimony from Richland *Monthly-Meeting in*
Pennſylvania, *concerning* E D W A R D R O-
B E R T S.

HE was born in Merionethſhire, in the
principality of Wales, in the third
month 1687, and came into Pennſylvania
about the twelfth year of his age; was early
convinced of the principle of truth as held
forth by friends, with whom he joined in
communion, and by his godly life and converſation through the courſe of his time,
was nearly united to them. His miniſtry
was attended with divine ſweetneſs and energy, labouring faithfully therein to the comfort and edification of the living whilſt health
and bodily ability continued; being a lively
example of humility, plainneſs, temperance,
meekneſs and charity, and of juſtice and uprightneſs in his dealings amongſt men, which
gained him the love and eſteem of people of
all denominations. He was a tender affectionate huſband and father, earneſtly concern'd to train up his children and family
in the fear of God, and example and inſtruct them in the paths of virtue, and alſo
manifeſted a true zeal for promoting and

preſerving

preſerving peace and good order in ſociety, wherein he was often ſingularly ſerviceable. His bodily ſtrength gradually diminiſhing, he was reduced even to a child's ſtate, in which he quietly departed this life, without much ſickneſs, on the 25*th* of the eleventh month 1768, in the eighty-ſecond year of his age; a miniſter above 40 years.

A Teſtimony from Abington *Monthly-meeting in* Pennſylvania, *concerning* MARY KNIGHT.

SHE was the daughter of John and Mary Carver, who came from England in the year 1682, and was born in or near Philadelphia ſoon after her parents arrived, being one of the firſt children born of Engliſh parents in Pennſylvania. Her parents ſettled at Byberry in Philadelphia county, and educated her in our religious profeſſion. When about eighteen years old, ſhe married Iſaac Knight and became a member of Abington particular meeting: Some time after ſhe appear'd in meetings in a few words in ſimplicity and innocency, and in the exerciſe of her gift tho' ſmall, viſited divers meetings in ſome of the adjacent provinces, from whence ſhe generally produced accounts of friends acceptance of her ſervices: And continuing in a ſteady perſeverance, according to her talent, as ſhe advanced to old age, her zeal for the cauſe of truth and good

good of fouls manifeftly increafed; frequently recommending faithfulnefs, and a
daily watchfulnefs againft the enemy of
fouls, whom fhe often faid, ' Was un-
' wearied, and had followed her all her life
' long, being yet as bufy as ever, to draw
' her mind from off her watch;' fhe would
frequently exprefs, that fhe had great caufe
of thankfulnefs to the God and father of all
our mercies, who had fupported her through
many befetments, with his gracious promife,
that if fhe would be faithful according to
the meafure of grace beftowed, he would be
with her to the end.

Towards the clofe of her days, bodily
weaknefs increafed, yet fhe was remarkably
diligent in attending meetings, and with
ardency exhorted all, ' To come tafte and
' fee for themfelves that the Lord is good,
' for he had been good indeed to her foul,'
with other expreffions tending to encourage
well-doing. She feemed fo fill'd with love
to God, love to her friends, and love to her
fellow creatures in general, that we have
reafon to believe God was with her, and
that her laft days were her beft days. A good
end crowns all.

She departed this life, the 4th of the
third month 1769, and was buried at Abington the 6th of the fame month, aged near
eighty-feven years.

A Teftimony

A Teſtimony from Abington *Monthly-Meeting in* Pennſylvania, *concerning* THOMAS WOOD.

OUR ſaid friend was born in England, of parents not profeſſing with us, who brought him over with them when very young, and reſided in New-Jerſey in the early ſettlement of that province. Soon after he became capable of religious conſideration, he was convinced of the principle of truth as profeſſed by us, on which account he underwent the diſpleaſure of, and ſome ſeverities from his father, but being ſteady and prudent in conduct, and faithful to his convincement, he at length ſo gained on his father's affections, that after ſome time he became reconciled and friendly to him.

He became a member of this monthly, and of Abington particular meeting, on or about the thirtieth year of his age, and ſo continued to the end of his life, being always, when at home and in health, a conſtant attender of thoſe meetings, tho' living at a conſiderable diſtance therefrom.

When about forty-eight years of age, he appeared in the miniſtry, and became a faithful labourer therein according to ability. He had little or no ſchool-learning, yet delighted much in hearing the ſcriptures read, and often promoted the reading of them in his family; by means whereof and a retentive memory, he ſometimes, thro' the aſſiſtance of divine grace, quoted texts

from

from them in his miniſtry, which was not in the enticing words of man's wiſdom, but in the demonſtration of the ſpirit, often adminiſtring comfort to, and true ſympathy with, the afflicted and mourners in Zion.

He divers times viſited moſt of the diſtant meetings of friends on this continent, and on his return produced ſatisfactory accounts of his ſervices in thoſe viſits. He often communicated good and wholeſome advice to his neighbours of other religious denominations, amongſt whom he was generally reſpected, as a good neighbour, and an honeſt, innocent, inoffenſive man.

Altho' he did not appear to be much gifted for the exerciſe of the diſcipline, yet being a conſtant attender of meetings appointed for that purpoſe, and a diligent waiter therein, there was a language intelligible in his ſolid ſilence, which communicated inſtruction to his friends, who were always well pleaſed with his company.

He was a promoter of that weighty ſervice of viſiting friends families, wherein he was uſefully engaged, even when thro' old age and bodily weakneſs, it appear'd to human probability too hard and arduous an undertaking; but having diſcovered a willingneſs to make trial, he joined with ſome other friends, and was ſupported with inward and outward ſtrength to go through the ſervice, to his own and his friends great ſatisfaction. After which his ſtrength and faculties declining, he was moſtly confined

at

at home. On being vifited by his friends, he appear'd much in the innocent and child-like ftate, retaining his wonted mark of difciplefhip, viz. love to his brethren, in which he continued to the laft, and departed this life, the 7*th* of the third month 1769; from the cleareft information we could obtain, he was in or about the ninety-fourth year of his age; having been a member of our meeting about 64 and a minifter upwards of 45 years.

A Teftimony from Abington *Monthly-Meeting in* Pennfylvania, *concerning* ISAAC CHILD.

THOSE who die in the Lord, ceafe from their labours and the troubles of this life, and afcend to the heavenly manfions, where they are forever bleffed: And all that can be faid on their behalf, cannot in any degree advance their happinefs nor add to their worth; yet there is fomething due to the memory of the righteous, fuch whofe lives have been confpicuoufly virtuous, who have laid down their heads in peace, are gone from works to rewards, and left a fweet favour.

Our dear and well efteemed friend Ifaac Child, having departed this life, we find a freedom to give the following teftimony concerning him while amongft us.

In

In the year 1764, he, with his wife and
two children, came well recommended to us
from Buckingham monthly-meeting; when
he found a draught and freedom to come
and fettle amongft us, and a favourable opportunity prefenting, he was not hafty in
his determination, but, agreeable to the
good and wholefome rule of our difcipline,
laid the matter before the monthly-meeting
he then belonged to, for their advice.

This worthy friend approved himfelf to
be one who had fubmitted to the yoke and
crofs of Chrift in his youth, and by the influence and operation of truth upon him,
was made fenfible of the neceffity of living
a circumfpect and felf-denying-life; and as
he yielded obedience to the dictates of grace,
being thereby fubjected to the divine will
and requirings, the Lord was pleafed to
employ him in his vineyard, and to qualify
him for fervice therein, both in the exercife
of the difcipline of the church, and as a
minifter of the gofpel.

He was exemplary in life and converfation, his deportment being meek, humble
and innocently cheerful, yet guarding againft
any thing that would tend to lightnefs in
behaviour, his company was pleafant, and
his words favoury and edifying: A tender
affectionate hufband and parent, a kind
friend and neighbour; not of a murmuring
difpofition when he met with difappointments and afflictions, but freely fubmitted
to what was permitted to come upon him.

He

He was zealous for the caufe of God, and the fupport of chriftian difcipline in its various branches, not hafty in giving his fentiments on matters relative thereto; but after deliberately waiting for a proper qualification, he moftly fpake clofe and pertinent, with clearnefs and foundnefs of judgment. He was concern'd for the clofe and due exercife of the difcipline againft offenders, not willing that any part of it fhould be difpenfed with, through partial favour or affection, but that true judgment, according to their tranfgreffions, fhould be placed upon them, the church cleanfed from defilements and reproaches, and that the libertine profeffor and the circumfpect walker might be truly diftinguifhed. Yet he was at times, led into fympathy and travel of foul for fuch who through inadvertency had miffed their way, and were in fome meafure fenfible of their error; to thofe he fome times extended private admonition and counfel, in love to their fouls, and with defires for their reftoration. It may truly be faid, he was endowed with a large fhare of natural underftanding, which being fanctified by divine grace, he became well qualified for fervice in the church.

As a minifter, he approved himfelf one rightly called to the work, having experienced a growth from a good beginning to a large advancement, and at times, thro' divine aid was enabled to deliver much excellent doctrine to the comfort and edification

tion of fuch whofe minds were gathered into a true inward worfhip of God in fpirit:
And the negligent were exhorted to more attention in the great work of religion and
their fouls falvation.

He often founded an alarm to the rebellious and gainfayers, with a warning to repent and amend their ways, that their fouls
might be faved in the day of trouble. He
had a clear delivery and ready utterance, his
ftile being familiar to the loweft capacities,
his matter well connected, his doctrine
found, his powerful miniftry having a great
reach upon the people. He frequently attended burials, both within the compafs of
our own meeting, and fome more diftant,
faying, ' It was better for him to go to the
' houfe of mourning than the houfe of
' mirth;' at which times there was often
large gatherings of divers forts of chriftian
profeffors, where he frequently appeared in
teftimony, much to their fatisfaction; being
favour'd with a clear fight of the ftates of
the people, and enabled faithfully to fpeak
what was given him, in a clofe fearching
manner, without affectation, and in that
univerfal love which wifhes well to all men.

He travelled abroad but little, except to
fome neighbouring yearly-meetings and
fome other meetings adjacent. In his laft
public teftimony, which was in our monthly-meeting, he was led to fpeak of the val-
lies that were to be raifed and the hills
brought down; that when the Lord was
pleafed

pleafed to raife fome as out of the low val-
lies and adorn them with his jewels, it made
them appear above their brethren ; but when
thofe jewels were taken off, they were then
on a level; this was agreeable to his own
experience, he having at times witnefled a
being baptifed into lowlinefs of mind and
nothingnefs of felf; under which he appeared
much refigned to the divine will, often fitting
in filence, as one who had neither call nor
commiffion to fpeak ; for he never difcovered a defire to be heard in words, until he
had received a renewed qualification, in
pure love, to fpeak to the people, and, as
upon the walls of Zion, to proclaim the
everlafting gofpel of peace, and the means
of falvation through Chrift our Saviour.

In the time of his laft ficknefs (which was
about nine days) he was preferved in patience and refignation of mind; and near the
morning before his departure, being clear
in his underftanding, and fenfible of death
approaching, he was drawn forth in fervent
fupplication to the Almighty : After which
laying ftill for fome time, he departed like
a lamb, without figh or groan, on the *5th*
of the fourth month 1769, aged thirty-five
years, having been a minifter about 11 years,
and a member of our meeting near 5 years.
A large number of friends and others paid
their laft office of love towards him, in attending his interment at friends burying-
ground at Abington, on the *8th* of the faid
month, at which time a folid meeting was
held.

An

An additional Teſtimony concerning I s a a c
C h i l d, *from* Buckingham *Monthly-
Meeting in* Pennſylvania.

NOTWITHSTANDING our much e-
ſteemed friend Iſaac Child, removed
himſelf and family from within the compaſs
of our monthly-meeting near five years before his deceaſe, yet we find freedom to give
this ſhort teſtimony concerning him, having
been favoured to ſit under many living and
powerful teſtimonies deliver'd by him whilſt
among us.

We are fully ſatisfied he was one whom
the Lord in his wiſdom ſaw meet to make
uſe of for the work of the goſpel, having
fitted, qualified and called him forth when
but young, to publiſh the glad tidings thereof; to which divine call and holy requiring,
he gave up in obedience, and ſuffered not
the things of this world to take up his mind,
but in true fervency of zeal and love for the
cauſe of truth, he ſpent much time in its
ſervice. His teſtimony was living, ſound
and delivered with divine authority; for he
handled not the word deceitfully, nor endeavoured to pleaſe itching ears; but as a
true ſervant of Jeſus, waited to be renewed-
ly endowed with power from on high, whereby he was directed to divide the word aright,
and ſpeak home to the ſtates and conditions
of the people: He was alſo zealouſly concerned for the promotion of diſcipline and

good

good order in the church; and for the management of the affairs thereof, he appeared remarkably well qualified; his weighty admonitions being enforced by a pious life and converfation. May we, under the confideration of the great lofs the church has fuftained by his and fome others deceafe, be excited fo to follow their footfteps, that with them we may be partakers of that incorruptible inheritance which is referved for the righteous, when time here fhall be no more.

A Teftimony from Buckingham *Monthly-Meeting in* Pennfylvania, *concerning* J O H N S C A R B O R O U G H.

H E was born of honeft parents, and educated within the compafs of this meeting; in his youth was fomewhat airy, but when arrived to riper years he embraced the truth and appeared clofely to follow the dictates thereof to the end of his life.

About the year 1740 he appeared in the miniftry and experiencing a growth therein, he at different times vifited moft of the northern colonies, in which fervices he always had our concurrence, and at his return produced certificates of friends unity with his miniftry and labours of love; the remembrance whereof yet lives as a memorial in the minds of many.

He

He earneſtly laboured for the good and ſalvation of men, and tho' not learned, ſpoke with great propriety, yet plain and familiar, his doctrine being found, lively and edifying, which being adorned by a pious life and innocent converſation, ſeaſoned with true charity, made him juſtly eſteemed by people of all denominations.

He was ſteadily concern'd to promote good order and diſcipline, and therein to act uprightly for truth's cauſe without partiality. With great cheerfulneſs giving up much of his time, and labouring for the reſtoration of ſuch who had miſs'd their way; and altho' he uſed great plainneſs in admoniſhing tranſgreſſors, ſeldom gave offence; being a man of remarkable ſelf-denial and endued with much mildneſs, made him very ſerviceable in the affairs of the church in general, and tended to ſupport the authority of truth.

In his declining years he was affected with bodily weakneſs, yet his zeal for the cauſe of truth did not abate, but the life and power uſually attending his miniſtry rather increaſed. In his laſt teſtimony at our meeting, he was highly favoured, the power of truth riſing into dominion; with much ſalutary counſel and fatherly admonition he ſeemed to take a final farewell of his brethren, and fervently prayed for our preſervation. As his departure drew nigh, he often expreſs'd his willingneſs to leave this world, ſaying, ' He did not know any

T 2   ' thing

' thing that remained undone to compleat
' his days-work, and that no cloud nor any
' thing appeared in his way.' He departed
this life, the *5th* of the fifth month 1769,
in the fixty-fixth year of his age; and as a
good and faithful fervant, we doubt not, is
entered into everlafting joy and happinefs.
The frefh remembrance of his loving and
kind deportment and many faithful fervices,
imprefs our minds with a deep fenfe of his
worth and our great lofs.

A Teftimony from Gwynedd *Monthly-Meeting in*
Pennfylvania, *concerning* MARY EVANS.

SHE was born in Philadelphia, in or
about the year 1695, her father dying
when fhe was young, fhe was educated by
her mother in the principle of truth as profeffed among us; in her young years fhe
was fober and grave in her behaviour and
deportment; and about the time fhe came
forth in the miniftry, fhe went through
clofe trials and deep conflicts, as we have
frequently heard her relate, in which the
divine arm was her fupport, brought her
through, and qualified her for religious fervice.

In the year 1736, fhe was married to our
worthy friend Owen Evans, and thereby became a member of this meeting. Her public appearances were not very frequent, but
when

when fhe fpoke, her teftimony was fervent, found and edifying, her conduct and converfation being agreeable to her religious profeffion. She was feveral times drawn forth in the love of the gofpel, to vifit friends in moft of the provinces on this continent, alfo the Ifland of Tortola, which fhe undertook with the unity of her friends at home, and returned with clear and fatisfactory accounts of her labours amongft thofe whom fhe vifited. She was a lover and promoter of peace and good order in the church and amongft her neighbours, and was frequently engaged in that weighty fervice of vifiting friends families, to good fatisfaction. In the year 1757, fhe met with a clofe exercife, in the lofs of her hufband, who was removed from her by death, which fhe bore with becoming refignation. After which, fhe lived fome years with her daughter, who was married and fettled in Philadelphia; but returned back again within the compafs of this meeting, frequently faying, ' She apprehended it to be her duty, ' to fpend the remainder of her days a- ' mongft us;' labouring faithfully, as one that forefaw her time was fhort. Her laft illnefs was lingering, which fhe bore with becoming refignation; a few days before her death, fome friends had a fitting with her in her chamber, when notwithftanding fhe was weak in body, fhe was enabled to fpeak for a confiderabie time, in a lively and inftructive manner, much to their fatisfaction.

faction. She departed this life, the 20*th* of the fifth month 1769, and was interr'd in friends burying-ground at Gwynedd, the 22*d* of the fame.

A Teſtimony from Middletown *Monthly-Meeting in* Pennſylvania, *concerning* GRACE CROASDALE.

AS memorials of the virtuous lives and acts of the righteous when deceaſed, may afford matter of help and encouragement to furvivors to follow their pious examples; we are therefore engaged to give this fhort teſtimony concerning our eſteemed friend Grace Croafdale.

. She was born the 6*th* of the eighth month 1703, of reputable parents, members of this meeting, who brought her up to induſtry and plainnefs in fpeech and habit; being married young, fhe early entered into the cares of a family; and being religiouſly inclined, and of a cheerful active difpofition, approved herfelf well qualified for fuch a charge; inſtructing her children and family both by precept and example, in piety and plainnefs, as well as the neceſſary cares of life. As fhe advanced in years, fhe grew in religion, and became very ferviceable in divers ſtations in the church. About the year 1745 fhe firſt appear'd in the miniſtry, in the exerciſe whereof fhe was acceptable and edifying,

fying, exhortimg all to the true love and fear of God, and a humble attention to the divine principle of truth in themfelves; adorning her doctrine by a life and conver-fation anfwerable thereto. The latter part of her time, when more difengaged from the cares of a family, fhe was much devoted to the fervice of truth, and occafionally vi-fited many of the meetings of friends in our own and feveral of the neighbouring pro-vinces.

She was a peaceable kind neighbour, a vifitor and fympathizer with the fick and afflicted whether in body or mind; and ap-pear'd eminently qualified for that weighty fervice of vifiting families, in which fhe was often engaged, not only within the compafs of our own particular meeting, but of di-vers others, to general fatisfaction.

Having lived in much love and unity with friends, fhe had to reflect thereon with great peace and fatisfaction of mind in her laft illnefs, during which fhe was fig-nally favoured with the incomes of divine love and heavenly confolation; in the a-boundings whereof, fhe was frequently drawn forth in thankfgivings and living high praifes to the Lord.

She departed this life, the 23d of the tenth month 1769, and was buried the 24th of the fame, in friends burying-ground at Middletown.

A Teftimony

A Testimony from Evesham *Monthly-Meeting in* New-Jersey, *concerning* Josiah Foster.

HE was born in Rhode-Island, of honest parents, who died whilst he was young, from which time until he came to man's estate, we have no account of him, only that some of us have heard him say, he was much delighted with mirth and vanity. Soon after his arrival at manhood, he came into New-Jersey, where he married, and settled at Evesham; not long afterwards he was convinced, and effectually reached with the power of truth, through the living ministry of that eminent minister of Christ Jesus, Thomas Wilson; and by the operation of divine grace in his heart, he gradually experienced a growth therein. Thus advancing in true obedience, he witnessed an overcoming of his own strong will (as some of us have heard him relate with awful gratitude to the divine hand) and in due time he became a father and elder in the church; being tenderly concerned for the promotion of the truth, which had in measure set him free from the body of sin and death, communicating suitable advice and counsel to such as were tender, and a sharp reprover of obstinate sinners; his advice being much enforced by his upright uniform conduct.

In conversation he was free and open, and easy of access: In meetings for worship and discipline difcipline (which he diligently attended whilft of ability) his deportment was awful, reverent and unaffectedly grave, waiting for the arifing of life, which qualified him to be of great fervice in the fociety. He was of a benevolent difpofition, his heart and houfe being open to entertain ftrangers, efpecially travelling friends; nor was his benevolence confined to thofe of our own fociety; for, being bleffed with affluence, many widows and fatherlefs received his hearty affiftance. He was well beloved by moft or all who were acquainted with him; his converfation and conduct truly demonftrated, that he had learn'd to do to others, as he would be done unto; which is truly worthy the imitation of all. Being defirous to retire from the cares of the world, he removed to Mount-Holly, where he refided until he was taken with a paralytick diforder, which much impaired his natural faculties, after which he return'd to his former fettlement at Evefham under the care of his fon. Altho' his diforder render'd him incapable of much converfation, yet he gave evident figns of a lively fenfe of divine goodnefs accompanying him to the laft; and quietly departed this life, the 9th of the firft month 1770, in the eighty-eighth year of his age, and was buried the 11th of the fame month at Evefham.

A Teftimony

A Teftimony from the Monthly-Meeting of Friends in Philadelphia, *concerning* DANIEL STANTON.

WHEN John the Divine was in exile in the ifle of Patmos, " He heard " a voice from Heaven, faying, write,— " bleffed are the dead, who die in the Lord, " from henceforth, yea faith the fpirit, that " they may reft from their labours, and " their works do follow them;" which we believe now is the portion of our worthy friend, concerning whofe faithful fervices we are engaged from the united motives of love and duty, to give this teftimony; defiring, that all who read it, and more efpecially the youth, may be excited, by his example, to feek an early acquaintance with the Lord, and to take up their daily crofs in the prime of their days. Thus, they alfo, may become fhining lights and inftruments of good to others.

He was born in this city, in the year 1708, and his father dying before his birth, and his mother a few years after, he fuffered great trials and hardfhips when very young: Being early concerned to feek the knowledge of God, he had a fervent defire to attend religious meetings, though fubjected to many difficulties and difcouragements, before that privilege was allowed him; yet, being earneft in his defires to obtain divine favour, he was eminently fupported

ported under great conflicts and probations, and, continuing faithful to the degrees of light and grace communicated, a difpenfati- of the gofpel miniftry was committed to him, fometime before the term of his ap- prenticefhip was expired; and abiding un- der the fanctifying power of truth, he grew in his gift, and became a zealous faithful minifter.

He was very exemplary in his induftry and diligence, in labouring faithfully at his trade, to provide for his own fupport, and after he married, and had children, for their maintenance; and was often concerned to advife others to the fame neceffary care; yet he continued fervent in fpirit for the promotion of truth and righteoufnefs, fo that he was foon engaged to leave home, and the neareft connections of nature, to publifh the glad tidings of the gofpel, and frequently vifited moft of the meetings of friends in this and the adjacent provinces, and feveral times as far as the eaftern parts of New-England. Having thus honeftly difcharged his duty among us above twenty years, and feeling his mind conftrained in the love of the gofpel, to vifit the few friends who remained in fome of the Weft-India iflands, and from thence the meetings of friends in general through Great-Britain and Ireland, he communicated his concern to a few of his moft intimate friends, who having unity therewith, he was encouraged to lay it before our monthly-meeting. Before he
entered

entered on this weighty fervice, he paffed
through a near trial and affliction in the
death of his beloved wife; under which
exercife he was gracioufly fupported by the
arm of divine ftrength, which had often
been revealed for his help, in times of inward conflicts and outward diftreffes.

His concern to travel in the fervice of
truth continuing, and the meeting having
full unity with him therein, he embarked
in the fifth month 1748, accompanied by
our dear friend, Samuel Nottingham, in a
veffel bound for Barbados, and having vifited the few meetings in that ifland, they
went by way of Antigua to Tortola, where
they continued fometime, having fome difficulty to get a paffage to Europe; and their
voyage thither was attended with fome fingular hazards and dangers, which occafioned their landing in Ireland; where our friend
Daniel continued fome months, vifiting the
meetings of friends in that kingdom; and
after he apprehended himfelf clear, went
over to England, and vifited the meetings
generally in that nation, and in Wales and
Scotland, where his meek circumfpect conduct and converfation, and lively edifying
miniftry, rendered his vifit very acceptable,
and his memory precious.

In his return home, and for fometime after, he was in a low afflicted ftate of mind;
being apprehenfive, that through diffidence,
and the want of perfect refignation to the
divine will, he had omitted fully performing

ing the fervice required of him, by not vifiting the few friends in Holland: Yet he
was mercifully preferved, and after a time
of deep exercife, raifed again to fing of the
mercies and loving-kindnefs of God on the
banks of deliverance.

He feveral times, with other friends appointed to that fervice, vifited the families
of friends in this city, and between the
years 1757 and 1760, being accompanied
by our friend John Pemberton, he vifited
the families of friends generally within the
limits of our meeting; which weighty exercifing fervice, he was enabled to perform
to our edification and fatisfaction. After
which, he was frequently engaged to excite
friends to this ufeful and edifying practice.

In the twelfth month 1760, he fet out on
a vifit to the meetings in the weftern parts
of this province, and from thence in Maryland, Virginia, and North and South-Carolina, and returned in the fixth month following; fince which he frequently vifited
many of the meetings near home, and fome
as far as Long-Ifland, and other parts of the
province of New-York. Within the laft two
years, he vifited the families of friends of fome
of the meetings in Weft-Jerfey, in the city
of New-York, and part of Long-Ifland; and
after his return from this fervice, with great
peace and fatisfaction, he exprefled his apprehenfion that he was now clear of all places,
and that his ftay here was near over; having

an

an evidence, that he had been faithfully concerned from his youth to fear and ferve
God.

His chief labour and religious exercifes
were in this city, where he was a diligent
attender of all our meetings, and often on
committees appointed on the fervices of the
church; in which he was folid and weighty
in fpirit, waiting for the fpringing up of
life, being fteadily concerned both in and
out of meetings, to live near the divine fountain: Thus he was very frequently qualified, and enabled to ftir up the pure mind,
and to recount the gracious dealings of God
to mankind, and as a faithful embaffador
to warn the negligent to flee from the wrath
to come, and to excite the people to bring
forth fruits anfwerable to the great mercies
gracioufly beftowed on us; and was fometimes conftrained to declare in a prophetic
manner, a day of trial, in divers inftances,
very fhortly before fuch a feafon came to
pafs.

He was of late deeply exercifed in confideration of the evils of the horfe races,
ftage plays, drunkennefs, and other grofs
enormities encouraged and increafing in this
city; clofely exhorting our youth againft
thofe pernicious and deftructive devices of
the enemy of mankind; and under the awful fenfe that God will judge and punifh the
wicked and evil doers, he was often fervent
in public fupplications, that the Lord would
lengthen out the day of his merciful vifitation,

on, and yet try the people longer; which feafons were folemn and humblingly affecting; manifefting, that although he was very clofe and fharp in reproof againft evil, yet moft tenderly concerned, that the tranfgreffors of the righteous law of God might be prevailed with to repent, return, and live.

His love for the rifing generation was very great; which he manifefted by his affectionate notice of them, and efpecially of thofe who were religioufly inclined, and his houfe was open to receive fuch, his converfation with them being feafoned with grace, and his counfel inftructive and helpful to thofe who had feeking defires after the knowledge of truth, often lovingly inviting them to come, tafte, and fee, that the Lord is good; greatly defiring, that all who profefs the truth, might walk agreeable to its dictates and be led thereby, as our worthy predeceffors were, into that meeknefs, humility, and godly fimplicity and plainnefs, which rendered them confpicuous and fhining examples, and that none might reft fhort of the enjoyment of the life of religion, his zeal being great againft fuch, who have the form of godlinefs, and by their actions manifeft they have not the power thereof; and he often fervently advis'd and cautioned thofe who are eagerly purfuing the world, and by the furfeiting cares, and grafping after earthly treafures, fruftrate the good purpofe of the vifitation of divine grace to them, and clofely reminded thofe, who

in

in their fmall beginnings were low and humble, that now they were abundantly favoured, they fhould not fet their affections on things below, but remember the rock from whence they were hewn; and his concern was great that thofe who had the glad tidings of the gofpel to publifh, might be true examples to the flock, and adorn the doctrine they had to deliver by a circumfpect life and converfation, and where any by not fteadily keeping to that which would have preferved them, had involved themfelves in difficulties, either by letting their minds out to the gains and profits of this world, or otherwife, his travail was great for fuch that they might be brought through, and every cloud and mift removed.

He was much employed in vifiting the fick and afflicted, to whom he adminiftered his fpiritual advice and experience, and often engaged in humble prayer for their fupport; and in the diftributing to the neceffitous according to his circumftances, he manifefted his benevolent difpofition.

As he had been many years under great exercife and fuffering of fpirit on account of the flavery of the poor Africans, and frequently bore teftimony againft that unrighteous gain of oppreffion, he was of late fomewhat relieved, as he found the eyes of the people become more open to fee the iniquity of the practice; and he died in faith, that the light of the gofpel will fo generally prevail, that the profeffors of chriftianity
will

will find it their duty to reftore to thefe people their natural right to liberty, and to inftruct them in the principles of the chriftian
religion.

On the 5th day of the fifth month, he
was violently feized with the bilious cholic,
and continued in great pain feveral days;
but afterwards being fomewhat eafier, he
was at our morning and evening meetings
on firftday, the 13th of the month, in which
he was much favoured in his public miniftry, and expreffed that he thought his time
would not be long with us. After this day's
labour, he was again confined, yet being a
little recovered he was at our meeting on fifth-
day, the 24th of the month, which being
fmall, he expreffed his forrow for it, and
encouraged friends to diligence in the attendance of week day meetings, the benefit
of a faithful difcharge of duty therein being great; the next day he was at our
monthly-meeting, and to his own and our
admiration was enabled to ftay through both
our fittings, though the laft of them was
longer than ufual, and he afterwards expreffed that he thought himfelf better in the
meeting than when out; it was a feafon of
divine favour, and fome weighty matters
being before the meeting, he with great
opennefs fpoke pertinently and clearly to
them, encouraging friends to the fupporting
and maintaining our chriftian teftimony,
againft all that is contrary to it: This was
the laft public meeting he was at, being the

U   next

next morning early feized with a renewed attack of the fame diforder, which increafed on him feveral days, and was fo fixed, that all the endeavours of feveral fkilful phyficians and tender nurfes, were not effectual to remove it, tho' in fome meafure to mitigate the pain, that he fuffered much, not being able to lie down in his bed feveral weeks, yet thro' all he was mercifully fupported, in much refignation, and patience, rather inclining, if it was the Lord's will, to be releafed.

For two or three weeks before his ficknefs, he appeared very defirous of fettling every thing he had to do refpecting the affairs of this life, and defired a friend to review and tranfcribe the fhort memoirs he hath left of his travels and religious fervices, and to write his will, which he executed the day before he was firft taken fick, and then appeared eafy in his mind.

During the time of his ficknefs he often expreffed his concern left his friends fhould be too anxious for his recovery, faying, if he fhould live longer, and thro' any human frailty or infirmity occafion any reproach, it would be a caufe of forrow to them.

By the defire of his friends who attended him, he rode out feveral times, tho' not without much difficulty, and fpent the two laft days of his life at the houfes of two of his intimate friends. As he drew near his end, the ftrength of his love to mankind in general, and his friends in particular, evidently

dently increafed, much defiring the profperity of truth, and when a meeting time came
had an earneft defire to be with friends, and
particularly the day before his departure.

During his ficknefs, he frequently expreffed himfelf in a very feafonable, inftructive, and affecting manner; and the evening of the firftday before he died, feveral
friends coming in to fee him, he fpoke a
confiderable time to them, having before
been defirous of fuch an opportunity of the
company of his friends, to fit down and
wait upon God, which was his great delight.

The laft day of his life he fpent at the
houfe of his friend Ifrael Pemberton, at Ger-
mantown, and was unufually free and cheerful, even till ten o'clock at night, when he
undreffed himfelf, and went into bed, remarking on lying down, that he had not
before been able to do fo, for five weeks or
upwards, and he foon after fell afleep, but
in a fhort time was awakened by the return
of pain and difficulty of breathing, which
thro' his illnefs he had been much afflicted
with, fo that he was oblig'd to fet up in bed,
and thus continued, at intervals freely converfing with our faid friend, who fat up
with him, and he expreffed his great thankfulnefs that his head was preferved free
from pain and his underftanding clear, and
that though it had been a time of clofe trial
and deep probation, he could fay he felt the
evidence of divine fupport ftill to attend
him. After which, his pains increafing he

got

got up and dreſſed himſelf, and walking about the room ſometime, ſat down in an eaſy chair, in which he fell into a ſweet ſleep, and in about three hours departed without ſigh or groan.

Thus died this righteous man, who having fought the good fight and kept the faith, finiſhed his courſe in full unity with us, and univerſally beloved by his fellow citizens, on the 28*th* day of the ſixth month 1770, in the ſixty-ſecond year of his age and 43*d* of his miniſtry. His body was the next day attended by a large number of people of divers religious denominations to our meeting-houſe, and afterwards interr'd in friends burial-ground in this city.

A Teſtimony from Warrington *Monthly-Meeting in* Pennſylvania, *concerning* JOHN THOMAS.

HE was born in Cheſter county Pennſylvania, in the year 1716, of believing parents, and being religiouſly inclined from his youth, he received a part in the miniſtry, whereto being faithful, he experienced a growth therein. In the year 1766, he removed with his family, and ſettled in Warrington Townſhip, York county, within the limits of our meeting: And tho' his time among us was ſhort, yet we have this teſtimony to bear concerning him; that his

labours

labours of love, accompanied with an exemplary conduct, were comfortable and inftructing to us.

In his laft illnefs (which was a confumption) he, at times in the beginning of it, complained to fome of his intimate friends, of great poverty of fpirit, and feemed deeply engaged to wreftle for ftrength, to bear with patience the prefent difpenfation: And in due time it pleafed the father of mercies who hears the fecret cries of his depending children, to caufe the mifts to be difpelled, fo that, in an opportunity which fome friends had with him fome little time before his departure, he was much favoured, and drawn forth to ‘ Declare of the tender deal-
‘ ings of the Lord with him, from his youth
‘ unto that time; earneftly exhorting friends
‘ to faithfulnefs, efpecially thofe on whom
‘ the Lord had beftowed a gift in the mini-
‘ ftry;’ faying, ‘ He had loved the Lord
‘ from his youth, that he had a fmall gift
‘ in the miniftry beftowed upon him, in
‘ which he had been concerned to be faith-
‘ ful, and now he felt the comfort of it;
‘ feeling the ownings of the divine prefence,
‘ whereby he was enabled to bear with pa-
‘ tience his bodily affliction; having an af-
‘ furance of immortal reft; and that tho’
‘ in the beginning of his illnefs, from the
‘ poverty of fpirit that attended him, he
‘ was ready to conclude that the Lord had
‘ forfaken him, but now he anfwered him
‘ to the joy of his heart, and he had to
‘ magnify

' magnify his goodnefs, feeing his wifdom
' therein, in weaning his affections more
' thoroughly from all lower enjoyments,
' and placing them on things above.'

He advifed friends to humility, faying,
' The time draws near, that my body muft
' go down to the grave, wherein is no ex-
' altation; and I have this teftimony to bear
' for the Lord, that as I have been engaged
' to love him and walk humbly before him,
' defiring he might give me ftrength, not
' having any dependance on my own wif-
' dom, I have found him to ftrengthen me,
' and now find him to be near me in this
' pinching time, and comfort me with the
' joys of his prefence.' Many and comfortable were the expreffions which flowed
from him, tho' weak in body, and fcarcely
able to fpeak intelligibly, yet ftrong and
lively in the inward man. In great fweetnefs of fpirit he departed this life, the 9th
of the fifth month 1771, and on the 11th
of the faid month, his corps, accompanied
by a large number of friends and others,
was interr'd in friends burying-ground at
Warrington, a folemn meeting being held,
and divers living teftimonies borne, to the
efficacy of that divine power which gives
victory over the world.

A Teftimony

A Teſtimony from Salem *Monthly-Meeting in* New-Jerſey, *concerning* MARY LIPPIN-COTT.

FROM a motive of love and eſteem, to the memory of this our ancient worthy friend, and that ſurvivors may be encouraged by ſuch pious examples, to embrace the truth and perſevere in the way to ſalvation, we give forth this teſtimony.

She was the daughter of Henry and Elizabeth Burr, by whom ſhe was religiouſly educated, we believe to good effect; for in her very young years, ſhe cloſed in with the love and mercy of God extended to her, and did not incline to vanity and lightneſs, but was a good example to other youths.

She married young, and with her huſband Jacob Lippincott, ſettled among us. Her exemplary conduct, as a wife and when a widow, both in the church, in her family, and her neighbourhood gained our great eſteem; being given to hoſpitality and liberal to the poor.

She was an earneſt traveller in ſpirit for the cauſe of truth on earth, ſolid and weighty in her deportment, affable and inſtructive in converſation, frequently imparting ſeaſonable admonition and counſel to her children and others, and tho' endowed with ſuperior natural underſtanding, was not exalted therewith.

In

In the decline of life, fhe underwent much bodily infirmity, yet diligently attended meetings when of ability, where fhe was a humble waiter for the arifing of the pure truth, travelling in the deeps for the exaltation thereof; well qualified for fervices in the church, a true mourner in Zion, being grieved for the corruptions, vain fafhions, and cuftoms of the times, and in obferving the gaiety and lightnefs apparent in fome, when they came to places for worfhip. It fell to her lot in the courfe of her time, to meet with a large fhare of exercifes and trials, which fhe bore with great refignation; and was a true fympathizer with thofe under affliction in body or mind whom fhe often vifited. Sometime before her laft ficknefs, fhe fignified her apprehenfion, that her day's work was near over; and departed this life, the 9*th* of the firft month 1771, and on the 12*th* was interr'd in friends burying-ground at Pilefgrove; in the feventy-third year of her age, having been an elder many years.

A Teftimony from New-Caftle *Monthly-Meeting in* Great-Britain, *concerning* W I L L I A M H U N T.

OUR dear friend William Hunt, of New-Garden, in Guilford county, North-Carolina, accompanied by his nephew

phew Thomas Thornborough, of the fame place, being on a religious vifit to friends of this nation, departed this life, at the houſe of a friend near New-Caſtle upon Tyne. The deep regard we bear to his memory and eminent fervices, engageth us to tranſmit the following teſtimony concerning him.

They arrived in London about a week after the yearly-meeting 1771, and attending feveral meetings in that city, proceeded northward, vifiting friends in divers counties in England, and alfo in Scotland. The enſuing winter was fpent in vifiting York-fhire, Lancaſhire and Ireland, returning to London in time to attend the yearly-meeting there in 1772; then attending the yearly-meetings in Eſfex, Suffolk and Norfolk, and proceeding through Lincolnſhire to Hull, they took fhipping for Holland, and after vifiting the few friends there, they embarked for Scarborough, but by contrary winds landed at Shields, the 25th of the eighth month, and after being at their meeting on the 26th came that afternoon to the houſe of a friend near New-Caſtle upon Tyne.

From accounts received, and our own knowledge of his conduct and miniſtry, we have good cauſe to believe, that in all his travels in Europe, he behaved as a faithful miniſter of Chriſt, exemplary and uniform in conduct, of a weighty deportment and retired fpirit, his converfation was grave and inſtructive, feafoned with love and fweetneſs, fweetnefs, which rendered his company both profitable and defirable, his miniftry was living and powerful, deep and fearching, an excellent example in patiently waiting for the clear manifeftation of the divine will, and careful to move accordingly, fo that his appearances in meetings were moftly accompanied with great folemnity,, in which he fkilfully divided the word, being to the unfaithful as a two edged fword, but to the honeft hearted travellers in Zion, and to fuch as were feeking the way to God's kingdom, his doctrine was truly refrefhing. He was a man of found judgment, quick of apprehenfion, and deep in religious experience; and altho' he was only in the thirty-ninth year of his age, yet fuch was his experience and ftability, that he ftood as an elder and a father in the church, worthy of double honour.

He attended the meeting at New-Caftle, on the 27*th* of the eighth month 1772, in which he delivered a fhort and living teftimony in the love of the gofpel to his friends of that place; that afternoon he was cheerful, and expreffed his fatisfaction in being there, and upon being afked what place they intended for next, he replied, he faw no further at prefent than New-Caftle. Next day he was taken ill, which was not apprehended to be the fmall pox 'till the fourth day of his illnefs; when the eruption appeared, he faid to his companion, ' This ficknefs is nigh ' unto death if not quite;' his companion figuified fignified his hope that it might not be fo, he replied, ' My coming hither feems to be ' providential, and when I wait I am in- ' clofed and fee no further.' At another time he made the fame remark to a friend, fay- ing, ' It will be a fore trial to my compani- ' on if I am now removed.' He alfo men- tioned in an affectionate manner his dear wife and children to a friend who attended him, and requefted fome counfel and advice (which he then communicated) might be tranfmitted to them, if it fhould pleafe the Lord to remove him, which was according- ly done.

On the third day of his illnefs, two friends from the country came to vifit him, to whom he thus expreffed himfelf, viz. ' I ' have longed to fee you and be with you, ' but was put by,' one of them faid, I hope we fhall have thee with us yet; he anfwered, ' That muft be left;' the friend faid, that whatever affliction we are tried with, we may yet fee caufe of thankfulnefs; he repli- ed, ' Great caufe indeed, I never faw it ' clearer, O the wifdom! the wifdom and ' goodnefs, the mercy and kindnefs has ap- ' peared to me wonderful, and the further ' and deeper we go, the more we wonder; ' I have admired fince I was caft upon this ' bed, that all the world does not feek after ' the truth, it fo far tranfcends all other ' things.' Two friends from Northumber- land coming to vifit him, he faid, ' The ' Lord knows how I have loved you from

' our

‘ our firſt acquaintance, and longed for your.
‘ growth and eſtabliſhment in the bleſſed
‘ truth; and now I feel the ſame renewed
‘ afreſh;’ and ſaid, ‘ He much deſired they
‘ might fill up the places Providence intend-
‘ ed, and lay up treaſure in Heaven,’ adding,
‘ What would a thouſand worlds avail me
‘ now?’

The diſorder was very heavy upon him,
having a load of eruption, under which he
ſhewed great fortitude and patience even to
the admiration of the phyſician and ſurgeon
who attended him; his mind being mercifully preſerved calm, and reſigned to his
maſter's will, whoſe preſence he found to be
near him in the needful time, ſaying, ‘ It
‘ is enough, my maſter is here;’ and again,
‘ He that laid the foundation of the moun-
‘ tans knows this, if it pleaſes him he can
‘ remove it;’ at another time he ſaid with
great compoſure, ‘ The Lord knows beſt, I
‘ am in his hands, let him do what he
‘ pleaſes.’

Perceiving a friend to be diligent and attentive to do what ſhe could for him, he ſaid,
‘ The Lord refreſh thy ſpirit, for thou haſt
‘ often refreſhed this body, and whether I
‘ live or die, thou wilt get thy reward.’

After the ſecond fever came on, finding
himſelf worſe, he ſaid, ‘ My life hangs upon
‘ a thread.’ The doctor being ſent for, he
ſaid, ‘ They are all phyſicians of no value
‘ without the great Phyſician.’ A friend ſaid,
I know thy dependance is on him, he anſwered,

fwered, ' Entirely.' Underſtanding that two friends who had ſat much by him, did not intend to leave him that night, he very ſweetly ſaid, ' And will you watch with me ' one night more?'

On being aſked how he did, he ſaid, ' I ' am here pent up and confined in a narrow ' compaſs, this is a trying time, but my ' mind is above it all;' which was evident to thoſe about him, who were ſenſible of praiſes and ſweet melody in his heart when few words were expreſſed.

A little before he died, he ſaid triumphantly, ' Friends, truth is over all;' ſo in great peace departed this life, the 9*th* day of the ninth month 1772, and was interr'd in friends burying-ground in New-Caſtle upon Tyne, the 11*th* of the ſame month, accompanied by many friends; upon which occaſion a ſolemn meeting was held, and divers teſtimonies borne to the truth, in the ſervice of which he lived and died, an example to many brethren. A miniſter 24 years.

A Teſtimony from Burlington *Monthly-Meeting in* New-Jerſey, *concerning* JOHN WOOL-MAN.

HE was born in Northampton, in the county of Burlington, and province of Weſt-New-Jerſey, in the eighth month 1720, of

of religious parents, who inftructed him very
early in the principles of the chriftian religion, as profeffed by the people called Quakers,
which he efteemed a bleffing to him, even in
his young years, tending to preferve him
from the infection of wicked children; but
through the workings of the enemy, and levity incident to youth, he frequently deviated
from thofe parental precepts, by which he
laid a renewed foundation for repentance,
that was finally fucceeded by a godly forrow
not to be repented of, and fo became acquainted with that fanctifying power which
qualifies for true gofpel miniftry, into which
he was called about the twenty-fecond year
of his age, and by a faithful ufe of the talents committed to him, he experienced an
increafe, until he arrived at the ftate of a father, capable of dividing the word aright to
the different ftates he miniftered unto; dif-
penfing milk to babes, and meat to thofe of
riper years. Thus he found the efficacy of
that power to arife, which in his own expreffions, ' Prepares the creature to ftand
' like a trumpet through which the Lord
' fpeaks to his people.' He was a loving
hufband, a tender father, and very humane
to every part of the creation under his care.

His concern for the poor and thofe in affliction was evident by his vifits to them;
whom he frequently relieved by his affiftance
and charity. He was for many years deeply
exercifed on account of the poor enflaved A-
fricans, whofe caufe, as he fometimes mentioned,

tioned, lay almoſt continually upon him, and to obtain liberty to thoſe captives, he laboured both in public and private; and was favoured to ſee his endeavours crowned with conſiderable ſuccefs. He was particularly deſirous that friends ſhould not be inſtrumental to lay burthens on this oppreſſed people, but remember the days of ſuffering from which they had been providentially delivered, that if times of trouble ſhould return, no injuſtice dealt to thoſe in ſlavery might riſe in judgment againſt us, but, being clear, we might on ſuch occaſions addreſs the Almighty with a degree of confidence, for his interpoſition and relief, being particularly careful as to himſelf, not to countenance ſlavery even by the uſe of thoſe conveniencies of life which were furniſhed by their labour.

He was deſirous to have his own, and the minds of others, redeemed from the pleaſures and immoderate profits of this world, and to fix them on thoſe joys which fade not away; his principal care being after a life of purity, endeavouring to avoid not only the groſſer pollutions, but thoſe alſo which, appearing in a more refined dreſs, are not ſufficiently guarded againſt by ſome well diſpoſed people. In the latter part of his life he was remarkable for the plainneſs and ſimplicity of his dreſs, and as much as poſſible, avoided the uſe of plate, coſtly furniture and feaſting; thereby endeavouring to become an example of temperance and ſelf-denial, which, he believed himſelf called unto; and was favoured ed with peace therein, altho' it carried the appearance of great aufterity in the view of fome. He was very moderate in his charges in the way of bufinefs, and in his defires after gain ; and tho' a man of induftry, avoided, and ftrove much to lead others out of extreme labour, and anxioufnefs after perifhable things; being defirous that the ftrength of our bodies might not be fpent in procuring things unprofitable, and that we might ufe moderation and kindnefs to the brute animals under our care, to prize the ufe of them as a great favour, and by no means abufe them; that the gifts of Providence fhould be thankfully received and applied to the ufes they were defigned.

He feveral times opened a fchool at Mount-Holly, for the inftruction of poor friends children and others, being concerned for their help and improvement therein: His love and care for the rifing youth among us was truly great, recommending to parents and thofe who have the charge of them, to chufe confcientious and pious tutors, faying, ' It is a lovely fight to behold innocent chil-
' dren,' and that ' To labour for their help
' againft that which would marr the beauty
' of their minds, is a debt we owe them.'

His miniftry was found, very deep and penetrating, fometimes pointing out the dangerous fituation which indulgence and cuftom leads into; frequently exhorting others, efpecially the youth, not to be difcouraged at the difficulties which occur, but prefs after

ter purity. He often expreſſed an earneſt engagement that pure wiſdom ſhould be attended to, which would lead into lowlineſs of mind and reſignation to the divine will, in which ſtate ſmall poſſeſſions here would be ſufficient.

In tranſacting the affairs of diſcipline, his judgment was ſound and clear, and he was very uſeful in treating with thoſe who had done amiſs; he viſited ſuch in a private way in that plainneſs which truth dictates, ſhewing great tenderneſs and chriſtian forbearance. He was a conſtant attender of our yearly-meeting, in which he was a good example, and particularly uſeful; aſſiſting in the buſineſs thereof with great weight and attention. He ſeveral times viſited moſt of the meetings of friends in this and the neighbouring provinces, with the concurrence of the monthly-meeting to which he belonged, and we have reaſon to believe had good ſervice therein, generally or always expreſſing at his return how it had fared with him, and the evidence of peace in his mind for thus performing his duty. He was often concerned with other friends in the important ſervice of viſiting families, which he was enabled to go through to ſatisfaction.

In the minutes of the meeting of miniſters and elders for this quarter, at the foot of a liſt of the members of that meeting, made about five years before his death, we find in his hand-writing the following obſervation and reflections. ' As looking over the mi-

X   ' nutes

' nutes made by perfons who have put off
' this body, hath fometimes revived in me
' a thought how ages pafs away ; fo this lift
' may probably revive a like thought in
' fome, when I and the reft of the perfons
' abovenamed, arc centered in another ftate
' of being. The Lord, who was the guide
' of my youth, hath in tender mercies help-
' ed me hitherto; he hath healed me of
' wounds, he hath helped me out of griev-
' ous entanglements ; he remains to be the
' ftrength of my life; to whom I defire to
' devote myfelf in time, and in eternity.'

Signed, John Woolman.

In the twelfth month 1771, he acquainted
this meeting that he found his mind drawn
towards a religious vifit to friends in fome
parts of England, particularly in Yorkfhire.
In the firft month 1772, he obtained our certificate, which was approved and endorfed
by our quarterly-meeting, and by the half
year's meeting of minifters and elders at
Philadelphia. He embarked on his voyage
in the fifth and arrived in London in the
fixth month following, at the time of their
annual meeting in that city. During his
fhort vifit to friends in that kingdom, we
are informed that his fervices were acceptable and edifying. In his laft illnefs he uttered many lively and comfortable expreffions, being ' Perfectly refigned, having no
' will either to live or die,' as appears by the
teftimony of friends at York in Great-Britain, in the fuburbs whereof, at the houfe

of

of our friend Thomas Prieſtman, he died of the ſmall-pox, on the 7th day of the tenth month 1772, and was buried in friends burying-ground in that city, on the 9th of the ſame, after a large and ſolid meeting held on the occaſion, at their great meeting-houſe, aged near fifty-two years; a miniſter upwards of 30 years, during which time he belonged to Mount-Holly particular meeting, which he diligently attended when at home and in health of body, and his labours of love and pious care for the proſperity of friends in the bleſſed truth, we hope may not be forgotten, but that his good works may be remembred to edification.

A Teſtimony from the Quarterly-Meeting at York in Great-Britain, concerning JOHN WOOLMAN.

THIS our valuable friend having been under a religious engagement for ſome time, to viſit friends in this nation, and more eſpecially us in the northern parts, undertook the ſame in full concurrence and near ſympathy with his friends and brethren at home, as appeared by certificates from the monthly and quarterly-meetings to which he belonged, and from the ſpring-meeting of miniſters and elders, held at Philadelphia, for Pennſylvania and New-Jerſey.

X 2

. He

He arrived in the city of London the beginning of the laſt yearly-meeting, and after attending that meeting travelled northward, viſiting the quarterly-meetings of Hertford-ſhire, Buckinghamſhire, Northamptonſhire, Oxfordſhire and Worceſterſhire, and divers particular meetings in his way.

He viſited many meetings on the weſt-ſide of this county, alſo ſome in Lancaſhire and Weſtmoreland, from whence he came to our quarterly-meeting in the laſt ninth month, and though much out of health, yet was enabled to attend all the ſittings of that meeting except the laſt.

His diſorder then, which proved the ſmall-pox, increaſed ſpeedily upon him, and was very afflicting; under which he was ſupported in much meekneſs, patience, and chriſtian fortitude; to thoſe who attended him in his illneſs, his mind appeared to be centered in divine love; under the precious influence whereof, we believe he finiſhed his courſe, and entered into the manſions of everlaſting reſt.

In the early part of his illneſs he requeſted a friend to write and he broke forth thus.

‘ O Lord my God! the amazing horrors
‘ of darkneſs were gathered around me and
‘ covered me all over, and I ſaw no way to
‘ go forth; I felt the miſery of my fellow
‘ creatures ſeparated from the divine har-
‘ mony and it was heavier than I could
‘ bear, and I was cruſhed down under it; I
‘ lifted up my hand, and ſtretched out my
‘ arm,

' arm, but there was none to help me; I
' looked round about and was amazed: In
' the depths of mifery, O Lord! I remem-
' bred that thou art omnipotent, that I had
' called thee father, and I felt that I loved
' thee, and I was made quiet in thy will,
' and I waited for deliverance from thee;
' thou hadft pity upon me, when no man
' could help me; I faw that meeknefs under
' fuffering was fhewed to us in the moft af-
' fecting example of thy fon, and thou waft
' teaching me to follow him, and I faid, thy
' will O father, be done.'

Many more of his weighty expreffions
might have been inferted here, but it was
deemed unneceffary, they being already
publifhed in print.

He was a man endued with a large natural capacity, and being obedient to the manifeftations of divine grace, having in patience and humility endured many deep baptifms, he became thereby fanctified and fitted
for the Lord's work, and was truly ferevice-
able in his church; dwelling in awful fear
and watchfulnefs, he was careful in his public appearances to feel the putting forth of
the divine hand, fo that the fpring of the
gofpel miniftry often flowed through him
with great fweetnefs and purity, as a refrefhing ftream to the weary travellers towards
the city of God: Skilful in dividing the
word, he was furnifhed by him in whom
are hid all the treafures of wifdom and knowledge, to communicate freely to the feveral

states of the people where his lot was cast. His conduct at other times was seasoned with the like watchful circumspection and attention to the guidance of divine wisdom, which rendered his whole conversation uniformly edifying.

He was fully persuaded that as the life of Christ comes to reign in the earth, all abuse and unnecessary oppression, both of the human and brute creation will come to an end; but under the sense of a deep revolt, and an overflowing stream of unrighteousness, his life has been often a life of mourning.

He was deeply concerned on account of that inhuman and iniquitous practice of making slaves of the people of Africa, or holding them in that state; and on that account we understand he hath not only wrote some books, but travelled much on the continent of America, in order to make the Negro masters (especially those in profession with us) sensible of the evil of such a practice; and though in this journey to England, he was far removed from the outward sight of their sufferings, yet his deep exercise of mind remained, as appears by a short treatise he wrote in this journey, and his frequent concern to open the miserable state of this deeply injured people: His testimony in the last meeting he attended was on this subject, wherein he remarked, that as we as a society, when under outward sufferings, had often found it our concern to lay them before those in authority, and thereby in

the

the Lord's time, had obtained relief, fo he
recommended this oppreffed part of the creation to our notice, that we may as way
may open, reprefent their fufferings in an
individual, if not a fociety, capacity to thofe
in authority.

Deeply fenfible that the defire to gratify
people's inclinations in luxury and fuperfluities, is the principal ground of oppreffion,
and the occafion of many unneceffary wants,
he believed it to be his duty to be a pattern
of great felf-denial, with refpect to the things
of this life, and earneftly to labour with
friends in the meeknefs of wifdom, to imprefs on their minds the great importance of
our teftimony in thefe things, recommending
to the guidance of the bleffed truth in this
and all other concerns, and cautioning fuch
as are experienced therein, againft contenting
themfelves with acting up to the ftandard of
others, but to be careful to make the ftandard of truth manifefted to them, the meafure
of their obedience; for faid he, ' That pu-
' rity of life which proceeds from faithful-
' nefs in following the fpirit of truth, that
' ftate where our minds are devoted to
' ferve God, and all our wants are bounded
' by his wifdom; this habitation has often
' been opened before me as a place of re-
' tirement for the children of the light, where
' they may ftand feparated from that which
' difordereth and confufeth the affairs of
' fociety, and where we may have a tefti-
' mony of our innocence in the hearts of
' thofe who behold us.'

We

We conclude with fervent defires, that
we as a people may thus, by our example,
promote the Lord's work in the earth ; and
our hearts being prepared, may unite in
prayer to the great Lord of the harvelt, that
as in his infinite wifdom he hath greatly
ftripped the church, by removing of late
divers faithful minifters and elders, he may
be pleafed to fend forth many more faithful
labourers into his harveft.

*The following Minutes of fome of his Expreffions
in the time of his ficknefs, were preferved by
our friend* Thomas Prieftman *and others
who attended him,* viz.

FOURTH-DAY morning, 30*th* of the
ninth month 1772, being afked how he
felt himfelf, he meekly anfwered, I don't
know that I have flept this night, I feel the
diforder making its progrefs, but my mind
is mercifully preferved in ftillnefs and peace :
Sometime after he faid he was fenfible the
pains of death muft be hard to bear, but if
he efcaped them now, he muft fometime pafs
thro' them, and he did not know that he
could be better prepared, but had no will in
it. He faid he had fettled his outward affairs to his mind, had taken leave of his wife
and family as never to return, leaving them
to the divine protection ; adding, and tho' I
feel them near to me at this time, yet I freely give them up, having a hope that they
will

will be provided for. And a little after faid,
This trial is made eafier than I could have
thought, my will being wholly taken away;
for if I was anxious for the event it would
have been harder, but I am not, and my
mind enjoys a perfect calm.

In the night a young woman having giv-
en him fomething to drink, he faid, My child
thou feems very kind to me a poor creature,
the Lord will reward thee for it. Awhile after he cried out with great earneftnefs of fpirit, Oh my father! my father! and foon after he faid, Oh my father! my father! how
comfortable art thou to my foul in this trying feafon. Being afked if he could take a
little nourifhment; after fome paufe he replied, my child I cannot tell what to fay to
it; I feem nearly arrived where my foul fhall
have reft from all its troubles. After giving
in fomething to be inferted in his journal,
he faid, I believe the Lord will now excufe
me from exercifes of this kind; and I fee no
work but one which is to be the laft wrought
by me in this world, the meffenger will come
that will releafe me from all thefe troubles;
but it muft be in the Lord's time, which I
am waiting for. He faid he had laboured to
do whatever was required, according to the
ability received, in the remembrance of
which he had peace; and tho' the diforder
was ftrong at times, and would like a whirl-
wind come over his mind; yet it had hitherto been kept fteady and center'd in everlafting love; adding, and if that be mercifully
continued,

continued, I aſk nor deſire no more. Another time he ſaid, he had long had a view of viſiting this nation, and ſometime before he came had a dream, in which he ſaw himſelf in the northern parts of it, and that the ſpring of the goſpel was opened in him much as in the beginning of friends, ſuch as George Fox and William Dewſbury, and he ſaw the different ſtates of the people, as clear as he had ever ſeen flowers in a garden; but in his going along he was ſuddenly ſtopt, tho' he could not ſee for what end; but looking towards home, fell into a flood of tears, which waked him.

At another time he ſaid, my draught ſeemed ſtrongeſt towards the north, and I mentioned in my own monthly-meeting, that attending the quarterly-meeting at York, and being there looked like home to me.

Fifth-day night, having repeatedly conſented to take medicine with a view to ſettle his ſtomach, but without effect; the friend then waiting on him, ſaid thro' diſtreſs, what ſhall I do now? He anſwered with great compoſure, Rejoice evermore, and in every thing give thanks; but added a little after, this is ſometimes hard to come at.

Sixth-day morning he broke forth early in ſupplication on this wife, O Lord it was thy power that enabled me to forſake ſin in my youth, and I have felt thy bruiſes for diſobedience; but as I bowed under them thou healed me, continuing a father and a friend; I feel thy power now, and I beg that in the approaching

approaching trying moment thou wilt keep
my heart ftedfaft unto thee. Upon his giving directions to a friend concerning fome
little things, fhe faid I will take care, but
hope thou wilt live to order them thyfelf;
he reply'd, my hope is in Chrift, and tho' I
may feem a little better, a change in the diforder may foon happen, and my little ftrength
be diffolved, and if it fo happens, I fhall be
gathered to my everlafting reft. On her faying fhe did not doubt that, but could not
help mourning to fee fo many faithful fervants removed at fo low a time; he faid all
good cometh from the Lord, whofe power is
the fame, and can work as he fees beft. The
fame day he had given directions about
wrapping his corpfe; perceiving a friend to
weep, he faid I would rather thou wouldft
guard againft weeping for me, my fifter, I
forrow not, tho' I have had fome painful conflicts, but now they feem over and matters
well fettled, and I look at the face of my
dear redeemer, for fweet is his voice and
his countenance is comely.

Firft-day, 4*th* of the tenth month, being
very weak and in general difficult to be underftood, he uttered a few words in comme-
moration of the Lord's goodnefs; and added, how tenderly have I been waited on in
this time of affliction, in which I may fay
in Job's words, Tedious days and wearifome
nights are appointed unto me, and how many are fpending their time and money in
vanity and fuperfluities, while thoufands
and

and tens of thoufands want the neceffaries of
life, who might be relieved by them, and
their diftreffes at fuch a time as this, in fome
degree foftened by the adminiftring fuitable
things.

Second-day morning the apothecary who
appeared very anxious to affift him, being
prefent, he queried about the probability of
fuch a load of matter being thrown off his
weak body, and the apothecary making fome
remarks implying he thought it might; he
fpoke with an audible voice on this wife,
My dependance is on the Lord Jefus, who I
truft will forgive my fins, which is all I hope
for, and if it be his will to raife up this body
again, I am content; and if to die, I am refigned; and if thou canft not be eafy without trying to affift nature, I fubmit. After
which his throat was fo much affected, that
it was very difficult for him to fpeak fo as to
be underftood, and frequently wrote when
he wanted any thing. About the fecond
hour on fourth-day morning he afked for
pen and ink, and at feveral times with much
difficulty wrote thus, I believe my being
here is in the wifdom of Chrift, I know not
as to life or death.

About a quarter before fix the fame morning he feemed to fall into an eafy fleep, which
continued about half an hour, when feeming
to awake, he breathed a few times with more
difficulty, and expired without figh, groan,
or ftruggle.

A Teſtimony

A Teftimony from Derby *Monthly-Meeting in* Pennfylvania, *concerning* W I L L I A M H O R N E.

H E was born in the county of Suffex, Great-Britain, in the year 1714, and came with his parents to Philadelphia about the year 1724; in 1736 he came to refide in this townfhip, where he continued the remainder of his life. He married in 1737, and in 1746 he appeared in public teftimony in our religious meetings, and being obedient to the heavenly call, became an able minifter of the gofpel.

In the year 1752 he vifited the meetings of friends in New-England; and in the fourth month 1763 embark'd for Great-Britain, where he vifited the meetings generally in England and fome part of Wales, returning home in the tenth month 1764, to the great fatisfaction of his family and friends. He alfo, at feveral other times, vifited moft of the meetings in Pennfylvania and New-Jerfey, and the back parts of Maryland and Virginia; it appearing, by certificates produced, that his labours of love were acceptable to friends.

His minifterial labours werefrequent, lively and edifying, adorning the doctrine he preached by a circumfpect life and converfation, being zealoufly concerned for the maintenance of good order in the church, a good example in his family, careful to bring

up

up his children in diligently attending religious meetings, and manifesting his care in divers respects for their present and future welfare. Kind and hospitable to friends, his house and heart being open for their reception.

He departed this life, at his own habitation, the 11*th* of the eleventh month 1772, in the fifty-ninth year of his age and the 26*th* of his ministry, and was interr'd in friends burying-ground at Derby aforesaid.

A Testimony from Little Egg-Harbour *Monthly-Meeting in* New-Jersey, *concerning* JOHN RIDGWAY.

HE was born in the county of Burlington, in West-New-Jersey, in the year 1705, and soon after came with his parents and settled within the compass of this meeting: He was religiously educated, which as he grew in years, had a good effect, by his yielding obedience to the heavenly vision of light and grace in his own mind, which weaned him from the vanities of the world. He was a steady and constant attender of meetings when at home and in health; and altho' his circumstances in life made him apprehend it necessary to follow the sea for a time, yet by attending to the divine principle of grace, he was preserved from that extravagance in his conduct and conversati-

'on

on too prevalent in men in that bufinefs. He was early in life appointed to the ftation of an elder in the church, in which he conducted with reputation; being of a benevolent fpirit, his heart and houfe were open to entertain his friends and others, cheerfully and liberally affifting the poor in many refpects; and in an extenfive commerce and converfation amongft men of various ranks, he demeaned himfelf with a becoming gravity, which render'd him truly worthy of efteem. He was carefully concerned that his children and other youth, might partake of the benefits of a fober education; and in his declining years, was much afflicted with bodily indifpofition, which he was enabled to bear with patience and refignation; often expreffing a defire to be contented in the divine will.

He quietly departed this life, on the 21/ℓ of the fifth month 1774, aged near feventy years, and was buried at Egg-Harbour.

A Teſtimony from Plainfield *Monthly-Meeting in* New-Jerfey, *concerning* JOHN VAIL.

OUR worthy and much efteemed friend John Vail, was born at Weft-Chefter, in the province of New-York, and removed from thence while young to Woodbridge, where he fettled and married. He was when a youth, reached by the power of truth, and

and fubmitting to the crofs, he became fober and religious; and continuing faithful
and obedient to what he believed to be his
duty, the Lord in infinite mercy, was
pleafed to beftow on him, a gift in the gofpel miniftry, and he proving faithful with
the one talent, witnelled an increafe and
growth in the truth, and was enlarged in
his public teftimony, whereby the church
was edified, and the faithful comforted.
Having a regard to the putting forth of the
divine hand, he waited in meetings for proper qualifications to minifter in the ability
that God gives, whereby he was often enabled, not only to reprove the unrighteoufnefs of men, but to fpeak comfortably to
thofe who mourned for the pride and abo-
minations of the times. He often mentioned the plainnefs and fimplicity which our
forefathers appeared in, and was forrow-
fully affected for many of the prefent generation, in that they flighted their good examples, and indulged themfelves in many
things which thofe worthy men bore a faithful teftimony againft. He was a diligent
attender of meetings, and very exemplary
in being early there, even to old age, when
of ability of body; often exciting friends
to that duty, not as formalifts, but patiently to wait for qualification to perform acceptable worfhip to the Almighty. His outward circumftances being low, he was very induftrious, labouring with his hands
for the fupport of himfelf and family, to

an

an advanced age, being very loth to be bur-
denſome to friends.

He lived to a good old age, and on his
death-bed, expreſſed his great ſatisfaction,
and reſignation to the will of the Almighty,
and ſaid he had often conſidered that paſſage of ſcripture, " If our hearts condemn
" us not, God is greater," adding, ' But
' my heart condemns me not, for I have
' walked in innocency from my youth up:'
He divers times ſignified his being ready
and willing to leave the world. As our dear
friend walked in righteouſneſs and humility, he increaſed in divine experience, and
his lamp ſhone bright to the laſt. He departed this life, on the 27*th* of the eleventh
month 1774, in the eighty-ninth year of
his age, much beloved by his friends, neighbours, and acquaintance in general, a large
number of whom attended his corpſe to the
grave, where, after a ſolid meeting on the
occaſion, it was interr'd in friends burying-
ground at Rahway.

A Teſtimony from Goſhen *Monthly-Meeting in*
Pennſylvania, *concerning* THOMAS GOOD-
WIN.

HE was born in the principality of Wales
in the year 1694, and came over to
Pennſylvania with his parents about the
year 1708; and according to the beſt ac-

counts

counts we can collect, he appeared in the miniftry near the fortieth year of his age; and became a faithful labourer in the Lord's vineyard. He fundry times vifited friends in the adjacent provinces, feveral of which vifits he performed even in old age; and about the fixty-ninth year of his age vifited friends in many parts of England and Wales; and fome years after, friends in Ireland; which vifits were acceptable, as appeared by feveral certificates given by friends amongft whom he laboured. He was zealous for the promotion of good order in the church, and often fervently engaged in our meetings for difcipline, to recommend friends to a humble waiting for the pointings of truth, as the alone fafe guide and qualifier for every good word and work.

He was exemplary himfelf, and careful to bring up his family in the practice of attending meetings on the firft and other days of the week; was zealous in promoting and faithful in performing that good work of vifiting friends families: His miniftry was found and edifying, being in the demonftration of the fpirit and power; and he may be faid to be of the number of them that through faith have obtained a good report.

The laft year of his life, he was prevented from travelling far abroad, by reafon of a lingering and painful diforder, but when able to attend his own meeting, he frequently appeared in the miniftry, tho' under much bodily infirmity. And altho' he was

a3

as a fhock of corn fully ripe, gathered in its feafon, yet we are fenfible of the lofs the church has fuftained by his removal; but we truft it is his everlafting gain, and that he now enjoys the fruits of his labours. His laft expreffions were, ' Lord Jefus receive ' my foul.'

He departed this life, the 16*th* of the fourth month 1775,. and was buried in friends burying-ground at Gofhen, on the 19*th* of the fame, aged eighty-one years, and a minifter about 41 years.

A Teftimony from Nottingham *Monthly-Meeting in* Pennfylvania, *concerning* J o h n C h u r c h m a n.

H E was born at Nottingham in Chefter county, Pennfylvania, the 4*th* of the fixth month 1705, of religious parents, John and Hannah Churchman; and by his own account, was remarkably reached and made fenfible of the inward appearance of grace and truth when very young; but through inattention thereto, fuffered lofs. About the twentieth year of his age, thro' the great loving kindnefs of a merciful God, the divine vifitation was again renewed wherewith he clofing in, became fubject to the Lord's hand, who was about to prepare him as a chofen inftrument for fervice. In his twenty-fifth year he married, and foon after was

Y 2 recommended

recommended to the ftation of an elder, wherein we find, he acted with great caution, humility and fear, and being qualified for the fervice of vifiting families, was employed therein.

His firft appearance in public miniftry, was in the year 1733, and by humble obedience to the giver, he improved in the gift, and became an able minifter of the gofpel; in which fervice he travelled much, having vifited the meetings of friends in this and feveral of the adjacent provinces, moftly feveral times; and in the fummer 1742, he perform'd a religious vifit to friends in New-England, and the year following to New-York and parts adjacent, which he repeated in 1774. In the year 1750 a concern ripened, which he expreffed had for fome years before, at times, refted with weight on his mind, to crofs the feas in the fervice of the gofpel, wherewith he had the free concurrence of his brethren at home (being always very careful in that refpect;) and fpent upwards of four years on a general vifit to the meetings of friends in England, Scotland, Wales, Ireland and Holland, and alfo to the particular families of friends within the compafs of divers meetings in different parts of Europe; and by feveral certificates produced to our meeting after his return, the unity and latisfaction of friends in thofe European countries with his exemplary conduct and religious labours were fully exprefied.

Although

Although he was of a weakly conftituti-
on, and often infirm, efpecially in the latter
part of his life, yet he appeared to be much
devoted to the fervice of truth and the good
of mankind, and gave up his time for that
purpofe, when he apprehended it was required of him, being favoured with a fufficiency
of outward things, and we believe he ftood
loofe from the world and its connections,
not feeking, but refraining opportunities he
might have had to get outward riches; he
vifited neighbouring yearly, quarterly, and
other meetings of friends at times to his laft
year, and was truly ufeful in the difcipline
of the church, being eminently qualified for
that fervice, and was a good example in a
diligent care to attend all the meetings both
for worfhip and difcipline to which he belonged, cautious of being forward in his
public appearances, and for the moft part
exampled us to filence in our meetings at
home, efpecially in the latter part of his
time; yet when he did appear in teftimony,
we think it may be truly faid, his doctrine
dropt as the dew, being lively and edifying
to the honeft hearted, tho' clofe and fearching
to the carelefs profeffors, as well as to the profane and hypocritical. The elders who have
ruled well are to be accounted honorable, fo
the remembrance of the fatherly, diligent,
humble, upright, honeft, and felf-denying
example of this our deceafed friend, as alfo
his various fervices in our meetings and
neighbourhood remain frefh, and of a pleafant favour to many minds.

In

In his last illness, which held him upwards of three weeks, he appeared mostly
sensible, and manifested much patience and
resignation, uttering many lively expressions
to those attending him, and to divers friends
who came to see him; some of which being
taken down in writing, are hereunto sub-
joined, viz.

*Some Account of the last illness of our friend
John Churchman, and of divers of his
weighty expressions, near the close of life.*

ON the 11*th* of the sixth month 1775,
he return'd home, after performing
his last journey, on a visit to most of the
meetings on the Eastern-Shore of Maryland,
and attending the yearly-meeting at Third-
Haven in Talbot county. On the 14*th* of
the same month, he went to the weekday
meeting at London-Grove, to meet with a
committee of our quarterly-meeting on particular business, and returned to our meeting at Nottingham the next day, on the first
day of the week following was there also, in
the same week he attended our preparative
and monthly-meetings, but a fever daily increasing upon him, he was afterwards chiefly confined at home.

On the 4*th* of the seventh month he expressed
himself thus, ' I am glad that I am at home,
' I have ever found it best when my service
' abroad was over, to get home as quick as
' might

' might be, and though I have felt great in-
' ward poverty and weaknefs fince my laft
' journey, fo that I can neither fee my be-
' ginning nor ending, but feem as if all
' were hidden, yet I hope if Providence fhall
' fee meet to remove me at this time, fome
' light will appear again, and that it will
' be otherwife before I go.'

At another time he fpake to this purpofe,
' I have found myfelf much ftripped as to a
' fenfe of good, and tried with poverty ma-
' ny days. I fuppofe I have been accounted
' by fome, as one of the better fort of peo-
' ple, but have feen great occafion to beware
' of a difpofition that would feek to feed up-
' on the praife or commendations of others;
' a carnal felfifh fpirit is very apt to prefent,
' and creep in here if poffible, and I have
' feen it hurt many who have had right be-
' ginnings, it always introduceth dimnefs,
' and oppreffion, to the pure, precious, in-
' nocent life of truth, which only groweth
' up into dominion, through deep abafe-
' ment of foul, and the entire death of felf.'

At feveral other times he fignified to this
effect, ' My prefent baptifm of affliction
' hath tended to the further refinement of
' my nature, and to the bringing me more
' perfectly into the image of my mafter.'

He frequently expreffed his full fubmiffion to the divine will either refpecting life or
death, feveral times faying, ' I now expe-
' rience my life and my will to be flain, and
' I have no will left.'

' In

In the two laſt weeks of his time it appeared that his deſire and hope, mentioned in the forepart of his illneſs, for light again to appear, was fully anſwered by the freſh influence thereof, ſo that altho' his pain was often great, he would many times in a day break forth into a kind of melody with his voice, without uttering words, which as he ſometimes intimated, was an involuntary aſpiration of his ſoul in praiſe to the Lord, who had again been pleaſed to ſhine forth in brightneſs after many days of poverty and deep baptiſm, which tho' painful, had proved beneficial to him, being a means of further purifying from the dregs of nature, ſaying he was at times afraid to diſcover that melody in the hearing of ſome that viſited him, left they could not comprehend its meaning, and might therefore miſconſtrue it.

On ſecond day morning the 17*th* of the ſeventh month, being aſked by a friend how he was, he replied, ' I am here in the body ' yet, and when I go out of it I hope there ' is nothing but peace,' and ſoon after further ſaid, ' I have ſeen that all the buſtles, ' and noiſes that are now in the world will ' end in confuſion, and our young men that ' know not an eſtabliſhment in the truth ' and the Lord's fear for a ballaſt, will be ' caught in a trying moment.' At another time he ſaid, ' I feel nothing but peace, having endeavoured honeſtly to diſcharge my-

' ſelf

' felf in public, and privately to individu-
' als as I apprehended was required, and if
' it be the Lord's will that I fhould go now,
' I fhall be releafed from a great deal of
' trouble and exercife, which I believe friends
' who are left behind will have to pafs
' through.'

On the 20*th* of the fame month he thus
exprefled himfelf, ' I love friends who abide
' in the truth as much as ever I did, and I
' feel earneft breathings to the Lord, that
' there may be fuch raifed up in the church
' who may go forth in humility, fweetnefs,
' and life, clear of all fuperfluity in expreffi-
' ons and otherwife, ftanding for the tefti-
' mony, that they may be ufeful to the
' church in thefe difficult times.'

About three days before his death, feveral
friends being in his room, he fpake as follows,
' Friends in the beginning, if they had
' health and liberty, were not eafily divert-
' ed from paying their tribute of worfhip
' to the Almighty on week days as well as
' firft-days, but after awhile when outward
' fufferings ceafed, life and zeal decaying,
' eafe and the fpirit of the world took place
' with many, and thus it became cuftoma-
' ry for one or two out of a family to attend
' meetings, and to leave their children much
' at home; parents alfo if worldly concerns
' were in the way could neglect their week
' day meetings fometimes, yet be willing to
' hold the name, and plead excufe becaufe
' of a bufy time, or the like, but I believe
' that

' that fuch a departure from primitive inte-
' grity ever did, and ever will, occafion a
' withering from the life of true religion.'

To a friend who came to vifit him on the
21ſt of the feventh month he faid, ' I feel
' that which lives beyond death and the
' grave, which is now an inexpreſſible com-
' fort to me after a time of deep baptifm
' that I have paſſed through, I believe my
' being continued here is in the will of Pro-
' vidence, and I am fully refigned.'

His illnefs increafing he faid but little on
feventh-day the 22d; in the afternoon he
was very low, and fpeechlefs about twelve
hours; early on firft-day morning he recruit-
ed a little, and gave directions about his
coffin to a friend who fat up with him, being
a joiner; continuing rather eafier the forepart of that day and appearing cheerful, he
expreſſed divers weighty fentences like farewell exhortations to fome who came to fee
him; on fecond-day morning he fat up a
confiderable time, in the afternoon he appeared lively and fenfible, tho' very weak,
thus expreſſing himſelf, ' I am much re-
' freſhed with my mafter's fweet air, I feel
' more life, more light, more love and
' fweetnefs than ever before,' and often mentioned the divine refreſhment and comfort
he felt flowing like a pure ſtream to his inward man, faying to thofe who were with
him, ' I may tell you of it, but you cannot
' feel it as I do.'

In the evening a young perfon coming into the room, looking at her earneſtly and affectionately,

fectionately, he faid, ' Deborah arofe a mo-
' ther in Ifrael,' and fhortly after, ' The
' fweetnefs that I feel;' then his difficulty
of breathing increafed, and being turned
once or twice, he requefted to be helped up,
and was placed in his chair, in which he expired about the ninth hour on fecond day
night the 24th of the feventh month 1775, being aged near feventy, and a minifter about 42
years, and was buried on the 26th in friends
grave-yard at Eaft-Nottingham, a large concourfe of people attending, after which a folemn meeting was held.

A Teftimony from New-Garden *Monthly-Meeting
in* Pennfylvania, *concerning* SARAH MIL-
HOUSE.

SHE was religioufly inclined from her
youth, and when married, was a good
example in her family as a wife and a parent,
of an inoffenfive life and converfation, and
a diligent attender of religious meetings,
until prevented by age and bodily infirmity:
Her appearances as a minifter were not frequent, but favoury and in few expreffions.

In her laft illnefs fhe feem'd refigned either to live or die, and by her fenfible expreffions and good advice to her children and
others, fhe appeared in a living humble
frame of mind, and fignified, ' She did not
' fee any thing in her way.'

She

She quietly departed this life, the 26*th*
of the eighth month 1775, aged about feventy-four years; and on the 27*th* was interr'd in friends burying-ground at New-
Garden.

After her deceafe, was found, wrote with
her own hand, as follows, ' Oh! that my
' children would walk in the truth, the pure,
' inward, everlafting truth, which is Chrift;
' feek unto him in fecret and great humility,
' who alone can preferve you in every try-
' ing time which muft be met with in this
' life, that we may be prepared for that life
' which is everlafting; feek it before any
' earthly treafure.'

A Teftimony from Gwynedd *Monthly-Meeting in*
Pennfylvania, *concerning* W I L L I A M
F O U L K E.

HE was born of religious parents, early
fettlers of Gwynedd, from whom he
received a pious education, to which, with
the vifitation of divine grace, he fo far attended from early youth, that in the feveral
characters of hufband, father, mafter, and
neighbour, with his hofpitality and charitable difpofition to the poor, he was much endeared to his family, friends and neighbours.
Being a man of integrity and a lover of peace,
he endeavoured to promote it in others, and
was remarkably endued with a happy talent
for

for compofing differences and reclaiming of-
fenders, in which fervices he was much exercifed.

In the ftations of an elder and overfeer
which he filled for a number of years, he
was exemplary and ferviceable. His health
gradually declined for feveral months; and
though his diforder proved lingering, he was
enabled to bear it with refignation and patience, expreffing the expectation of his change
with calmnefs.

The day before his deceafe, a friend who
vifited him, mentioned, what a comfortable
reflection it muft be to him, when drawing
near to the clofe of life, that he had filled
up the ftation alloted him in a good degree
of faithfulnefs; he replied, ' I have no fight
' when my change may be, I endeavour to
' be refigned, I have not any thing to boaft
' of, I have not any thing to expect from a-
' ny works I have done, it was but little;
' but I have experienced that the Lord is
' merciful, in whom I truft, having redeem-
' ed my foul from deftruction. I much de-
' fire to be within the pale of happinefs,
' fomewhere within the door where I may
' find a quiet habitation.'

He continued fenfible to the laft, and departed this life, on the 30*th* of the eighth
month 1775, in the fixty-feventh year of his
age, and on the 1*ft* of the ninth month, was
interr'd in friends burying-ground at Gwynedd.

A Teftimony

A Teſtimony from the Monthly-Meeting of Philadelphia, *concerning* SARAH MORRIS.

SHE was born in this city, being the
daughter of our ancient friends Anthony
and Elizabeth Morris, who were careful to
inſtruct her in the fear of the Lord, a diligent attendance of our religious meetings,
and an early acquaintance with the holy
ſcriptures; the advantage whereof ſhe at
times expreſſed to be a great comfort to herſelf, and of benefit to others. Her father died when ſhe was about ſeventeen years of
age, and near his end gave this teſtimony
reſpecting her, ' That ſhe had never diſobey-
' ed him, and was his comfort;' which we
inſert with deſires it may ſo impreſs the
minds of youth, that by duly regarding the
divine command of obedience to parents,
they may be their comfort, merit the like
teſtimony, and ſecure peace to their own
minds. She was endued with underſtanding ſuperior to many, which, with her ſoci-
able, agreeable diſpoſition, occaſioned her
converſation in the younger part of her life
to be ſought and acceptable to ſuch who were
accounted wiſe in the eſtimation of the world;
but from her religious inclination preferring
the company of thoſe who exceeded her in
age and experience, ſhe was mercifully preſerved from the ſnares and temptations to
levity and vanity by which many of the
youth are too readily captivated.

The

The state of mind and religious exercise she was brought under, through the early visitations of divine grace, being sensibly expressed in a short account written by herself, we think worthy to be preserved, directed as follows,

' To all to whose hands this may come, be
' it known,

' That, I having been one who was born
' of religious parents, was by that means fa-
' voured with a sober and virtuous educa-
' tion, but what was far beyond all outward
' blessings, the Lord in his mercy was pleaf-
' ed to make very early impressions of reli-
' gion on my soul, by his immediate grace
' and good spirit, and made me sensible of
' the touches of divine love when very
' young, and at times these merciful visita-
' tions were continued from my very infan-
' cy (and through every part of life) by
' which I was in a good degree preserved
' from the evils and vanities of the world,
' and not only so, but comforted and sup-
' ported in every time of trouble and diffi-
' culty, as there was a secret regard to that
' good hand which is, and ever will be the
' help of all those who put their trust in it.
' But tho' the Lord had so favoured me that
' I was made capable of being in some re-
' spects serviceable amongst my acquaintance
' and friends, from a propensity in my na-
' tural disposition (which is likewise a bless-
' ing from Heaven) to assist or oblige those
' with whom I conversed; yet after it pleaf-
' ed

‘ ed God, by the death of a fifter whom I
‘ entirely loved, to give me a frefh inftance
‘ of the uncertainty and unfatisfactorinefs
‘ of all temporal bleffings, he was pleafed
‘ to ftrengthen my defires after the enjoy-
‘ ment of that which is eternal and fadeth
‘ not away; and ftrong cries were raifed in
‘ my foul that I might be brought to a near-
‘ er acquaintance, and a more conftant a-
‘ biding with him who is the beloved of
‘ fouls, and who, by the fecret touches of
‘ divine goodnefs, had raifed fuch a hunger
‘ and thirft after righteoufnefs, that my foul
‘ could not be fatisfied fhort of it: I fay, af-
‘ ter it had pleafed God thus to incline my
‘ mind to feek after a more full enjoyment
‘ of that inward life and virtue which is
‘ communicated and conveyed to the foul
‘ through the illumination of the holy fpi-
‘ rit, I was vifited with ficknefs, in which
‘ I had fo a near a profpect of eternity, that
‘ I feemed juft entering into it; O! then,
‘ the emptinefs and vanity of all the world;
‘ the pleafures and friendfhips of it appear-
‘ ed in a clear and ftrong light; nothing
‘ then but the hope of an entrance into the
‘ kingdom of Heaven feemed of any value,
‘ and that hope the Lord was at that time
‘ pleafed in fome degree to afford me; but
‘ yet I thought I faw a great deficiency, and
‘ was made to defire of the Lord, that if it
‘ was his will to reftore me, he might ena-
‘ ble me to live more clofe to his teachings,
‘ and follow him more fully than I had hi-
                                    ‘ therto

' therto done; but in order to this, a work
' of greater mortification than ever had
' been experienced by me, was neceffary.
' Great diftrefs of foul and affliction of bo-
' dy was I brought into, infomuch that I
' knew not where, or what I was; fuch
' temptations and buffetings of Satan that
' I had till now been a ftranger to, were
' fuffered to befet me, in the abfence of fpi-
' ritual comfort and refrefhment, yet in all
' this the Lord was very merciful, and let
' me fee that his dealings with my foul were
' in order to qualify and fit for fome fur-
' ther fervice; O! then the folemn engage-
' ments my foul was willing to enter into at
' this Bethel! If thou O Lord! will be with
' me in the way that I go, and give me
' bread to eat and raiment to put on, in a
' fpiritual fenfe, and bring me to my hea-
' venly father's houfe in peace, thou fhalt
' be my God, and I will ferve thee! And
' the Lord, who knew the tendernefs of my
' heart (at that time, for it was his own
' work) was pleafed gracioufly to fhower
' down of the heavenly rain of his king-
' dom, by which my foul was greatly com-
' forted and refrefhed in his prefence; and
' in a true fight and fenfe of my own no-
' thingnefs and inability to do any thing
' that was acceptable in the fight of God
' without his affiftance, was my fpirit great-
' ly humbled before him, and a refignation
' wrought in my will to be given up in all
' things to him, who had thus enabled my

Z.   ' foul

' foul to praife his name upon the banks of
' deliverance from great and fore conflicts
' and troubles, which were unknown to
' any in that day, for then was the Lord my
' refuge and fure hiding place, and under
' the fhadow of his wing was I kept, and
' in the fweet enjoyment of divine love,
' light and life, at times was made to fay,
' furely nothing fhall ever be able to make
' a feparation from the love of God in Chrift
' Jefus: But alas! this lafted not long, for
' when it was clearly fhewn me what was
' required of my hands, which was to bear
' a public teftimony for God, and to declare
' unto others what he had done for my foul,
' then confultations with flefh and blood
' began, tho' the merciful vifitations of love
' were long continued unto me; yet doubts,
' fears and reafonings increafed, fo that
' great darknefs and diftrefs came upon me,
' nor could I now apply with that confi-
' dence and truft as formerly, to him a-
' lone who can help, but began to difclofe
' fomething of my condition to others,
' from which time I was fenfible that my
' ftrength decreafed; yet all this while I
' was willing to hope that a frefh vifitation
' might be fometime afforded, for without
' it, I faw my ftate very dangerous; what
' would I not then have done to have reco-
' vered my former condition? I went un-
' der great diftrefs and perplexity day and
' night for fome months, the comfortable
' refrefhments and divine openings with
' which

' which I had been fo plentifully favoured,
' were withdrawn, and I left in unfpeakable
' anguifh and diftrefs; under this fenfe of
' terror I cried to the Lord to fhew me his
' will and enable me to perform it, but the
' fenfe of his love was fo far withdrawn, and
' fears and doubts had fo prevailed, that I
' began to queftion every thing, and by de-
' grees the unwearied adverfary hath fo pre-
' vailed, or it is fo fuffered for ends I know
' not, that I am at this time, according to
' my weak apprehenfion, left very much to
' myfelf without the fenfation of divine love
' upon my foul, or the ability to feek after
' it, or rightly to wait for it, or to ftir or
' move any way as to my foul, but, in a
' ftupidity not to be defcribed, ftript of all
' inward comfort, and not able to take plea-
' fure in any thing this world can afford.'

Being, through the mercy of the Lord,
preferved under this clofe probation, and, in
his time, gracioufly relieved by the quickening virtue of his divine prefence and power,
fhe, in great abafement and humiliation, became refigned to his holy requirings, and
appeared in public teftimony in one of our
religious meetings; being thus brought forth
in the miniftry, through great mortification
of her own will, her appearance was much
to the comfort and fatisfaction of friends, it
being evident to the fenfible and judicious
members of the church, that fhe was rightly called to this weighty work; and divers
nearly fympathizing with her, were fpiritual

helpers

helpers, watching over her in much love and tenderneſs; and through faithfulneſs to her gift, ſhe increaſed in knowledge and experience, and became an able goſpel miniſter, being found in doctrine, pertinent in exhortation, clear and audible in utterance, and careful to adorn the doctrine ſhe preached by a pious exemplary life and converſation.

Her firſt journey in the ſervice of truth was to ſome adjacent meetings as companion to our valuable friend Margaret Ellis; being afterwards, through the efficacy of divine love, drawn forth to viſit many of the meetings in this province, New-Jerſey and the yearly-meetings in Maryland and Long-Iſland; and in the year 1764, in company with our friends Joyce Beneʒet and Elizabeth Smith, attended that at Rhode-Iſland; though her religious labours were chiefly in this city, manifeſting among us a ſteady uniform concern for the cauſe of truth, and preſervation of true chriſtian fellowſhip, not only in the exerciſe of her gift in the public miniſtry, wherein ſhe was eminently favoured, but alſo of our chriſtian diſcipline among friends of her own ſex, for which ſhe was well qualified and of real uſe.

After the deceaſe of her ancient mother, who, in the ninety-fourth year of her age, departed in a calm and peaceful ſtate of mind, toward whom ſhe had manifeſted a filial affection and care, an exerciſe which ſhe had many years been under to viſit friends

in

in Great-Britain now reviving, the weight
of the fervice, and her apprehenfion of being difqualified therefor, affected her fo
deeply, that fhe was reduced to fuch a low
ftate of mind and body, her recovery appeared doubtful; but after a diftreffing feafon
of conflict, fhe was favoured with ftrength
to communicate her concern to this meeting,
and obtaining a certificate of the near fympathy and concurrence of friends, fhe was
left to proceed, with their free approbation,
as the Lord might be pleafed to furnifh ability; and her affectionate niece Deborah
Morris's offer to accompany her, being alfo
concurred with, they embarked for London,
in the third month 1772, where being arrived, tho' continuing in a weak ftate of
health, fhe was enabled to perform her vifit
to friends in moft of the principal counties
and towns from Exeter in the weft as far
north as Cumberland, and thofe called the
Eaftern-Counties; attending two yearly-
meetings in London, and divers general
meetings in other parts of the nation; and
being favoured with ftrength beyond expectation, and with that wifdom which truth
gives to thofe who faithfully refign to its
holy requirings, difcharged her religious duty to the edification of the churches and her
own peace; returning home in the ninth
month 1773, accompanied by her faid niece,
who had been truly helpful to her, and three
friends from Great-Britain on a religious
vifit; her having been thus mercifully fuftained

ed through this weighty fervice, and under
fuch apparent infirmity, advanced to the feventieth year of her age, was both matter
of comfort, and occafion of grateful admiration to friends.

Having, foon after her return, attended
the general meeting at Shrewfbury, the quarterly-meeting of Bucks and fome other meetings, fhe united that winter with our valuable friends, M. Leaver and E. Robinfon,
from Great-Britain, in vifiting many of the
families of friends in this city, being eminently favoured with divine help therein,
as fhe had been at times before in the like
fervice.

In the fifth month 1774, fhe vifited friends
at New-York and Long-Ifland, attending the
yearly-meeting there, and divers others; and
in the fame fummer and fall, vifited fome
meetings in New-Jerfey and this province,
befides diligently attending thofe in this city
as fhe was enabled, being favoured in moft
of them with a lively edifying teftimony.

For about fix months before her departure,
a dropfical diforder fubjeded her to great
bodily weaknefs; yet her love to God, his
truth and people, was fo prevalent, that
when unable to walk to a meeting, fhe was
divers times carried to her feat; one of the
laft fhe attended in public, was on the 4*th*
of the fixth month 1775, to which fhe was
with great difficulty brought, and was enabled to bear a lively teftimony; affectionately expreffing her great concern for the
welfare

welfare of the people, that they might be gathered to God, and mentioning the paſſage of our bleſſed Saviour weeping over Jeruſalem, tenderly exhorted the riſing youth to embrace the call of the Lord, ſubmit to his teaching, and thereby experience preſervation.

During her illneſs, ſhe had to endure great bodily pain, and at times, depreſſion of ſpirit; yet was at ſeaſons much favoured, and uttered many comfortable and edifying expreſſions, ſome of which being noted down, are as follows, viz. ſixth month 1775. On hearing the ſound of a drum paſſing, it being a time of great commotion, ſhe ſaid, ‘ Oh, it is the ſpirit of Chriſt that is the ‘ chriſtians glory and ſtrength! It makes us ‘ humble, meek and wiſe, it is this teacher ‘ that cannot be removed; a guide into that ‘ righteous way, which if but lived in, ‘ would have kept off this impending ſtorm. ‘ O! that they would even now but humbly ‘ ſeek to learn the chriſtian warfare, and be ‘ earneſtly engaged to fight under the ban— ‘ ner of Chriſt, to know their own hearts ‘ luſts totally ſubdued.’ At another time being in great pain, ſhe cried out, ‘ O ſweet ‘ Lord Jeſus, that thou wouldſt be pleaſed to ‘ give me a little eaſe, who am an unwor— ‘ thy creature, undeſerving thy ſweet pre— ‘ ſence; but thou art merciful, and thou, ‘ O Lord! knoweſt that nothing leſs can ‘ eaſe and comfort me; thy living preſence ‘ is all I want.’ And after the favour was

granted,

granted, which for an hour she enjoyed, she
said, ' Oh! how good is my God, thus to
' hear my feeble cry ; O how sweet is this
' case! All my pains are eased by one secret
' look from thee ; O! that I could be thank-
' ful enough for this favour; this sweet tho'
' short quiet, which we cannot get at but
' when thou, O father! pleases. O! that
' the people would but believe, that in thy
' peace their strength consists; and that they
' would more generally seek to know it be-
' fore it is too late; but too many are con-
' tented without witnessing the frequent re-
' newings of divine love, in which only
' there is life, if they are but preserved
' from gross evils and go on in prosperity,
' they sit down easy and think all is well;
' but O! that they may not too late find
' their mistake, and that they have pleased
' themselves with favours which they have
' unthankfully received, and so stopt short
' of greater, by not desiring them, and
' more frequently than the day, waiting to
' know the renewings of that life, without
' which there is no life to the truly begotten
' children, and which would shew them,
' not only what they ought to do, but
' would give them strength to do it.

Seventh month 2d; in a quiet sitting of
some friends in her room, she said in sub-
stance, ' If I may take the freedom to ex-
' press my experiences of the Lord's graci-
' ous dealings with me, when in a land of
' darkness and drought, where no water is,
a land

‘ a land of pitts and deferts, befet as with
‘ noxious creatures, and amongft ferpents
‘ and fcorpions, from whence none could
‘ deliver but him who can open and none
‘ can fhut; I have feen the neceffity, after
‘ having done the will of God, to wait
‘ with patience to receive the promife of
‘ him who is the fame to-day. as yefterday,
‘ and will fo continue forever. Many are
‘ the comfortable affurances in holy writ to
‘ thofe who keep the word of his patience;
“ I will keep fuch in the hour of temptation,
“ which fhall come upon all the earth, to try
“ them that dwell therein;” I have many
‘ times, my dear, may I not fay my beloved
‘ friends, for fo at feafons you have been
‘ to me, tho’ at other times I hardly dare
‘ fay fo; I have many times been glad to
‘ feel a little opening of ftrength with my
‘ friends, and may fay, I am thankful for
‘ this quiet folemn opportunity, for great
‘ have been and ftill are my trials, and clofe
‘ may be your provings; I don’t fpeak it to
‘ difcourage any, but I find without the re-
‘ newings of divine love and life, we are
‘ incapable of keeping the word of his pa-
‘ tience, being fo frequently befet and fur-
‘ rounded with weaknefs and infirmities;
‘ O! may you, my dear friends, who have
‘ been called and anointed for fervices, wit-
‘ nefs a renewed fupply of holy oil, where-
‘ by your lamps may be kept burning, and
‘ your lights fhining; and experience the
‘ law to go forth from Zion, and the word
of

' of the Lord from Jerufalem, and remem-
' ber your covenants made in the day of
' deep diftrefs; may you be fupported thro'
' every future difficulty and trial, and I
' thro' the prefent conflict; that when eve-
' ry pool and channel of comfort fhall be
' dried up, and all human help found un-
' availing, we may witnefs him to be near,
' who hath promifed, for the cry of the
' poor and for the fighing of the needy he
' would arife; therefore, cry mightily to him,
' that we may know him to do fo for us;
' for I find, without fenfibly feeling the
' drawing cords of his love, which opens
' and enlarges the heart, we cannot apply
' thofe gracious promifes to our comfort;
' and when he draws, let not the cares of
' this life, nor flavifh and unneceffary fears,
' prevent your following him faithfully,
' whatever afflictions may attend; O! may
' we be fo preferved in his holy hand, as
' that nothing may be fuffered to pluck us
' out of it, and fo aflifted to conduct, as to
' be found among that happy number who
' have come through many tribulations,
' where all forrows and fighing will be done
' away and all tears wiped from our eyes,
' to join thofe who can acceptably fing the
' fong of praife, having had their robes
' wafhed in the blood of the lamb and made
' white.' And on the 3d, tho' with fome
difficulty of utterance, faid, ' Though the
' floods beat high at times, and the waves
' roared, fhe was then fenfible of the divine
' love

' love being prefent, and in that love faluted
' her friends, as fhe hoped each one there
' had in a greater or leffer degree, known
' the fanctifying power of religion on their
' minds; fhe very earneftly and affection-
: ately urged them to a more clofe and fo-
' lemn attention to this important work,
' not to reft fatisfied fhort of witneffing
' daily advancing forward on the way; that
' when this earthly tabernacle was diffolved,
' we might have a well grounded hope of a
' houfe eternal in the Heavens, whofe maker
' and builder was God. That our bleffed
' Saviour had told his immediate followers,
' in his father's houfe were many manfions,
' and that he went to prepare a place for
' them, that where he was they might be
' alfo; and that tho' the fenfible enjoyment
' of divine love was much withdrawn from
' many who had formerly been eminently
' favoured with its living influence; yet not
' to be difcouraged, as living faith in Chrift
' Jefus (tho' but in a fmall degree) was
' abundantly fufficient for our ftrength and
' fafety; and as his divine love ftill continu-
' ed with thofe who are far advanced and
' as on the verge of time, it would alfo be
' the guide and bleffed guardian of the
' younger in years, as they humbly and
' fteadily kept upon their watch, and paid
' a due obedience to the divine inftructions
' of his holy fpirit.'

The laft night of her life, being in bodily
pain, and under fome difcouragement of
mind,

mind, fhe was reminded of fome late favours of divine love extended to her; after
laying fometime in awful filence, fhe replied,
' Now I fee it to my comfort, that the Lord
' hath been with me through all this illnefs,
' and I, at times, knew it not, fuch was my
' diftreffed fituation, it was hard for me to
' believe it.' Afterwards falling into a fweet
fleep, fhe in about two hours awaked much
refrefhed, and remarked, fhe had not flept
fo fweetly in all her illnefs, for fhe had been
in company with her father's God, mother's
God and her God; afked her niece (Deborah
Morris) who had with abundant care attended on her, if fhe thought life would hold
all night, who anfwering, fhe thought it
might, as the night was far fpent, fhe defired her faid niece would fit by her until
the Lord came, (meaning to clofe her life)
then flumbered again, and awakening, admired, faying, ' It is ftrange I fhould
' fleep at fuch a time as this.' Being told
her work was done, and it was a favour to
her fhe could fleep, fhe replied, ' I believe
' it is, and am thankful;' inquiring what
time it was, on being told it was after three
o'clock, fhe lifted up her hands as engaged in
mental prayer; foon after uttered fome words
but not intelligibly, and feeming again to
drop into a fweet fleep, neither ftirred or fpoke
more, but continuing till between eight and
nine o'clock, paffed eafily away, on the
24*th* of the tenth month 1775, in the feventy-fecond year of her age, and 31*ft* of
her

her miniftry, fitted, no doubt, for the enjoyment of that reft, which is prepared for
the righteous, having accomplifhed her warfare in the church militant.

Her burial on the 26*th*, after a folemn
meeting, was refpectfully attended by many friends and others of her fellow-citizens, to our grave-yard in this city.

A Teftimony from Wrights-Town *Monthly-
Meeting in* Pennfylvania, *concerning* ZEBU-
LON HESTON.

HE appeared early in the miniftry, continued faithful, and died in good unity with the church. His miniftry was lively and edifying, in the exercife whereof, he
feveral times travelled through this and the
neighbouring colonies: And at the age of
near feventy-years, performed a religious
vifit to the Delaware Indians, refiding to the
weftward of Pennfylvania, which vifit was
cordially received, as appears from a copy
of a fpeech made by one of their chiefs
(captain White Eyes) and the delivery of a
belt at the fame time in token of friendfhip,
at a meeting for worfhip in their town on
the river Mufkingum, which were produced
to our meeting at his return.

In his laft illnefs, he expreffed his fatisfaction with the dutiful deportment of his
children towards him as a parent, and gave
them

them falutary advice; exhorting them, ' Not
' to give their minds too much to temporal
' things, nor feek after worldly enjoyments,
' but learn to get wifdom and underftand-
' ing, which would make them fhine as
' ftars in the firmament; and to remember
' their feveral duties, and be ready at the
' cock-crow, or at midnight; praying his
' God and father to be with them and blefs
' them.' After a time of filence, he faid,
' I am at peace with all men. Lord thou
' haft been with me in times paft, be with
' me in my laft moments, and I pray my
' God and father, that he will bear me up
' as in the hollow of his hand, to my ever-
' lafting home.'

In regard to outward affairs, he expreffed
himfelf in the following manner, ' If the
' world would have lived in love and unity
' one with another, it appears to me, that
' no good thing would have been withhold-
' en from us, but it feems to be dark times,
' and things lay very wide. But it looketh
' to me, there will be a gathering home
' from off the barren mountains and defert
' hills, of them that are little thought of at
' this time. Lord, let thy will be done and
' not mine. If it be thy will that I muft
' depart from my brethren in the time of
' their trouble, I willingly yield in obedi-
' ence. If it be thy will that I fhould be
' fpared a while longer, I willingly bear
' my part of the burdens whatfoever thou
' pleafeft to lay upon me.' Many more
fimilar

fimilar expreffions, he frequently uttered during his laft illnefs, under which he was fupported in a truly pious and refigned ftate of mind.

He departed this life, the 12*th* of the third month 1776, in the feventy-fourth year of his age.

———————

A Teftimony from Kingwood *Monthly-Meeting in* New-Jerfey, *concerning* MARY HORNER.

SHE was born at Mansfield, in the county of Burlington, New-Jerfey, in the year 1736, of parents in memberfhip with friends, and was educated in the profeffion of the truth as held by us. Her tender mind while in her minority, was fenfibly reached with a divine vifitation of the love of God, and as fhe grew to riper years, fhe was preferved in a good degree of circumfpect walking in the fear of the Lord; her converfation being ferious, fenfible and guarded, and oftentimes her grave deportment was ufeful as a check to her companions. In the year 1757 fhe was married to Ifaac Horner, and filled the ftation of a faithful and prudent wife and mother. In the beginning of the year 1768, fhe appeared in public as a minifter, her teftimony being fhort and lively. In the year 1770, fhe removed with her hufband and family, to fettle within the compafs of this meeting,

and

and has fince refided among us. She was remarkable for her unreferved charitable opennefs and innocent freedom of deportment towards all; and through the influence of the love of God fhed abroad in her heart, by a life of unaffected piety, and a godly circumfpection of conduct and deportment, fhe obtained a good report. She was divers times, with the concurrence of her friends, engaged in gofpel love, in vifiting meetings abroad, and had good fervice in vifiting families, not only within the compafs of this monthly-meeting, but others.

Having taken a cold, it brought on a decay, under which fhe languifhed upwards of eight months, near half of which time fhe neverthelefs attended meetings. During her indifpofition, her quiet compofure of fpirit, and cheerful refignation to the will of her heavenly mafter was truly edifying. She told a friend who vifited her not long before her departure, that ' Though death appear-
' ed a dark paffage, yet all was light beyond
' it.' And to another, who at parting, bid her farewell, fhe faid, ' I fhall fare well
' when I am rid of this body.' She was remarkably clear in her underftanding, and faid, ' Though bodily weaknefs prevail-
' ed, yet her fpirit felt no diminution of
' ftrength;' and exhorted thofe about her, to place their reliance on the Lord alone,
' A confidence,' faid fhe, ' In which I have
' never been difappointed.'

One

One evening near her clofe, fhe broke forth
into expreffions of praife to the Almighty,
and humble acknowledgments, ' That he
' had to her, performed all his promifes,
' had prepared and fanctified her, and
' brought her to that hour; and that fhe
' fhould praife him as long as fhe continued
' in the body, and at the conclufion, cheer-
' fully furrender hufband and children, and
' all that he had given her, into his hands.'

In or near her laft hour, fhe beckoned her
hufband, to come and take his leave of her,
and then compofedly faid, ' Thou art a
' welcome meffenger, thou art welcome,
' take me quickly.'

She died the 31ſt of the fifth month 1776,
in the fortieth year of her age, having been
engaged in the miniftry upwards of 8 years.

A Teſtimony from Salem *Monthly-Meeting in*
New-Jerſey, *concerning* JAMES DANIEL.

HE was born of pious parents, and thereby knew the advantage of a religious
education, which he frequently expreffed
by way of encouragement to parents and
youth, as a means by which he had in a
good degree been guarded in the time of his
youth, from the vanities of the world.
Yet as he grew in years he clearly faw he
wanted the experimental part of the chriſtian religion, without which he could not at-

A a   tain

tain to that which his foul exceedingly longed for; and under a fenfe of this want, was
brought at times very low, and for fome
years had to pafs through a ftate of mourning and deep exercife, being baptized as under the cloud and in the fea in a fpiritual
fenfe; which brought him to a paffive fubmiffion to the divine will, fo that it pleafed
the Lord, in the returns of his favour, to
vifit him with the day fpring from on high;
and having learned obedience through the
things that he fuffered, he gave up to the
heavenly vifion, and came forth in the miniftry in a few words, moftly in fcripture
language, in great fimplicity; and altho'
not eloquent, yet being faithful in the little,
he became much enlarged in his gift, having
clear openings in the fcriptures, and at times
much favoured with clear profpects of the
ftates of meetings and individuals, that he
had to fpeak to fecret and hidden things, in
the demonftration of the fpirit and with
power, which reached the witnefs in many
hearts. He was a father to the young in
experience, and zealous to reprove lightnefs
and vanity where he faw occafion.

He travelled in the work of the miniftry,
in feveral of the American provinces, and
once to England, of which fervices we had
comfortable accounts. He was zealous for
the fupport of our chriftian difcipline, was
favoured with a good underftanding, exemplary in his life and converfation, and lived
much in the fimplicity of the truth, which
made

made him near to his friends, and a ufeful member in fociety. Being weak in body, a confiderable time before his deceafe, he faid, ' It feemed as if his day's work was ' done, and nothing lay upon him;' obferving that fome worthy friends had of late been removed without much forefight of their latter end, and had not much to communicate, he faid, ' If it fhould be his cafe, ' he would not have it looked upon as in ' difpleafure, for he was clear and eafy in ' his mind, and that he believed his ftay ' would not be long;' which proved according to his profpect; for being taken with fomething of a quinfy followed by an ague, he faid, ' He thought that would be his laft ' illnefs,' adding, ' I have never been de- ' firous to know when my time was near at ' an end, but have long been defirous to ' live fo as to be ready, and I think I am ' ready. I have endeavoured to be faithful ' in the difcharge of my duty in every re- ' fpect, and have nothing lies againft me, ' but feem at quiet. I have in other illneffes ' been pretty much refigned, yet there feem- ' ed fomething of a choice to live, but in ' this I have not that choice, but I am rea- ' dy.' He quietly paffed away, after a fhort illnefs of about fifteen hours, on the 18th of the twelfth month 1776; aged feventy-two years. Having been a minifter about 40 years.

A Teftimony

A Teſtimony from Eveſham *Monthly-Meeting in* New-Jerſey, *concerning* HANNAH FOSTER.

SHE was the daughter of Enoch and Sarah Core, of Eveſham aforeſaid, and was born the 17*th* day of the tenth month 1710; her father dying while ſhe was very young, left her and three other children under the care of their mother, whoſe religious concern for them was very great; as ſome of us have heard our ſaid friend often expreſs both in public and private.

She was naturally of a cheerful diſpoſition, and at times when young in years, ſhe ſuffered an airy ſpirit to prevail ſo far as to lead her into lightneſs, yet, thro' divine favour, the ſolid inſtruction and example of her mother, had ſuch influence on her mind, as to preſerve her from groſs evils; which we have often heard her expreſs with awful reverence.

In the year 1729, ſhe was married to our friend William Foſter, and entered into the care of a family, at which time, the cares of this world had great effect on her mind, as ſome of her laſt expreſſions herein after mentioned will more clearly evince.

Some time after her marriage, it pleaſed the Lord to renew his viſitation of love to her ſoul, and to ſhew her the vanity of all temporal enjoyments without his love; and ſhe yielding obedience to the heavenly viſion, and being given up to ſerve the Lord, had

a gift

a gift in the miniftry committed to her, in which we have reafon to believe, fhe was in a good degree faithful to improve, and through divine aid, became a lively minifter.

She vifited moft of the meetings on the continent of America, except fome part of Virginia and Carolina; and the accounts received of her religious labour in the miniftry, were comfortable and fatisfactory. Her humble awful waiting in religious meetings was edifying; fhe was much concerned that good order might be preferved, and careful to example and admonifh her offspring in the fear of the Lord, more than to influence their minds to feek after the treafures that are tranfitory and perifhing. A near fympathizer with the afflicted, either in body or mind, often vifiting fuch and adminiftring to their relief.

Towards the latter part of her time, her health was much impaired, yet fhe grew more lively in the miniftry, and in fome of the laft meetings fhe attended, was enabled in a folemn manner, to invite the youth to join the heavenly call of God, and to be faithful in their gifts, and then they would be raifed like an army in his power, to fubdue the works of darknefs, which fhe faw much prevailed amongft them; remarking fome parts of the epiftle from our laft yearly-meeting, refpecting fome hopeful youths who attended that folemn fervice.

In

In her laſt ſickneſs, which tho' ſhort, was
ſharp, ſhe was preſerved in much patience
and ſtillneſs; and when it was apprehended
ſhe was near expiring, a friend who came
to viſit her, taking leave of thoſe attending
her, ſhe held out her hand to the ſaid friend
and deſired to be raiſed up, when with conſiderable difficulty ſhe ſaid, ' That there was
' a time when her heart and mind was
' much ſet on the world and the things of
' it, and it proſpered with her according to
' her deſire; but ſhe bleſſed the name of
' the Lord, who ſoon let her ſee the vanity
' and emptineſs of all worldly treaſure, and
' that ſhe was thankful he had enabled her
' to yield obedience to the heavenly viſitati-
' on, and in ſome degree to anſwer his re-
' quirings, for it now yielded her more
' peace, than if ſhe had poſſeſſion of the
' whole world, if it was of tenfold more
' value than it is; and that her prayers had
' often been to the Lord, that he might yet
' favour the riſing generation with the like
' viſitation of his love,' with ſome other
words which could not be underſtood. She
appeared in a ſweet frame of mind, and after a ſhort pauſe, took her ſolemn leave of
the ſaid friend; after which ſhe lay ſtill,
and in a few hours quietly departed this life,
on the 14*th* of the firſt month 1777, and
was buried in friends burying-ground at
Eveſham the 17*th* of the ſame, where a ſolemn meeting was held; aged ſixty-ſix and
a miniſter upwards of 40 years.

A Teſtimony

A Testimony from the Falls *Monthly-Meeting in* Bucks *county, concerning* JOSEPH WHITE.

AS the memory of the just is pronounced blessed, we think it expedient to give forth a testimony concerning this our e-steemed friend.

He was born at the Falls the 28*th* of the eleventh month 1712-13; being young when his father died, he was brought up under the care of his relations and friends: And through the early extendings of hea-venly regard whilst young, and attending to the teachings of divine grace, he was led and preserved from many of the follies and extravagances incident to unthinking youth. About the twentieth year of his age he ap-peared in public testimony in our religious meetings, and continuing in a good degree faithful to the measure of light and grace communicated, he grew in his gift, and be-came a lively and able minister.

He was naturally of an open cheerful disposition, and honestly concerned for the promotion of piety and virtue, and for the support and maintenance of good order in the church; for which service he was emi-nently gifted, and truly serviceable amongst us, being often concerned that the authority of truth might be kept up in all our meet-ings of discipline, and that true judgment might be placed upon the disorderly and irreclaimable. He was exemplary in his

life

life and converfation, a diligent and timely
attender of our religious meetings when
health of body permitted; and was often
favoured therein in public teftimony and
fupplication, much to the comfort and edification of the truly humble waiters. And
altho' he had a large gift in the miniftry,
he many times fat meetings in filence, waiting upon the Lord, not being hafty or forward in the exercife of his gift; but careful
not to minifter without the heavenly life
and power that firft raifed him up in the
miniftry, whereby his public fervice was
greatly to the confolation and refrefhment
of many.

He feveral times had a concern to vifit
the churches abroad, and with the concurrence of this meeting, vifited many of the
meetings of friends in this and feveral of the
adjacent provinces, and once through fome
parts of Maryland, Virginia and North-
Carolina: And having for fome confiderable time been under a weighty concern to
pay a religious vifit to friends in feveral
parts of Europe, he with the concurrence
and unity of his friends took fhipping for
that purpofe in the year 1758, and after a
fhort paffage landed in England, and having
pretty generally vifited friends meetings in
England and Ireland, and fome parts of
Wales, he returned to his family and friends,
having been from home in truth's fervice
near three years: And at his return from
thefe

thefe vifits produced certificates of friends unity and good fatisfaction with him, and his public fervice amongft them.

He was divers times appointed and engaged in the fervice of vifiting families, being well qualified for that weighty fervice.

He much loved the company and converfation of his friends; was a loving and affectionate hufband, a tender parent and a good neighbour, generally beloved by his friends and others that knew him, being in feveral refpects ufeful and ferviceable in the neighbourhood where he lived.

He was attended from his youth at times, with a pain at his breaft, with intermiffions of health, fometimes for years, and at other times but fhort; but as he advanced further in age, intermiffions of health grew fhort and pain increafed, which brought on other bodily infirmities, which he bore with patience and refignation, often craving he might not be off his watch when his pains were exquifite, nor his faith fail in the time of trial, believing it to be the goodnefs of God, through his thus dealing with him, more and more to wean him from all outward connections and neareft ties of nature, that being as the pure gold, refined through the furnace, he might with triumph join the redeemed that were gone before, which he at times had a foretafte and evidence of; but the time when, as he himfelf fometimes expreffed, he did not then fee, believing it to be confiftent with divine wifdom to keep it hid from him.

The

The latter part of his time for feveral months, he flept but litte in the night feafon, being at times engaged in reverent interceffions and divine contemplation, and appeared to be waiting for the folemn moment.

He lived in the compafs of the Falls particular meeting until a few years before his death, and then removed to Makefield, (a branch of the fame monthly-meeting,) and having for fome months felt ftrong defires (if favoured with health) to go to the Falls meeting, and on a monthly-meeting day fet out to go there; but the weather being cold and he in a weak ftate of health, foon found himfelf unable to perform the journey, and returned home. But fometime after feeling his bodily ftrength fomewhat reftored, and love renewed, he fet out, in company with his wife, one firft-day morning, and got to the meeting where he was favoured with an open time in public teftimony, much to the fatisfaction of thofe prefent. After the meeting was over and friends gone out, a friend being defirous of fpeaking to him, not feeing him out of doors, returned into the houfe, and found him fitting on a feat, unable to move without help; the friend affilted him, and took him to his houfe, where he was taken care of: The fit being of the paralytick kind, was much more favourable than at fome other times, tho' it continued ebbing and flowing for feveral hours; in which time

time he expreffed feveral things, fome of
which being then taken down, are nearly as
follows.

Being afked by his fon Samuel how it was
with him; he anfwered, ' I dont know but
' that I am near my end. My defire at this
' time for thee is, that thou feek unto the
' Lord for affiftance, to govern thee in thy
' conduct in this fluctuating life, for I have
' found him to be a fure help and counfellor
' to me; and if thou follow after him in
' truth and fincerity, as I have endeavoured
' to do, he will be unto thee a fufficient
' director, a teacher that cannot be removed
' into a corner: I have not been anxious to
' gather a portion of this world, nor make
' to myfelf mammon of unrighteoufnefs,
' for I think I have feen a fnare that has at-
' tended many young people on thefe ac-
' counts. I have ever from my youth had
' a defire to be more in fubftance than in
' fhew: Let me appear as I might in the
' fight of men, their praife I fought not
' for; but I have fought the honour of God,
' therefore there is a place where no trouble
' fhall annoy, prepared for me as a reward
' for obedience: You that ftay, be more
' humble, and when trouble awaits you,
' look not upon nor truft to the arm of flefh
' for affiftance, but ftay yourfelves upon
' him who fuffered for you, for me, and
' for all mankind; for I have for fometime
' believed, and lived in the hopes thereof,
' and am now in meafure confirmed, of
' more

‘ more glorious things yet to be revealed to
‘ the church of Chrift, and that further and
‘ greater difcoveries will yet be made, with
‘ refpect to the chriftian religion than ever
‘ yet has been fince the apoftafy.’

And after a fhort paufe he broke forth in
thefe expreffions, ‘ The door is open, I fee
‘ an innumerable company of faints, of an-
‘ gels, and of the fpirits of juft men, which
‘ I long to be unbodied to be with, but not
‘ my will, but thy will be done O Lord! I
‘ cannot utter nor my tongue exprefs, what
‘ I feel of that light, life and love that at-
‘ tends me, which the world cannot give,
‘ neither can it take away from me. My
‘ fins are wafhed away by the blood of the
‘ Lamb that was flain from the foundation
‘ of the world: All rags and filthinefs are
‘ taken away, and in room thereof love and
‘ good will for all mankind: O that we may
‘ become more united in the church mili-
‘ tant, and nearer refemble the church
‘ triumphant! O that we all might make
‘ fuch an end as I have in profpect, for its
‘ all light, all life, all love and all peace,
‘ the light that I fee is more glorious than
‘ the fun in the firmament; come Lord Je-
‘ fus Chrift, come when thou pleafes, thy
‘ fervant is ready and willing; into thy
‘ hands I commit my fpirit, not my will,
‘ but thy will be done O Lord! Let this
‘ mortal body be committed to the duft, be
‘ with me, with my children and my grand-
‘ children; be with all them that love thee,
‘ that

‘ that love thy appearance. O the pains
‘ that I feel, that attend this mortal body,
‘ they are more comely to me than jewels!
‘ I rejoice in my fighs and groans, for to
‘ me they are moft melodious; I am near
‘ to enter that harmony with Mofes and the
‘ Lamb, where they cry holy, holy, holy,
‘ I cannot exprefs the joy I feel. My heart
‘ (if it were poffible) would break for joy:
‘ If any inquire after me, after my end,
‘ let them know all is well with me.’

Many more weighty expreffions he fpoke,
which not being taken down, cannot be re-
collected.

The next day his pain abating, and finding himfelf fomewhat relieved from his diforder, he was taken to his own houfe, where
he remained in a weak ftate of health for
fometime, being unable to go much abroad.
And one night fome fhort time before his
death, his pain had been fharp the forepart
of the night, but the latter part it abating,
his wife lay down by him, and fell afleep,
but he as ufual flept not, but after fometime called to his wife in thefe words: ‘ My
‘ dear, I believe I muft take my leave of
‘ thee. I have never feen my end till now,
‘ and now I fee it is near, and the holy an-
‘ gels enclofe me around, waiting to receive
‘ me;’ his wife afked him if fhe fhould call
up the children, he faid, he did not fee any
thing further he had to fay to them, except
to his fon Jofeph, who being called, and he
having expreft what he had on his mind,

was

was much fpent, and appeared as tho' he was near his defired port; but after fome-time he revived, with thefe words, ' Life ' is yet ftrong in me and will not yield;' thus he continued the few concluding days, waiting in refignation and retirednefs of mind, until the repeated returns of the pa-ralytick complaint reduced his faculties and fenfes fo, that he knew not what was done for fome days, and departed in much ftill-nefs as in a fleep, the 10*th* day of the third month 1777, and was decently interr'd in friends burying-ground at the Falls meet-ing-houfe, the 12*th* of the fame; his body being attended to the grave by a number of friends and neighbours.

May we under the confideration of our great lofs of him, and many other faithful labourers in the Lord's vineyard, now re-moved from us, be excited fo to follow their footfteps, that with them, we may be par-takers of that incorruptible inheritance, which is referved for the righteous, when time here fhall be no more.

Aged fixty-four, and a minifter about 44 years.

A Teſtimony

A Testimony from Haddonfield *Monthly-Meeting in* New-Jersey, *concerning* JOSEPH GIBSON.

PRECIOUS is the memory of the righteous, thofe who have been bright examples of holinefs in their day, and therein preachers to others in life and converfation: It lives in our hearts to give this fhort teftimony, that fuch was our ancient and beloved friend Jofeph Gibfon, an elder of this meeting. He was born at Woodbury in the year 1690, and became early acquainted with the feafoning virtue of truth, which preferved him in a good degree, from the vanities of youth, and made him in love with plainnefs and fobriety while young; by a watchful attention to this divine principle, he attained a pious and innocent ftability of conduct through life, not often equalled; that it may be juftly faid, he was " An If- " raelite indeed in whom there was no " guile." A diligent attender of meetings, and a lively example there, in awful humble labour for that bread which ftrengthens and nourifhes the foul; wherein he continued fteadfaft to his concluding period. We could enlarge, but conclude with the words of the Pfalmift, " Mark the perfect man, " and behold the upright, for the end of " that man is peace;" which we believe was in an eminent degree the cafe of this our friend, who " Being dead, yet fpeaketh."

He

He departed this life, after a fhort illnefs,
on the 9th of the fourth month 1777, and
was buried the 11th, in friends burying-
ground at Woodbury aforefaid; aged about
eighty-feven years.

———————

A Teftimony from Pipe-Creek Monthly-Meeting
in Maryland, concerning RACHEL FAR-
QUHAR, late wife of William Farquhar
junr.

SHE was born at Caftlefhane, in Ireland,
in the year 1737, and removed to Pennfylvania with her parents, John and Elizabeth Wright, who, after fome years, fettled
in York county, within the compafs of Warrington monthly-meeting, of which fhe was
a member, till her marriage and removal
with her hufband to Pipe-Creek.

She was religioufly inclined when young;
and about the fifteenth year of her age, by
a frefh vifitation of divine love, was engaged to feek after divine wifdom; fo that
fhe became an early example of piety and
virtue; an encourager and promoter of virtuous inclinations in her companions and
acquaintance; her fteady conduct, and kind
and exemplary converfation, gained the love
and efteem of her friends and neighbours.

After her marriage, which was near the
beginning of the twenty-third year of her
age, fhe continued a diligent attender of
meetings

meetings for worſhip and diſcipline when
ability of body would admit; and when
there, was of an exemplary ſolid deportment,
ſo that ſhe was favoured to become a uſeful
member of ſociety, of ſound judgment.

She firſt appeared in the miniſtry in the
ſecond month 1771, and tho' not large was
pertinent in teſtimony; often admoniſhing
ſuch as were forgetful of their known duties,
and ſharply reproving where a wrong ſpirit
prevailed: Yet frequently ſpeaking comfortably to the bowed down mourners in
Zion, with whom ſhe often travelled in ſpirit, endeavouring according to her ability,
to lend a hand of help to ſuch.

The laſt meeting ſhe was at, was on a
firſt-day, about a week before ſhe died, in
which ſhe was much favoured, and ſpake
concerning Iſrael's journey from Egypt to
Canaan, adviſing not to ſettle ſhort of a poſſeſſion in the promiſed land. As ſhe was
walking home with her huſband in a ſolid
frame of mind, ſhe ſaid, ' In my father's
' houſe are many manſions;' ſignifying,
' If ſhe might be favoured with one of the
' leaſt of them, ſhe would be content.'

She departed this life, the 19th of the
fourth month 1777, and was interr'd in the
family burying-ground on the 21ſt of the
ſame month; in the fortieth year of her
age and 7th of her miniſtry.

A Teſtimony

A Testimony from the Monthly-Meeting of Philadelphia, *concerning* MARY EMLEN.

THIS our beloved friend arrived in Pennsylvania, with her parents Robert and Susannah Heath, from Great-Britain, about the year 1701, in the ninth of her age; and in 1716, was married to George Emlen and settled in this city.

About the year 1728, a remarkable visitation being extended to friends in this city, the hearts of divers were humbled, and, in the efficacy of divine love, several were constrained to open their mouths in our religious assemblies, in public testimony, and acknowledgments of the Lord's goodness and gracious dealings with their souls.

Our worthy friend Daniel Stanton, in his journal, mentions this as a memorable time, and names the several friends who then came forth in the ministry, of which number this friend was one; who being faithful, grew in her gift, and not only laboured in this city, but divers times was drawn forth in the love of the gospel, to visit the meetings in other parts of Pennsylvania and New-Jersey. And in the year 1744, in company with our dear friend Mary Evans, visited the meetings of friends in New-England; and was several times engaged with others in the weighty and profitable work of visiting the families of friends in this city, and through divers meetings in the country;

in

ʼn which ſervices, her labours were acceptable, being qualified in a peculiar manner
for that work.

Her miniſtry was lively, and delivered
in much innocency and brokenneſs of ſpirit.
Being a woman of integrity, ſhe loved chriſtian candor and plain dealing, and was
preſerved clear in her underſtanding, and
in her love to truth. During her illneſs,
which was ſhort, ſhe was favoured with an
earneſt of that divine peace and reſt which
is prepared for the righteous.

She departed this life, in this city, on the
1ſt of the ſixth month 1777, and was interr'd
in friends burial-ground the 3d following,
attended by many friends and others; aged
eighty-four years.

A Teſtimony from Wilmington *Monthly-Meeting
in the county of* New-Caſtle *on* Delaware,
concerning ELIZABETH SHIPLEY.

OUR beloved friend Elizabeth Shipley,
daughter of Samuel Levis, was born
in the Townſhip of Springfield, and county
of Cheſter in Pennſylvania, on the 26th day
of the tenth month 1690. She was led in
the prime of youth to deny herſelf, take up
her croſs, and follow Chriſt; and being
found walking in a good degree, in obedience to the meaſure of grace received, about
the twenty-fourth year of her age ſhe ap-

peared

peared in the miniftry; and being faithful
in the improvement of her talent, it pleafed
the Lord to make her an able and fkilful
minifter of the gofpel. She travelled in the
fervice thereof in this land, both fouthward
and northward in the early part of her time,
and vifited Barbados in company with Jane
Fenn, in the year 1725; but as fhe kept
few minutes, we have little account of her
labours abroad.

In the year 1728, fhe was married to
William Shipley, near Springfield aforefaid,
where they lived until the year 1736, about
which time they removed with their family
to this place; and we believe fhe was an inftrument in the Lord's hand, to fettle a
meeting here, and gather many to it. In
1743, fhe embark'd for England with our
friend Efther White, and the veffel going
by way of North-Carolina, while there,
they vifited fome meetings in that province;
after which they failed again, and arrived
at Liverpool on the 26th of the feventh
month, and in gofpel love, vifited generally the meetings of friends in England, Scotland and Ireland, to their own fatisfaction;
and, as appears by accounts from friends
there, to the comfort of many. She alfo
made feveral fhort vifits to the neighbouring
provinces; and in the feventieth year of her
age, in company with our friend Hannah
Foiter, vifited feveral of the northern provinces. She was feveral times exercifed in
that

that important fervice of vifiting families, in which her company and labour was very acceptable.

Her deportment in meetings was grave and folid, her gift in the miniftry lively and edifying, in prayer awful and weighty, not being forward in appearing.

Although her natural ftrength was much abated in the latter part of her time, yet her faculties remained bright, and her miniftry accompanied with life and power.

In the time of her laft illnefs, as feveral friends who came to vifit her were fitting by her, fhe appeared filled with divine pow-er, and fpoke in a lively manner, of the drawings of the father's love to bring her to fettle in this place, and faid, that his pro-mifes had been fulfilled to her; advifing to faithfulnefs in doing the work of their day; that for her own part, fhe was as a fhock of corn fully ripe, and fhould fhortly be gathered to the haven of reft.

In a little time after this, fhe was remov-ed to Weft-Marlborough; at which place fhe finifhed her courfe, on the 10th day of the tenth month 1777, in the eighty-feventh year of her age, a minifter about 63 years. She was interr'd in friends burying-ground on the 12th of the fame month, where a folemn meeting was held on the occafion.

A Teftimony

A Testimony from Wilmington *Monthly-Meeting in the county of* New-Castle *on* Delaware, *concerning* ESTHER WHITE.

OUR beloved friend Efther White, daughter of Thomas Canby, of the county of Bucks in Pennfylvania, was born in the fecond month 1700. In her young years fhe loved to attend religious meetings, and to fee friends behave folid therein, being herfelf an example of piety. She married John Stapler, of the county aforefaid; and being called to the work of the miniftry, fhe became a faithful labourer. About the thirty-fourth year of her age, her hufband was removed by death; after which fhe married John White, and in the year 1739 removed with their family to this place.

In the fpring of the year 1743, fhe, in company with our friend Elizabeth Shipley, failed for England by way of North-Carolina, and while there, vifited fome meetings in that province, then embarked, and arrived at Liverpool in the feventh month following, and in gofpel love, vifited the meetings of friends generally through England, Ireland and Scotland, to their own fatisfaction, and, as appears by accounts received, to the comfort and edification of many; and returned home in the latter part of the year 1745, to the joy of her friends and family.

In the year 1750, fhe vifited moft of the meetings of friends in Maryland, Virginia and

and the Carolinas; and in 1756, in company with Grace Fiſher, thoſe in New-Jerſey, and New-York Government: And in 1760, in company with Hannah Foſter junr. thoſe on the Eaſtern-Shore of Maryland, and the counties on Delaware: She alſo often viſited the neighbouring meetings; and in 1776, and the ſeventy-ſeventh year of her age, after a long time of ſickneſs, ſhe, in great bodily weakneſs, attended the quarterly-meeting at Fairfax in Virginia, much to her own peace and friends ſatisfaction.

She was an uſeful member of ſociety, and a woman of uncommon cheerfulneſs of ſpirit, although largely experienced in afflictions; through which ſhe was mercifully ſupported by divine ſufficiency; and being inſtructed in ſorrow, had a ſympathizing heart with the afflictions of others, and was ready to communicate to their relief both in ſpirituals and temporals. Her deportment was grave and ſolid, her miniſtry lively and edifying, even to old age. She was frequent in exhorting and encouraging friends to faithfulneſs in theſe times of great trial and outward commotion; that they might, with the wiſe builder, dig deep, and experience their foundation to be laid ſure, that neither winds nor floods might move them. She was careful to maintain brotherly love, ſometimes ſaying, that ' Love was her life, ' that ſhe could not live without it;' and being livingly ſenſible of the preciouſneſs thereof, was deſirous to promote it in others.

After

After a life in which she had to endure several long and trying seasons of sickness, and to pass through many deep baptisms of sorrow, through which she was supported with becoming cheerfulness, patience and resignation; she departed this life, on the 5th day of the twelfth month 1777, in the seventy-eighth year of her age, having been a minister upwards of 50 years; and on the 7th of the same month and 1st of the week, was interr'd in friends burying-ground in Wilmington; being much beloved by her neighbours, her funeral was accompanied by many friends and others, and was a solemn opportunity.

May the great Lord of the harvest, who is removing many eminent ministers from his churches, be pleased to raise up others to stand faithful witnesses for his name and truth in the earth.

A Testimony from Deer-Creek *Monthly-Meeting in* Maryland, *concerning* JOSEPH JONES.

HE was born in the city of Worcester, in Old-England, in the year 1686. His parents being of the church of England, educated him in that way during his abode with them, which was until he was about fourteen years of age. In the year 1700 he
arrived

arrived at Philadelphia, and going into New-Jerfey, there refided until twenty-one years of age.

He was convinced of the truth about the year 1708, and in 1712 appeared in the miniftry, being then in the twenty-fixth year of his age: Having, fince his convincement, undergone many fore conflicts, by reafon of a backwardnefs to comply with the Lord's requirings whereunto he had divers times been difobedient through diffidence and weaknefs, but at length he gave up, and therein found peace.

After his marriage, he refided about twelve years at Nottingham, in Chefter county Pennfylvania, and then removed to Deer-Creek where he continued. He was of an innocent life and harmlefs converfation; and in him were blended thofe truly chriftian virtues which render religion lovely and defirable; even the irreligious efteemed him an ornament to the chriftian profeffion. Being very converfant in the holy fcriptures, and favoured with a retentive memory, he was enabled to quote them with propriety, and very often fuitably apply them to inftruction and edification.

Divine love, as witneffed by the believers in Chrift, was a fubject upon which he frequently expreffed himfelf, in engaging and perfuafive terms; inviting others to come and be made partakers of fo glorious a treafure; adding, ' It had been the crown and
' joy

' joy of his life, the comfort and fupport of
' his old age, and was prefuaded would not
' forfake him in death.'

Of earthly treafure he poffeffed little, but
he appeared to be one of thofe poor of this
world, whom the apoftle James mentions, as
" Chofen by God, rich in faith, and heirs
" of the kingdom, which he hath promifed
" to them that love him." In this happy
fituation he was fupported with chriftian
fortitude, through times of adverfity and
deep affliction.

His wife dying in the ninth month 1777,
to whom he had been an affectionate companion upwards of fixty years, he did not
long furvive her, but, about four months
afterwards, was vifited with his laft illnefs,
in which he fuffered much pain, but was
compofed; fome days before his departure
he grew eafy, and in his latter moments,
when exhaufted nature fcarcely left him
ftrength to utter himfelf intelligibly, he lamented the ftate of the carelefs and uncon-
cerned, who did not duly and timely confider their latter end.

He feemed very defirous to be diffolved
and be with Chrift; and on the 8th of the
firft month 1778, as a fhock of corn fully
ripe, he was removed from works to rewards,
in the ninety-third year of his age; leaving
behind him the favour of a good name, being generally beloved by people of all ranks
and denominations who knew him. On the
11th of the fame month, he was interr'd in
friends burying-ground at Deer-Creek.

A Teftimony

A Teſtimony from Uwchlan *Monthly-Meeting in* Pennſylvania, *concerning* G R I F F I T H J O H N.

H E was born (by his own account) in Pembrokeſhire, in the principality of Wales, in the year 1683, and was in his youth an earneſt ſeeker after righteouſnefs among divers forms of religion, until he became meaſurably convinced of the principle of truth as held by friends, by peruſing William Penn's key to chriſtian knowledge, before he had much if any outward acquaintance with them : And coming over to this country when a young man, he ſoon after joined with friends in religious fellowſhip; and being faithful to the manifeſtations of divine grace in his heart, he had a gift in the miniſtry beſtowed upon him; and tho' not large, was ſavoury and edifying; which, together with his exemplary life and converſation, manifeſted him to be an heavenly minded man, much redeemed from the love and ſpirit of this world.

He was not anxious about the increaſe of outward riches, but eaſy and content with a ſmall ſhare thereof; ſo much as ſerved for bodily ſupport in great ſimplicity and plainnefs, he thankfully received; having a teſtimony againſt all ſuperfluity, and every thing tending to exalt the mind of man, or

promote

promote worldly greatnefs in any degrees
feeking above all, the kingdom of Heaven
and the righteoufnefs thereof.

He was a lover of peace amongſt brethren
and in his neighbourhood; and by precept
and example, laboured to promote it; being
at times concerned to travel about on foot,
even in advanced age, to his friends houfes,
and pay ſhort viſits in true chriſtian love,
and drop weighty and edifying hints, tending to ſtir up the pure mind; and ſcarcely
any thing was ſaid by him at any time but
what had a tendency that way.

He was a remarkable and worthy example, in conſtantly and early attending our
religious meetings, until upwards of ninety
years of age; when through weaknefs and
infirmity, he was confined at home, and
underwent great bodily afflicion with true
chriſtian fortitude and refignation to the divine will, patiently waiting his change;
which was on the 29*th* of the ſixth month
1778; aged about ninety-five, and a miniſter near 70 years.

A Teſtimony from the Monthly-Meeting of Friends
of Philadelphia *for the* Southern-Diſtrict,
concerning JOHN HALLOWELL.

HE was exemplary in a diligent attendance of our religious meetings and ſolid patient waiting therein, and ſerviceable
among

among us according to ability, in the fupport of the difcipline; of a meek and quiet fpirit, careful not to give juft occafion of offence to any. He was appointed an elder in the year 1772, in which ftation he conducted to good fatisfaction.

In the early part of the eighth month 1777, he was taken unwell, and being under great bodily pain, often begged for patience, faying, he was afraid to afk for any thing elfe. After he had been confined about two weeks, his pain fomewhat abating, he called his children together, and fpoke to them as follows: ' It looks as if I may
' fhortly be taken from you, and I think I
' have nothing to charge myfelf with, in
' regard to bringing you up; I have with
' great care watched over your morals, and
' anxioufly endeavoured by example, to
' teach you to walk in the fear of the Lord;
' but a backward difpofition prevailing,
' which I fear, has fometimes kept me from
' doing the good I might have done in the
' world, has at times, when my heart has
' been earneftly engaged for you, caufed me
' to keep filence, when it might have been
' profitable to have thus addreffed you:
' Look to the Lord my children, and afk of
' him to direct your ways. He muft be the
' fupport of youth as well as of old age. It is
' him, and him alone you muft cleave to,
' if ever you expect to find peace that will
' be lafting. It is not moral rectitude, go-
' ing to meeting, or any outward acts of
' devotion

'devotion only, that will do for you. Reli-
'gion is an inward work, and true worfhip
'muft be performed in the heart, by quiet-
'ly waiting on him who is the rock of ages.
'I know by experience what I fay, there-
'fore earneftly defire you to look to the
'Lord, live near him, and let his fear di-
'rect you in all you undertake. Keep out
'of the noifes and confufions that are in
'the world, 'tis all delufion. To be bleft
'with the prefence of the Lord in a dunge-
'on, is preferable to liberty enjoyed in
'palaces without it. And if it fhould pleafe
'the Lord to take me from you, tho' we
'may part for a feafon, yet if we walk in
'his ways, we fhall hereafter meet in eter-
'nal blifs.'

His diforder increafing, his pain at times
was very great, which he was enabled to
bear with a good degree of chriftian refignation; often defiring he might be endued
with patience to hold out to the end. And
altho' his outward tabernacle gradually de-
cayed, yet the feafonable and lively expreffions which he at times uttered, evidenced
that his inward man was frequently renewed.

'A few weeks before his departure, feveral
friends coming to vifit him, after a feafonable time of filence, he fpoke as follows.

'I have often of late been led to examine
'myfelf, to fee what it is that keeps me
'back, fometimes I think I fee death ad-
'vancing fwift, and at other times quite
'gone;

' gone; at this time in particular, I have
' been led to confider whether there remains
' any thing for me to do, and if I have any
' thing in my heart againft any perfon, that
' my love is not yet perfect; and upon a
' ftrict examination, I find nothing but love
' to mankind univerfally. I have been great-
' ly tried with pain of body, and poverty
' and barrennefs of fpirit, but through mer-
' cy have been preferved from murmuring;
' and I have a hope, that when I put off
' this body, I fhall be at reft; and that hope
' is an anchor to the foul.'

A day or two before his departure, his
pain much abated, and tho' he was reduced
very low, yet was preferved in much calmnefs and ferenity of mind, faying, ' He
' thought his diffolution was near; that he
' had done with every thing below, and ex-
' pected the change to him would be a hap-
' py one, believing a place of reft was pre-
' pared for him.'

He quietly departed this life, the 26*th* of
the feventh month 1778, in the fixty-fourth
year of his age, and his body was interr'd
the day following in friends burying-ground
in this city.

A Teftimony

A Teſtimony from Pipe-Creek *Monthly-Meeting in* Maryland, *concerning* W I L L I A M F A R Q U H A R.

HE was born in Ireland the 29*th* of the ſeventh month 1705, and came to America about the ſixteenth year of his age, and ſettled in Pennſylvania, where he was convinced of the truth, and married among friends. In the year 1735, he removed and ſettled at Pipe-Creek, when there were very few inhabitants in thoſe parts. Some years afterwards he was concerned that a meeting might be ſettled, which was allowed to be held at his houſe at times for ſeveral years ; when the number of friends increaſing, they concluded to build a meeting houſe, which our ſaid friend zealouſly promoted. His houſe was much reſorted to by travelling friends and others, both in that early period and ſince, to whom he was courteous and kind.

Some years after the ſettlement of a monthly-meeting at Fairfax, of which he was a member, he was appointed to the ſtation of an elder, which he filled with propriety and reputation ; being an example of plainneſs, and anxiouſly careful for the education of his children. He was, at times, concern'd in meetings, to exhort friends to keep to the teſtimony of truth, and particularly the youth, for whom he ſeemed zealouſly concerned, that as they grew in years they might grow in grace.

For

For fome months before his deceafe, he was in a weak ftate of body, yet frequently attended meetings, and the laft time of his being there was about four days before he died; the night following being in much pain, he feveral times cried out, ' O Father! ' mitigate my pain if it be thy will;' and was favoured to keep in the patience and refignation, waiting for his change. The day before he died, his wife leaning over him mourning; he faid to her, ' Weep not ' for me, but for thyfelf and others. The ' Lord is near.'

He departed this life, the 21*st* of the ninth month 1778, and was buried in the family burying-ground on the 23*d* of the fame month; aged near feventy-three years.

P. S. I am willing to communicate a few hints of what has often paffed through my mind concerning my dear hufband, whofe memory, to me, remains precious. He was much concerned for the welfare of the young and rifing generation, often cautioning and exhorting friends in their feveral ftations, ftrictly to examine the great duty and charge committed to their truft; and in a particular manner, his offspring, that they would mutually live in love with each other, and that they might be careful to bring up their children in the nurture and admonition of the Lord.

ANN FARQUHAR.

C c   *A Teftimony*

A Teſtimony from the Monthly-Meeting of Philadelphia, *concerning* MARY PEMBERTON.

SHE was the daughter of Nathan and
Mary Stanbury, of this city, who were
removed by death in her tender age, after
which ſhe was put under the care of our
friends Richard and Hannah Hill, by whom
ſhe was religiouſly educated: She was endued with good natural underſtanding, and
being obedient to the diſcoveries of divine
grace in her own mind, ſhe experienced a
growth and advancement in the life of religion, and through its gradual work, became a uſeful and active member in the
church, being many years in the ſtation of
an elder and overſeer. Her converſation
was lively and inſtructive, her deportment
ſolid and exemplary, and in our religious
meetings, it was often apparent ſhe was favoured with the preparation of a broken
heart and contrite ſpirit for the ſolemn performance of divine worſhip. She felt the
affliction of others with tender ſympathy,
and was enabled through divine help to bear
her own, which were various and proving,
with great reſignation and chriſtian fortitude. She was firſt joined in marriage to
Richard Hill; and ſometime after his deceaſe, to our worthy friend Robert Jordan;
and laſtly, in the year 1747, to our valued
friend Iſrael Pemberton lately deceaſed; and
through

through the feveral viciffitudes of life, fhe was
favoured to perfevere with great ftability
and prudence.

The following was found among her papers after her deceafe, by the date whereof
it is fuppofed to have been wrote on an occafion of very deep and uncommon affliction.

' Fourth month 16*th* 1761. This being
' a day of great falvation, wherein the di-
' vine power hath manifeftly appeared in
' bringing relief and fuccour to my diftreff-
' ed foul, and working deliverance for me
' which no human means could have effect-
' ed; I earneftly defire, in the depth of hu-
' mility and awful reverence, that it may
' be a day never forgotten by me, but that
' thankfgivings and living-praifes may fill
' my heart to the Lord Jehovah, in whom
' is everlafting ftrength, whofe arm alone
' hath brought falvation, bleffed be his
' name, his faithfulnefs faileth not thofe
' whofe truft and confidence is in him.'

The removal of her dear hufband, into a
ftate of exile in the ninth month 1777, was
a renewed affliction to her, which fhe apprehended, as fhe expreffed to a friend,
might tend to fhorten her ftay in this world.

She fell into a gradual decline and weaknefs of body during his abfence, which,
though it increafed upon her, fhe did not
keep her bed but about four or five weeks,
in which time fhe often expreffed herfelf in
a lively manner. On the 23*d* of the ninth

C c 2   month

month in the morning, her hufband fitting
with her, fhe faid, ‘ It is now evident to
‘ me, my dear, we muft foon part, we have
‘ paffed through many deep trials; there is
‘ nothing between us but true love and
‘ great affection, I hope thou wilt be kept
‘ in true refignation; I had fome hope of
‘ continuing fometime longer, both on thy
‘ account and for the fake of our dear
‘ grand-daughter, but I am not folicitous
‘ about it, not very folicitous.’

The afternoon of the fame day, being in
a fweet frame of mind, fhe faid, ‘ They
‘ who live near the fpring of life, are fenfi-
‘ ble their change will be for the better, a
‘ happy change from a ftate of deep afflic-
‘ tion;’ and fometime after faid, ‘ The
‘ fpring of life is often opened for the re-
‘ frefhment of the weary travellers.’

Tenth month 17th. Being low in body
and mind, one of her daughters prefent, fhe
faid, ‘ Whenever my mind is turned to
‘ think of getting better, I am engaged to
‘ defire to be kept under the Lord’s notice,
‘ who hath been good to me; the wonder-
‘ ful counfellor, the everlafting father, the
‘ prince of peace; few women, have had
‘ fuch fcenes to pafs through as I have had,
‘ but I have been favoured beyond what I
‘ expected.’ About an hour before her departure, fhe faid, ‘ Bleffed father, look down
‘ upon me if it be thy holy will.’ And
fhortly after faid, ‘ Deareft Lord, take me
‘ to thyfelf; there is joy in Heaven, there
‘ is

' is joy in Heaven.' After which fhe fell into a fweet fleep, and peacefully breathed her laft, on the 25*th* of the tenth month 1778, aged feventy-four years. And on the 27*th* was interr'd in friends burying-ground in this city.

A Teſtimony from Mount-Holly *Monthly-Meeting in* New-Jerfey, *concerning* RACHEL LIPPINCOT.

A FEW years before fhe died, fhe removed from Haddonfield to live within the limits of this meeting. She was an exemplary fympathizing friend; her teftimony in public meetings was fhort, yet favoury and feafonable. She was afflicted with a cancer in her breaft, and in her illnefs expreffed herfelf on this wife, ' Oh! if it be ' thy will, dear father, remove me before I ' be offenfive to my friends, and grant me ' patience to bear all that thou in thy wif- ' dom may fee meet to afflict me with.' To a friend prefent, fhe faid, ' Oh! that love ' may increafe and abound in this day of ' outward trials, and faithfulnefs be kept ' to, is my fincere defire; my trials through ' life have been many, but bleffed be the ' Lord's holy name, when he has appeared, ' all darknefs has vanifhed.'

She departed this life, the 29*th* of the ninth month 1779, and was interr'd in friends

friends burying-ground in Mount-Holly; aged eighty years.

———————————

A Teſtimony from Wilmington *Monthly-Meeting in the county of* New-Caſtle *on* Delaware, *concerning* DAVID FERRIS.

HE was the ſon of Zachariah and Sarah Ferris, and was born in Stratford, in Connecticut government, New-England, the 10*th* of the third month 1707. His parents being preſbyterians, brought him up in that way, his mother being religiouſly diſpoſed, and much concerned for her offspring, frequently gave them good advice and admonition, which had ſome good effect with this our friend, as he hath often been heard to expreſs.

We find by ſome remarks he left, that about the twelfth year of his age, he was frequently viſited and called unto by the divine monitor in his heart, to forſake evil and youthful vanities which he delighted in, and by being in a good degree faithful thereto, was for a time, preſerved from them; but for want of attending to that which would have continued to preſerve him, the pleaſures and vanities of this world got hold of his mind, ſo that he took much delight in airy and vain company, muſick and dancing, and ſuch like amuſements, until about the twentieth year of his age; when

it

it pleafed the Lord to vifit him with a fore
fit of ficknefs, which proved of lafting advantage to him, as it occafioned him to take
up a frefh refolution, to forfake the evil of
his ways, and turn to the Lord with full
purpofe of heart, which he was, thro' mercy, favoured with ability in meafure to
perform.

He ftill continued in profeffion with the
prefbyterians, not having any knowledge of
friends; although by attending to the teachings of divine grace, he became convinced
of the principle we profefs; and hearing of
a yearly-meeting of friends to be held on
Long-Ifland, went to it, with defires to dif-
cover whether they were a living people or
not, for fuch he defired to find; where he
met with what he often longed for, (a people that worfhipped God in fpirit and in
truth) which was a great ftrength and con-
firmation to him, in forfaking the errors of
his youth, and by yielding obedience to
thefe inward motions, he gained ftrength,
and was more and more enabled to bear a
faithful teftimony to the truth as it was
made known to him.

In the fixth month 1733, he removed to
Philadelphia, where he joined in religious
fellowfhip with friends; in 1735 he married
Mary the daughter of Samuel and Sarah
Maffey; and in 1737 removed to Wilmington in New-Caftle county, where he refided
the remainder of his days.

He

He made fome appearance in the miniftry about the year 1734, but through unfaithfulnefs to the divine call, he from time to time put it off, and remained in a neglect of duty therein upwards of twenty years; altho' he was often warned both immediately and inftrumentally in a remarkable manner, which at length produced a fubmiffion to the divine will, fo that in the year 1755, he was made willing to give up thereto, and therein found great peace.

He travelled thro' divers parts of this continent in the work of the miniftry, and by certificates produced on his return home, it appeared, that his conduct, converfation, and labours abroad were exemplary and edifying, tending to the advancement of truth and righteoufnefs. His doctrine was found, and acceptable to the honeft hearted, tho' fharp againft the hypocrite and rebellious, yet tender to the mourners and difconfolate.

He was very ferviceable in our meetings for difcipline, which, with other meetings, he diligently attended, not fuffering his outward affairs to hinder him from what he believed to be his religious duty. And altho' he followed fhop-keeping for a living, it was his practice to fhut up his fhop and take his family with him to week day meetings, often expreffing for the encouragement of others, that he believed it was attended with a bleffing. He was free and open hearted to entertain friends, and concerned to bring

up

up his children in plainnefs, and inftruct them in the fear of the Lord, believing that to be the beft portion they could inherit; remarkably charitable to the poor, and often adminiftred to their neceflities.

Bodily weaknefs attended him during the laft three years of his life, and near the clofe of his days, he was much afflicted with ficknefs, which he bore with patience, often exprefling his profpect of his approaching end, and his refignation therein; faying, ' All is well.' Several friends being prefent, after a time of filence, he in a lively manner repeated the exprefsions of the apoftle, " To " me, to live is Chrift and to die is gain."

He departed this life, the *5th* of the twelfth month 1779, aged upwards of feventy-two, a minifter about 24 years; on the *7th* of the fame month, his corps was interr'd in our burying-ground in Wilmington.

A *Teftimony from* Chefter *Monthly-Meeting in* Pennfylvania, *concerning* NATHAN YAR-NALL.

HE was born in the Townfhip of Edgemont, in Chefter county Pennfylvania, the *27th* of the twelfth month 1707-8, and continued a member of this monthly-meeting to his end. In the days of his youth he had a ftrong bias to the diverfions of the times,

times, which when given way to, he felt
the fecret reproofs of divine grace accompanied with great fervency of fpirit, to witnefs forgivenefs through Chrift Jefus, by the
operation of whofe fpirit, he obtained fo
great a victory, that he was (after a feafon
of probation) entrufted with a difpenfation
of the gofpel miniftry, in the exercife of
which, his doctrine was fharp againft a ftate
of lukewarmnefs about religion as well as
open profanenefs, feafonably inftructive to
the fincere feekers, exhorting them not to
be fatisfied fhort of witneffing a ftate of regeneration. He was often led to fympathize
with the afflicted in fpirit, unto whom his
doctrine dropt as the dew, and was by many efteemed a nurfing father in the meeting
to which he belonged. He feveral times,
with the concurrence of his friends, vifited
the churches in this and the adjacent governments; was zealoufly concerned that
meetings for difcipline might be maintained
in the fame authority wherein they were
firft eftablifhed; and divers times was engaged in vifiting families, for which weighty fervice he was well qualified. His concern for his children was great, which at
times he expreffed under the power of divine love, adopting the language of David,
viz. " My children, know ye the God of
" your fathers, and ferve him with a per-
" fect heart and willing mind; if ye feek
" him, he will be found of you, but if ye
" forfake him, he will caft you off forever."

For

For feveral years of the latter part of his life, he was afflicted with weaknefs of body, but not fo as wholly to prevent his attending meetings, in which he was at times, power-fully drawn forth in teftimony, and public-ly expreffed at Middletown a few weeks be-fore his confinement, an apprehenfion that his work was nearly over. He was confined at home near three months, in which time he was vifited by many friends, often had refrefhing opportunities in his room; in one of which, (being about a week after his confinement) he was led to fpeak of the precious effects of unity; at another time, divers friends being prefent, after fome fi-lence, he expreffed himfelf on this wife, ' How many opportunities of this fort I ' may yet have is unknown to me; this ' morning as I lay in bed, meditating on ' the things of God, it appeared to me as ' tho' my time in this world would be but ' fhort;' earneftly exhorting thofe prefent, to labour that they and their children might be prepared to meet with death. At feveral times he fignified, ' He was like one that ' was waiting for his change,' expreffing his refignation, and faid, ' Whenevei he turn-' ed his mind inward he felt great peace, ' and that the thoughts of the grave was ' no terror to him.' He gradually weaken-ed without much pain, till about two days before his departure, and continued fenfible to the laft, which was on the 10*th* day of the firft month 1780, and on the 13*th* his

body

body was interr'd in friends burial-ground at Middletown, attended by a large number of friends and neighbours; aged near seventy-two, a minister about 35 years.

A Testimony from Nottingham *Monthly-Meeting in* Pennsylvania, *concerning* R A C H E L B R O W N.

S H E was the wife of Thomas Brown, of West-Nottingham, in Chester county Pennsylvania, and daughter of Ralph and Phebe Needham, of Kent county on Delaware, educated amongst friends, shewing in her younger years an inclination towards piety, and after her marriage was concerned at times to speak in testimony in our religious meetings, and tho' not large, yet frequently, especially in the latter part of her time, her appearances were attended with a lively favour, which, with her exemplary conduct, and zeal for the attendance of our meetings for public worship and maintaining good order in the church, rendered her services useful and acceptable among us; and towards the conclusion of her life, she appeared to be favoured with an increase of solidity and weight.

In her last illness which continued about three weeks, we believe she was much blessed with the incomes of divine love, uttering many weighty expressions, some of which
being

being wrote down, are in fubftance as follows; ' Oh! that I had but power to ex-
' prefs the love I feel to flow towards the
' church, and thofe who are really joined
' thereto. Oh! the wonderful love of the
' father which I feel to flow even to the out-
' cafts of the houfe of Ifrael.' At another
time, ' Oh! the ftraitnefs and refinednefs of
' the path that leads to life and happinefs,'
repeating her fenfe of the wonderful love of
our Lord Jefus Chrift to his church, which
feemed then remarkably opened to her, in
an explanation of thofe expreffions in the
eighth verfe of the fourth chapter of Solomon's Song, " Come with me from Leba-
" non, my fpoufe, with me from Lebanon;
" look from the top of Amana, from the
" top of Shenir and Hermon, from the
" Lions dens, from the mountains of the
" Leopards;" the myftery of which invitation, we underftand fhe fpoke of at divers
times in her ficknefs in a lively manner, as
it appeared to her applicable to the divine call
of our Saviour to his followers, to come out
of all high things, and for his fake who was
plain, meek and lowly, to leave or forfake
the loftinefs and grandeur of this world,
things defirable to the proud flefhly part in
us, to ceafe alfo from fpotted things, and
thofe of a fierce devouring nature: And, as
her laft teftimony againft the fuperfluity
crept in among friends in relation to coffins
and dreffing the bodies of the dead, fhe
earneftly

earneftly defired that her coffin might be
quite plain, and that no needlefs things
might be put on or about her.

She defired her love to her friends, faying,
‘ I have frequently defired your prayers for
‘ me, that I might have an eafy paffage,
‘ and now I am refigned, and defire to have
‘ no will of my own, but to wait with pa-
‘ tience the Lord's time, and alfo for his
‘ falvation.’ Remaining fenfible after her
fpeech failed, fhe quietly departed this life,
the 11*th* of the fifth month 1780, in the
fifty-third year of her age, and was interr'd
in friends burying-ground at Eaft-Nottingham on the 13*th* of the fame month.

A Teftimony from Haddonfield *Monthly-Meeting in* New-Jerfey, *concerning* EPHRAIM
TOMLINSON.

OUR faid friend was born the 29*th* day
of the eighth month 1695, and his
parents fettling fomewhat remote from the
then fettlement of white inhabitants, it appears by a manufcript account he has left,
that he ufed to walk on foot about ten miles
to meeting, and being faithful to the manifeftations of truth in his young years, was
enabled to encourage his brothers to go with
him to wait upon the Lord.

He makes mention of divers befetments
and exercifes he met with in his fpiritual
journey,

journey, but by waiting in ftillnefs upon the Lord, he was pleafed to appear for his help; and he was often drawn to retire in the woods and folitary places, when his mind was at times enlarged in prayer for himfelf and mankind univerfally.

He was a diligent attender of religious meetings whilft of ability of body, feldom fuffering the extremity of weather or his temporal concerns to prevent him from the difcharge of his duty in this refpect, altho' he lived at a confiderable diftance from the particular meeting to which 'he belonged, and was an exemplary humble waiter there-in, for the arifing of that life which is the crown of our affemblies.

He was an appointed elder for the meet-ing at Haddonfield, and conducted upright-ly in his ftation, which rendered him ac-ceptable to his friends, being often employed in the affairs of truth; and was feveral times engaged in that weighty fervice of vifiting families, in the performance whereof, he was fometimes fervently and awfully drawn forth in fupplication to the father of mercies.

He was juft in his dealings among men, remarkably cautious in expreffion, which, joined with a meek and pious life, rendered him a pattern among his fellow-believers worthy of imitation; and his light fo fhined forth before men, that others feeing his good works, were made to acknowledge he had attained the marks of a true difciple and believer in Chrift.

He

He departed this life, on the 2d of the
eighth month 1780, having left a good favour, and we doubt not is made an inherit-
or of that incorruptible crown of righteoufnefs, which is laid up for all thofe who keep
the faith, and love the appearance of our
Lord Jefus Chrift.

He was buried in friends burial-ground
at Haddonfield, attended by a confiderable
number of friends and others, on the 4*th*
day of the fame month; being in the eighty-
fifth year of his age.

—————

A Teftimony from Uwchlan *Monthly-Meeting in*
Pennfylvania, *concerning* SUSANNA LIGHT-
FOOT.

B Y accounts we have had, fhe was born
at Grange, in the county of Antrim,
in the North of Ireland, the 1c*th* of the firft
month (old ftile) 1719-20, defcended of religious parents profeffing the truth (John
and Margaret Hudfon.) Her father dying
in low circumftances when fhe was young,
fhe was placed out by her mother to earn
her living by her own labour; who neverthelefs fought a portion in the truth for her
daughter, efteeming it the beft riches; and
lived to fee the defire of her heart in that
refpect in a degree accomplifhed; for the
tendering vifitations of divine love being
mercifully extended to this our dear friend

early

early in life, fhe happily clofed in therewith,
and witneffed an advancement in piety and
godlinefs; fuch was her love to the truth
and zeal for the attendance of meetings
when young, fhe would go many miles on
foot to them, and being an honeft fervant,
laboured hard to make up the time to her
employer. In thefe times, her cup was often made to overflow with the goodnefs of
the Lord to her* foul, which fhe has frequently been heard to fpeak of with tendernefs of fpirit, for the encouragement of fervants and others in low circumftances; and
that the rich and full who have horfes to
ride on, and are bleffed both with the neceffaries and conveniencies of life, might
prize their time and privileges, and bring
forth fruits adequate to the favours conferred on them.

A difpenfation of the gofpel was committed to her to preach, to which fhe gave up
in the feventeenth year of her age; and we
have reafon to think, fhe grew therein as a
willow by the water courfe; for in the exercife thereof, with the unity of her friends
at home, fhe came over to this country with
Ruth Courtny, in the latter part of the year
1737, and paid a religious vifit to friends
generally on this continent, we believe to
good fatisfaction; fome of us having caufe
to remember her, and the fweetnefs of her
fpirit at that time. With the fame friend
fhe alfo travelled in England and Wales, in

1740, fpending upwards of fifteen months
there in the fervice of truth.

On the 25th of the ninth month 1742,
fhe was married to Jeffe Hatton; in which
ftate, fhe for many years, underwent great
outward difficulties, as well as inward exercifes and trials on account of the caufe and
teftimony of truth which fhe had efpoufed,
and was favoured with firmnefs to hold her
integrity thereto; which fhe has been heard
to commemorate with thankfulnefs to the
Lord her deliverer, rendering the praife to
him alone, who, even during that trying
difpenfation, opened her way to labour con-
fiderably in his caufe in many places, as in
Ireland, Scotland, and again in England.

About the year 1754, fhe removed with
her hufband and family, and fettled in Wa-
terford, where fhe was made truly near to
friends and ufeful in the Lord's hand.

In the year 1759 her hufband died; and
in 1760, being conftrained by the love of
truth, and having the concurrence of her
friends at home and of the meeting of minifters and elders in London, fhe entered on
a fecond vifit to America, which for many
years had relted weightily on her mind. In
the ninth month of the fame year fhe arrived here, and vifited friends meetings ge-
generally throughout this continent, as far
fouthward as Charlefton, in South-Carolina, and to the eaftern parts of New-England, to the comfort and fatisfaction of
friends, leaving feals of her miniftry in
many

many places; and after a labour of upwards of two years, embarked for England. In the fummer following fhe vifited Munfter province in Ireland. And on the 25th of the ninth month 1763, fhe was married to our friend Thomas Lightfoot; and continuing fervent in fpirit for the difcharge of her religious duties, finifhed her vifit to that nation by midfummer following.

In the beginning of the eighth month 1764, fhe embarked at Cork with her hufband and family in order to fettle here, and arrived in the ninth month following, from which time fhe belonged to our monthly-meeting, whereof fhe was a ferviceable member; likewife was engaged in the love of the gofpel, to vifit many of the meetings of friends in this and the adjacent governments, alfo the neighbouring yearly-meetings, and in the year 1774, went into New-England, with our friend Elizabeth Robinfon from Great-Britain; in which vifits her company and fervices were weighty, ftrengthening and eftablifhing to friends.

At divers meetings previous to the breaking forth of the prefent calamity, fhe had, in an awful manner, to proclaim the approach of a ftormy day, which would fhake the fandy foundations of men; and many of the formal profeffors in our fociety fhould be blown away.

The laft journey fhe took, was to the yearly-meeting at Third-Haven, in Maryland, held in the fixth month 1779, wherein deep

wading

wading and wasting exercise, with feeble-
ness of body was her lot. Soon after her
return home, a fit of illness contributed
much to the breaking of her constitution;
but the balm of sweet peace of mind was
still her comfort and support. She recovered so as to get abroad again to her own and
many other meetings about the country,
and to our last yearly-meeting in Philadelphia, tho' in a weak state of health; the last
she attended was our select meeting at
Uwchlan, the 27*th* of the first month 1781,
under an increasing weakness of body, but
to the comfort of friends then assembled.

She was an excellent example of steady
waiting upon the Lord in silence, and out
of meetings solid and grave in her deportment, instructive and weighty in conversation, watchful over her own family for their
good, bearing her testimony against wrong
things in them as well as others; of a difcerning spirit; and when her lot was cast in
families as well as meetings, was often led
to feel for and sympathize with the hidden
suffering seed. Having passed through the
deep waters of affliction herself, her eye
was not unused to drop a tear for, and with
others in distress either in body or mind,
and she rejoiced in comforting and doing
them good.

She was a living and powerful minister
of the word, careful not to break silence in
meetings, until favoured with a fresh anointing from the holy one, whereby she was
preserved

preferved clear in her openings, awful and weighty in prayer, her voice being folemn and awakening under the baptizing power of truth.

Many were the heavenly feafons with which fhe was favoured during a lingering illnefs, in fome of which fhe was led to ex- prefs herfelf in a lively edifying manner, and often, with divine pertinence to the ftates of thofe who were prefent; as alfo her belief that fhe fhould join the fpirits of the juft made perfect, in that city whofe walls are falvation, and her gates praife.

One evening, after a folemn filence, fhe broke forth in a fweet melody, faying, ' I ' have had a profpect this evening, of join- ' ing the heavenly hoft, in finging praifes ' to Zions king, for which favour my foul ' and all that is fenfible within me, magni- ' fies that arm which hath been with me ' from my infant days, and caft up a way. ' where there was no way, both by fea and ' land.' She then fignified what an exercife fhe had laboured under for the good of fouls, and how it wounded her very life, to behold the profeffors of chriftianity acting incon- fiftent with the example of a crucified Sa- viour.

She frequently fupplicated the Lord for the continuance of his help, and that fhe might be endued with patience, adding, ' Oh! what would become of me now, if ' I had a wounded confcience? The work ' with me is not now to do: This winnow-
' ing

' ing day muſt come cloſer to the dwellings
' of ſome than ever it has done, even to the
' ſhaking of them from the gods of ſilver
' and of gold, hay or ſtubble.'

The quarterly-meeting being nigh, ſhe
urged her huſband to leave her, ſaying,
' There is nothing yields ſuch comfort on
' a languiſhing bed as an evidence of hav-
' ing performed our religious duties to the
' beſt of our underſtanding, I can ſpeak it
' at this time by experience.' She ſpoke of
the neceſſity there was for friends to guard
againſt keeping in their families perſons
of corrupt morals and evil communication,
which hath a tendency to poiſon the tender
minds of their children; and ſignified her
apprehenſion, that ſome parents were ſtain-
ed with the blood of their offspring thereby. At another time, ſhe encouraged ſome
that were preſent, to be faithful to the Lord,
and to keep to their gifts, adding, ' Oh!
' what a fine thing it is to ſit lively in meet-
' ings, and to witneſs the holy oil to run as
' from veſſel to veſſel.' Feeling herſelf grow
worſe, ſhe gave directions about the laying-
out her body, that it ſhould be with exemplary plainneſs.

One morning, in the hearing of a few
friends, ſhe cautioned againſt a light chaffy
ſpirit getting up in a ſhew of religion, and
was led in a remarkable manner, to utter
reproofs againſt the ungodly Quaker, ſignifying a terrible day would ſooner or later
overtake ſuch.

She

She expreffed herfelf one day nearly as
follows, ' When I have fat down in our
' meetings, and caft my eye over the peo-
' ple, how have I been grieved to fee the
' haughtinefs of the young men, and the
' folly of the young women, looking one
' upon another, as if there was nothing to
' do; coming to meetings juft to fee and be
' feen: Oh! will not the Lord vifit for thefe
' things? Yea, furely he will, and call to
' an account thofe haughty fons and for-
' getful daughters; I have been grieved
' with it when I have fat as with my lips
' fealed; and yet there is a remnant that are
' near to my life among the youth.

At another time, being raifed by divine
aid from great weaknefs, fhe thus expreffed
herfelf, " The Lord will fearch Jerufalem,
" he will blow away the chaff; but the
" wheat, Oh! the weighty wheat he will
" gather into his holy garner. It feems to
' me, that many of the better fort are haft-
' ening to their graves. I do not repine at
' my afflictions, for how fmall are they,
' compared with his who fuffered for us all,
' when he faid, " My God, my God, why
' haft thou forfaken me?" Oh the profeffors
' of truth! How often have I thought of
' their great privileges! How often have
' they been called unto and watered! And
' yet remain unredeemed; there is much
' impurity about the fkirts of fome; if they
' refufe they will be rejected and others
' called in; he will have his table filled, he
'will

' will have a people that will ſtand for his
' name.' After ſometime, aſking for a
friend, ſhe ſaid, ' I have ſomething to ſay
' to thee about the city; the folly, I would
' not willingly call it iniquity, but upon a
' ſtrict examination I believe it may be ſo
' called, of laying out their dead, has been
' a burden to me many times of late when
' I have been there, I have wondered at the
' pomp and vanity, and the coſt, how much
' for no good purpoſe at all, but to be buri-
' ed with the mouldering body. How much
' better it would be, to ſpare this expence
' for the benefit of ſome poor families? I
' did not know but I ſhould have mention-
' ed it at the yearly-meeting, but I got en-
' feebled, and I prayed it might reſt on
' ſome others, that it might be done then
' or at ſome other time.'

In the afternoon of the ſame day, ſhe
mentioned ſome of the words of Amos,
" I was no prophet, nor a prophet's ſon,
" but I was a gatherer of ſycamore fruit;"
' low employments, ſaid ſhe, " But the Lord
" raiſeth the poor out of the duſt, and lifteth
" up the beggar from the dunghill to ſet
" them among princes. I have been one
' of ſorrows, and much acquainted with
' grief. It is true, this has been a pleaſant
' ſpot to live in, and with an agreeable
' companion, and it was nothing ſhort of
' the good hand that thus provided for me,
' but I have never forgot the wormwood
' and the gall.'

She

She continued quiet and fenfible the remainder of her time, faying, ' Oh deareft
' Lord! take me to thyfelf, even into thy
' heavenly kingdom; take me into Paradife,
' for I long to be with thee there.' After
expreffing the defire of her foul refpecting
one of her fons, fhe took leave of her hufband and others prefent with a look of en-
dearing love, and expired about the fourth
hour in the morning, like one falling into
an eafy flumber, on the 8*th* of the fifth
month 1781, and was interr'd the 11*th* at
Uwchlan, attended by a very great concourfe of people; on which occafion a meeting was held, and was indeed a good meeting, agreeable to a profpect fhe had in the
early part of her illnefs; aged fixty-one,
and a minifter 44 years.

A Teftimony from Evefham *Monthly-Meeting in*
New-Jerfey, *concerning* THOMAS EVANS.

HE was born the 12*th* day of the fecond
month 1693, and defcended from parents profeffing the truth, whofe religious.
care over him, co-operating with the principle of divine grace implanted in his mind,
was the happy means of fixing his attention,
not on a corruptible inheritance, but on that
which is incorruptible, eternal in the heavens, and fadeth not away. And as he was
in a good degree faithful to the manifeftation

on of light afforded him, about the twenty-
fifth year of his age, he entered on the work
of the miniſtry, in which he diligently laboured, viſiting, with the concurrence of
his friends, divers parts of this continent.
He was often led ſenſibly to declare of the
love and goodneſs of the Lord to thoſe who
diligently wait upon and ſeek him; and is
worthy of remembrance for his ſteady example in the attendance of meetings.

In his advanced years, he had divers painful times of illneſs, but was admirably preſerved through them without the help of
medicine. He was temperate in his living;
and that innocency of life, meekneſs and
love which attended him in his early years,
ſhined clear in his latter days, being often
favoured (when his underſtanding in worldly matters appeared to fail him) in a lively
manner to ſpeak to the ſtates of the people
when religiouſly aſſembled, which made
him near to many friends. He was a peacemaker amongſt his neighbours and friends,
and earneſtly engaged for the univerſal advancement of true peace amongſt mankind;
bearing a faithful teſtimony againſt war,
and againſt the unneceſſary diſtillation and
uſe of ſpirituous liquors, and the prevailing and fooliſh cuſtoms and faſhions of the
world.

In his laſt illneſs, he was preſerved in
great patience and reſignation through much
bodily pain, ſignifying his ' Satisfaction in
' having diſcharged his religious duty; and
' that

' that all looked pleafant before him, and
' nothing remained for him to do, unlefs
' the Lord fhould again pleafe to raife him,
' which was hid from his fight, but that
' he was quite refigned to his will in all
' things.'

In thefe trying hours, wherein he was enabled to drop many comfortable and edifying fentences to thofe who vifited him, he appeared to be favoured with a foretafte of that true peace which is laid up in ftore for all them who hold out to the end in well-doing.

He departed this life, the 21/t of the firft month 1783, and was interr'd at Evefham on the 24th, aged near ninety, and a minifter about 65 years.

A Teftimony from the Monthly-Meeting of Philadelphia, *concerning* ANTHONY BENEZET, *an elder, deceafed.*

ON this occafion, we may pertinently adopt the lamenting 'addrefs of the difciples at Joppa, to the apoftle Peter, on the death of Dorcas their fifter, who had been " Full of good works, and alms deeds " which fhe had done. And all the widows " flood by him weeping, and fhewing the " coats and garments which Dorcas had " made while fhe was with them," Acts ix. 37. 39.

Ho

He was born in France, at a town named
St. Quintin, in the province of Picardy, on
the 31/t of that now called the firft month,
1713. At which time romifh bigotry and
fuperftition fubjected the proteftants in
that kingdom to very rigorous perfecutions,
which occafioned many thoufands of them
to leave it, among whom were the parents
of our deceafed friend, who removed from
thence on the 3d of the fecond month called
February, 1715, and after fpending a few
months in Holland, proceeded to London,
where they refided about fixteen years, and
in the month called November, 1731, they
arrived in this city, being well recommended by divers friends.

In the fifth month, 1736, he was married
to our friend Joyce Marriott, of this city, in
whom he experienced a truly religious help-
meet, almoft to the end of forty-eight years.
Being diffatisfied with following mercantile
bufinefs, to which he was brought up, he
declined that occupation and fought other
employments for the maintenance of his
family, and they alfo engaging more of his
time and attention than he found confiftent
with his peace of mind, he willingly embraced an opportunity which offered favourable to his inclination and concern for the
inftruction of youth in ufeful learning, by
fupplying a vacancy which happened in the
year 1742 in the Englifh-fchool under the
direction of friends in this city; which by
their encouragement he undertook, and continued

tinued in this employment through the remaining part of his life, except a fmall in-
termiffion of lefs than two years which he
fpent at Burlington, where he fought for
greater retirement, and more leifure to attend to his religious concern for the general
good of mankind: But did not find his
mind at the eafe he defired, until he returned to refume his employment of fchool-
keeping in this city; where he experienced
greater opportunity of extenfive ufefulnefs,
in which he was affiduoufly diligent, fuffering a fmall portion of natural reft to fa-
tisfy him; employing his pen day and night
in the compilation of books and other writings for profitable inftruction on religious
fubjects, chiefly extracted from various au-
thors of eminence, particularly to inculcate
the peaceable temper and doctrines of the
gofpel, in oppofition to the fpirit of war and
bloodfhed, as alfo to expofe the flagrant in-
juftice of flavery and the abomination of
the African-trade; lamenting the forrowful
defection of profeffed chriftians in thefe refpects, which deeply grieved his tender
heart. The diftribution of his labours have
been found productive of much good, to
render which more extenfive, he held a cor-
refpondence with fuch perfons in various
parts of Europe and America, as united
with him in the like concern, or were fo
circumftanced as to be likely to promote his
pious well-meant views.

On

On the late ceſſation of war betwcen
Great-Britain and America, apprehending
the revival of commerce would be likely to
renew the ignominious trade to Africa for
ſlaves, which had been in ſome meaſure ob-
ſtructed, among other endeavours to diſuade
from this cruel traffic, and having entertained a favourable opinion of the diſpoſition and ſentiments of the queen of
Great-Britain, hoping her influence might
be uſeful to diſcourage it, he was religiouſly
induced to tranſmit her a letter in 1783 on
the ſubject, with a preſent of a few books
of a pious tendency, which he committed
to the care of two of his friends in London,
to deliver in ſuch manner as they ſhould
judge to be moſt ſuitable; this ſervice being
performed ſoon after his deceaſe; one of
them, by a letter received within a few days
paſt, informs his friend here, that the letter
from him with the books. had been delivered to the queen, who on her reading it, expreſſed her perſuaſion, ‘ That the writer
‘ was truly a good man, and that ſhe kind-
‘ ly accepted his preſent,’ engaging alſo to
read the books.

(A copy of the letter is hereunto annexed.)

He was employed the two laſt years of
his life, as teacher in the ſchool for the inſtruction of the black-people and their off-
ſpring, eſtabliſhed and ſupported by the
voluntary contributions of friends in this
city, which by the indiſpoſition of the former

er teacher, had lain fometime vacant, undertaking this employment from an apprehenfion of religious duty, and an earneft folicitude that they might be better qualified rightly to enjoy the freedom to which great numbers of them had been of late reftored; for which purpofe he furrendered, with the confent of his friends, his other fchool, though to the manifeft difadvantage of his worldly intereft.

His confinement by his laft illnefs was not of long continuance, although he had not been in perfect health for more than a year before, but being of a lively difpofition, and remarkably temperate in his food, which was principally vegetables, he attended his fchool and other affairs until the increafe of his diforder difabled him.

He endured the bodily pains he fuffered with much patience, and was favoured with great calmnefs and compofure, being fenfible of his approaching diffolution, receiving his numerous vifitors with much kindnefs, but expreffed little to any of them concerning himfelf, abiding under that humble diffidence which was confpicuous in his conduct through life, confidering himfelf but as an unprofitable fervant. A fhort time before his confinement, in a familiar converfation, he took occafion to remark, that had he attended with due care to the profpects of duty given him in his younger years, he thought it was probable he might
have

have been made inftrumental for more extenfive ufefulnefs to mankind.

On the day preceeding his death he took
an affecting farewell of his wife, who was
then alfo in a weak infirm ftate, when he
reminded her of the affection and concord
which had been maintained between them
through the courfe of their union; and
having fometime before reviewed and executed his will, in which he had devifed his
whole eftate to her during her natural life,
(excepting his fmall library and other books)
and on her deceafe to certain truftees, the
income thereof to be applied to the ufe and
fupport of the Negro-fchool. He had in the
time of his illnefs added a codicil, confirming the fame, with a refervation of fome
fmall legacies to a few of his relations, indigent widows, and other poor perfons; and
having copies tranfcribed, with inftructions
for the diftribution of the books he had on
hand, and for binding divers tracts on religious fubjects which remained in fheets,
he delivered them to fome of his executors
for their government; the laft of which he put
into the hands of one of them not more than
three hours before he departed, which was
about fun-fet on the 3d day of the fifth
month 1784, being the day of our quarterly-meeting; and on the 5th day of the fame
he was buried in our grave-yard in this city; on which folemn occafion, a great
concourfe of inhabitants of all ranks and
profeffions attended, manifefting the univerfal

verfal efteem in which he was held, among
whom alfo feveral hundred black-people in
like manner teftified the grateful fenfe they
had of the benefits derived to them, through
his acts of friendfhip and pious labours on
their behalf.

Unwearied in his endeavours to promote
the effential intereft and well-being of men,
it feemed as his ' Meat and drink' to tread
the path of his divine mafter, in ' Going
' about, doing good.' His labours for the
relief of the afflicted and oppreffed, particularly that much injured people, the enflaved
Africans and their defcendants, having been
unabated and fuccefsful, beyond almoft any
advocate they have had in his time, devo-
ting no fmall portion of his life and worldly
fubftance, in vindication of their violated
rights as men, and their inftruction in things
relating to their temporal and everlafting
intereft.

By an innocent unreferved affability, he
gained efteem and acceptance among all
claffes of men; that love of his neighbour
which was confpicuous throughout his communication, having a foftening effect, even
on rough untractable fpirits, and fo generally did his ufeful life and inoffenfive de-
meanour engage the affections and regard
of all ranks of the people among whom he
dwelt, that at his deceafe, they feemed to
unite in one common fentiment and declara-
tion, of " Bleffed are the dead which die
" in the Lord."

E e

He

He wanted neither abilities nor opportunity for ufing endeavours in the acquirement of wealth; but his moderation in this as in other refpects, was uniformly manifeft to all obfervers; being with little more than a bare competency, rich and liberal beyond moft of thofe who are encumbered with the fuperabundant goods of this life.

This is a fummary narrative of the ufeful life of our valuable friend, and as we mean not to extol the inftrument, but to render to the Lord our creator the praife of his own works; let this account fuffice, and excite in each mind a due obfervance of that gofpel monition, " Go and do thou like-
" wife."

The following is a copy of his letter to the queen, mentioned in the foregoing teftimony, viz.

To CHARLOTTE, *Queen of Great-Britain.*

IMPRESSED with a fenfe of religious duty, and encouraged by the opinion generally entertained of thy benevolent difpofition to fuccour the diftreffed, I take the liberty, very refpectfully, to offer to thy perufal fome tracts which I believe faithfully defcribe the fuffering condition of many hundred thoufands of our fellow creatures of the African race, great numbers of whom, rent from every tender connection in life, are annually taken from their native land, to endure in the American iflands and plan-
tations,

(419)

tations, a moſt rigorous and cruel ſlavery,
whereby many, very many of them, are
brought to a melancholy and untimely end.

When it is confidered, that the inhabitants of Britain, who are themſelves ſo eminently bleſſed in the enjoyment of religious
and civil liberty, have long been, and yet
are, very deeply concerned in this flagrant
violation of the common rights of mankind,
and that even its national authority is ex-
erted in ſupport of the African ſlave-trade,
there is much reaſon to apprehend, that this
has been, and as long as the evil exiſts will
continue to be, an occaſion of drawing down
the divine diſpleaſure on the nation and its
dependencies. May theſe confiderations in-
duce thee to interpoſe thy kind endeavours
on behalf of this greatly oppreſſed people,
whoſe abject fituation gives them an additional claim to the pity and aſſiſtance of the
generous mind; inaſmuch as they are altogether deprived of the means of ſoliciting
effectual relief for themſelves. That ſo thou
may not only be a bleſſed inſtrument in the
hand of him " By whom kings reign, and
" princes decree juſtice," to avert the awful
judgments by which the empire has already
been ſo remarkably ſhaken, but that the
bleſſings of thouſands ready to periſh, may
come upon thee, at a time when the ſuperior
advantages attendant on thy fituation in
this world, will no longer be of any avail
to thy conſolation and ſupport.

E e 2   To

To the tracts on the fubject to which I
have thus ventured to crave thy particular
attention, I have added fome others, which
at different times, I have believed it my duty to publifh, and which I truft will afford
thee fome fatisfaction; their defign being
for the furtherance of that univerfal peace
and good-will amongft men, which the
gofpel was intended to introduce.

I hope thou will kindly excufe the freedom ufed on this occafion, by an ancient
man, whofe mind for more than forty years
paft, has been much feparated from the
common courfe of the world, and long pain-
fully exercifed in the confideration of the
miferies under which fo large a part of mankind equally with us the objects of redeem-
ing love, are fuffering the moft unjuft and
grievous oppreffion, and who fincerely defires the temporal and eternal felicity of the
queen and her royal confort.

ANTHONY BENEZET.

Philadelphia the 25th of the eighth month 1783.

———————

A Teftimony from Concord *Monthly-Meeting in*
Pennfylvania,*concerning* PHEBE TRIMBLE.

THE memory of the juft is pronounced
" Bleffed ;" which we wifh to be verified in the following memorial of this our
efteemed

efteemed friend, by affording an excitement to furvivors to walk in her fteps.

The days of her youth and early periods of maturer age, were attended with clofe trials, ftripping feafons, and deep baptifms, through all which the Lord her gracious helper (whofe tender regard is ever manifeft-ed towards his humble depending children) preferved her, and raifed her up to be a veffel in his houfe. About the forty-fecond year of her age, being in 1759, fhe fettled with her hufband William Trimble within the limits of this meeting, to which fhe was recommended by certificate from Gofhen monthly-meeting, as an approved minifter, which charadter fhe juftly retained during her ftay in mutability.

Her public appearances, tho' generally in few words, were truly acceptable and edify-ing, being clear, pertinent, comprehenfive and favoury, and accompanied with deep humility and gravity of deportment. She was not forward in the exercife of her gift, but appeared defirous to proceed therein under divine diredtion. At two different times fhe vifited friends in Maryland and Virginia, and once in North and South-Carolina, in which vifits her gofpel labours were well received.

Her common deportment was inftrudtive; evidencing lowlinefs, meeknefs and felf-de-nial; that it may juftly be faid, her ' Adorn-
' ing was that of a meek and quiet fpirit.'
Her converfation, tho' pleafant and cheer-ful, was accompanied with that fweetnefs

and

and gravity which rendered it both agreeable and profitable. Her heart and houfe were open to the reception and entertainment of her friends; nor was her benevolence and humane feelings circumfcribed to thofe in religious communion with her; but the poor, we believe, of all denominations in the neighbourhood where fhe lived, partook of her kindnefs, and by her removal have loft a fympathizing friend.

During the time of her laft illnefs, fhe was much given to ftillnefs and retirednefs of mind, being fometimes uneafy with friends converfing on temporal fubjects in her prefence. Her hope and faith in her dear redeemer, we believe did not fail her in this her laft and trying period; though fhe was very lowly and humble in her own eftimation, and at times almoft diffident of her being worthy of divine regard: Thus in her cafe may be applicably revived, the ancient interrogation, " If the righteous fcarce- " ly be faved, where fhall the ungodly and " finner appear?" May this awaken profitable reflections in the minds of all, efpecially the carelefs and indifferent.

On the 14*th* of the fixth month 1784, fhe quietly departed this life, in the fixty-feventh year of her age; and on the 16*th* was buried at Concord, attended by many friends and others, at which time was held a large and folemn meeting. And we doubt not but fhe is gone from works to an happy reward.

A Teftimony

A Teſtimony from the Monthly-Meeting of Friends of Philadelphia *for the* Southern-Diſtrict, *concerning* JOHN REYNELL.

THOUGH none of us were acquainted with him whilſt he reſided in Great-Britain, the land of his nativity, yet we have cauſe to believe, from what himſelf has ex-preſſed, that he was early viſited with the offers of divine love, and by wiſely cloſing in therewith, he came to experience preſer-vation from many temptations and allure-ments wherewith the minds of unwary youth are liable to be enſnared.

To ſeveral of his particular friends, he, at times, mentioned ſome tranſactions pre-vious to his coming to this country, which containing matter of encouragement to faithfulneſs in others, we apprehend may not improperly be here inſerted, viz.

When about eighteen years of age, pur-poſing to embark on a voyage to Jamaica, and being thoughtful leſt he might lay down the body at that place, as had been the caſe with many, he received, as he believed, a divine aſſurance that his life ſhould be pre-ſerved. During his reſidence there, he had a ſight given him, of a grievous calamity by means of a violent hurricane, to befall the inhabitants of the Iſland as a chaſtiſe-ment for their iniquities, which came to paſs according to his proſpect. Soon after-wards an occurrence happening which occaſioned

cafioned his being called upon to give evidence in a court of judicature, he was required to take an oath, which he confcientioufly refufing, it proved for a time, no fmall trial of his faithfulnefs; and although he had few or none outwardly to look to for ftrength and encouragement under that exercife, he was neverthelefs favoured to experience divine fupport to be near, fo that neither threatning nor perfuafion could prevail on him to deviate from our chriftian teftimony in that refpect. Very few of the members of our religious fociety then refided on that Ifland, yet a meeting-houfe belonging to friends ftill remaining in Kingfton, he was not eafy to omit attending at the times appointed for meeting, though he fometimes fat alone therein.

About the twentieth year of his age he came to Pennfylvania, and after fettling in this city, he became a ferviceable member among us both in a religious and civil capacity, cheerfully employing his talents and much of his time to beneficial and laudable purpofes, and was often engaged as a peacemaker in reconciling differences.

As an elder, he approved himfelf in faithfulnefs and uprightnefs in the difcharge of that important truft, being well qualified for the ftation he filled. A good example in diligently attending our religious meetings as long as ability of body permitted, and very ufeful in the exercife of the difcipline. A man of integrity and found judgment.

Being

Being favoured with an affluence of temporal riches, he endeavoured to fulfil his duty as a good steward, by liberally communicating of his subftance to fuch as ftood in need. Befides his repeated acts of liberality throughout the courfe of his life, the many charitable legacies he bequeathed by his will, are further proofs of his benevolent difpofition. So that we believe it may juftly be faid, he was one that " Feared " God and hated covetoufnefs."

In the fpring of the year 1784, his natural ftrength evidently impairing, he beheld the profpect of his approaching diffolution with the ferenity and compofure of a chriftian; and continued gradually declining for feveral months, during which time he did not impart much refpecting his own fpiritual ftate, being defirous to be more in fubftance than fhew, yet found it needful to keep up a fteady watch until his warfare fhould be accomplifhed. Two friends vifiting him one evening, he mentioned, ' That on look-
' ing over his paft life, he was fenfible of
' many deficiencies,' yet expreffed ' A hope
' that all would be well.' On the evening previous to his departure, he faid, ' I am
' ready. I feel myfelf happy, and furround-
' ed with divine glory;' and expired the 3d of the ninth month 1784, aged feventy-fix years. His corps being interr'd the day following in friends burying-ground in this city, a folemnity covered the minds of many at the grave which was truly confolatory.

A Teftimony

A Teſtimony from New-Garden *Monthly-Meet-ing in* Pennſylvania, *concerning* WILLIAM *and* KATHARINE JACKSON.

THEY were born in Ireland, came into this country with their parents, and ſettled within the limits of New-Garden meeting. About the year 1733 they were joined in marriage, proving true help-meets to each other; and as they advanced in age, grew in grace, and a qualification for ſer-vice in the church in the prime of life, be-ing of a meek and inoffenſive diſpoſition, well beloved and truly uſeful members in the meeting to which they belonged; in dealing with offenders, endeavouring to con-vince and reſtore, yet careful that the teſti-mony of truth might be preſerved blamelefs. Notwithſtanding their beginning in the world was ſmall, a bleſſing attending their induſtry and frugality, they got a comfort-able ſubfiſtance for themſelves, and to bring up their family; cheerfully and kindly en-tertaining many friends in thoſe early days, and having a near ſympathy with the meſ-fengers and ſervants of the Lord, who were tried and proved with humbling baptizing ſeaſons, were often enabled to ſpeak a word of comfort and encouragement to ſuch; af-fectionate and helpful to thoſe in affliction, charitable and conſiderate to the poor, many partaking of their bounty, they were nearly united with friends.

Their

Their care over their family, and concern to bring up their children in plainnefs, fimplicity, induſtry, and the attendance of religious meetings, was great. Katharine thro' weaknefs and infirmity, particularly in old age, often endured much pain in riding to meetings, yet when there, her folid innocent countenance and deportment therein were edifying. When near her end, during feveral weeks painful ficknefs, ſhe retained her innocent fweetnefs of difpofition, expreffing refignation to her allotment; often advifing her children and thofe about her to live in love. Some of her laft expreffions that could be underſtood, were, ‘ There is reſt and ‘ peace prepared for me, where I ſhall fing ‘ hallelujahs to the higheſt!’ And after a little paufe, faid, ‘ Thy fweetnefs, O Lord! ‘ is great.’ She quietly departed the 2d of the fourth month 1781, in the fixty-eighth year of her age, and on the 5th was interr'd in friends burying-ground at New-Garden.

William was fupported under the trial of this feparation, with becoming refignation to the divine will; having through life been an example of punctuality, juſtice, temperance and brotherly kindnefs.

On account of bodily infirmity, which at times made riding hard to bear, he often went on foot, when above feventy-five years of age, upwards of four miles to meeting; his faithfulnefs and example wherein, the becoming manner of his fitting there, evidencing a watchful folid frame of mind,

was

was very inftructive. On the 22d of the
tenth month 1785 (having been for fometime much confined at home) he was taken
ill, and tho' afflicted with much pain of body, his underftanding was preferved found,
and faculties clear. In the morning of the
23d to two of his children he faid, ' There
' is always fomething comes to take us out
' of the world, and if we are but prepared it
' is the lefs matter;' one of them expreffing a
hope that he did not feel any thing to the
contrary; he replied ' No, no, I don't, I have
' a comfortable hope and belief that all will
' be well.' Remarking fome little time after, on the fettlement of his affairs, his fmall
beginning, and how he had been favoured
through life; he expreffed his concern and
fympathy for divers friends in ftraitened
circumftances, and that he had been much
exercifed at times on account of many in
fociety who appeared forward and zealous,
but thro' neglect or mifmanagement of their
outward affairs, had miniftered caufe of reproach; obferving that it was wifdom not
to appear in fhew more than in fubftance,
either in our religious or temporal concerns.
The night of the 25th he communicated to
fome of his children much feafonable and
heart-tendering advice; recommending a-
bove all things to ftrive for an everlafting
inheritance, whereinto they might enter
when done with time; concluding in thefe
words, ' Love truth, love one another, love
' friends and all good people, even all man-
' kind,

' kind, and be careful to hurt none, no not
' the very meaneſt, if ye can do them no
' good, ye ſhould do them no harm.' Then
mentioning the uncertainty of his continuance here, gave directions that his coffin
ſhould be plain, no poliſh or ſtain upon it.

Being very low on the 28*th* and apprehenfive of his end being near, he ſpoke to ſome
of his children, defiring, when the change
came, all might keep ſtill and quiet; adding, it was an awful time, and ought to
be ſo to thoſe about him. Some hours after, ſaying, it would be a relief if he might
be favoured in his paſſage, his bodily diſtreſs being great; ' But I muſt not com-
' plain, it don't become us to complain, but
' we may tell each other of our afflictions
' without complaining or murmuring; for
' the Almighty has been good to me in my
' affliction, ſo that we have great cauſe to
' love him.' A few hours after ſaid, ' What
' manner of perſons ought we to be, to bear
' every diſpenſation of affliction and trial
' that comes upon us, as we ought to do?'
Saying at another time, ' Many tedious days
' and weariſome nights had been his lot
' theſe eighteen months paſt.' His ſon expreſſing his belief that reſt would be very
acceptable, he replied, ' Yes, an everlaſting
' reſt.' On the 13*th* of the eleventh month
he uttered the following ſupplication, ' O
' Lord God Almighty! if it be thy bleſſed
' will, mitigate my affliction, and relieve
' me in my diſtreſs; not my will but thine
' be

' be done.' And a little after faid, ' The
' appointed time will come, and it muft be
' waited for, he knows beft the right time;
' his wifdom is very great, and care and
' providence over his poor creatures very
' great indeed.' To one of his children,
taking leave of him, he faid, in fubftance,
' There is great corruption in the world
' amongft mankind, and need there is of
' care in bringing up children, and young
' people, to reftrain them; for many are
' running as the wild affes upon the moun-
' tains.' A few days before he departed he
faid, ' It is a comfort to me to have my
' children with'me, and it may be a fatis-
' faction to them to fee me go; I feel eafy
' in mind on looking backward and for-
' ward, I fee nothing in my way, the Lord
' has been good to us, and efpecially to me
' in my affliction.' Much more he expreffed at fundry times, continuing fenfible, but
gradually weakening, he departed this life,
on the 24*th* of the eleventh month 1785, in
the eighty-firft year of his age, having been
an elder upwards of 40 years, and having
ruled well was worthy of double honour,
his memory being of good favour. On the
27*th* he was interr'd in friends burying-
ground at New-Garden; attended by a large
number of people, with whom a folid meeting was held.

Some

Some expreſſions of JOSEPH HUSBAND, *before and in his laſt ſickneſs, read and approved in the Monthly-Meeting of Friends at* Deer-Creek *in* Maryland, *and directed to be forwarded to the* Weſtern *Quarterly-Meeting.*

A CONSIDERABLE time before his deceaſe, when in health, he ſometimes mentioned to his friends, and frequently to his wife, his profpect that his time would not be long here, and in or near his laft ſickneſs, told her that he felt eafy, and believed he ſhould foon be taken from her. Some days before his death he appeared exceeding low in mind attended with many doubts reſpecting his paſt and then ſituation, remaining ſeveral days in great diſtreſs; after which it pleaſed the Lord to manifeſt himſelf to him in ſo extraordinary a manner, that his wife perceiving a change, aſked him how he was; he anſwered I am better than I expected ever to be, my mind is now relieved, and, as a morning without clouds, all appears ſuſhine, mentioning to her and a friend preſent, many trials and temptations he had experienced; at another time ſaying, deep has been the baptifm I have paſſed through, my foul hath been dipt into a feeling fenſe of the ſtate of unbelievers, yea, I have paſſed through the valley of the ſhadow of death, which I am now convinced we muſt do before we can experience a glorious reſurrection unto eternal
nal

nal life. And frequently faid, my dear I feel thy fympathy and love, and ah! how precious do I feel the unity of the church; often mentioning divers of his near friends, and continuing in a fweet frame of mind, not complaining of pain (tho' the nature of his difeafe muft have occafioned much) his countenance remaining ferene and pleafant to the laft; a few minutes before his death he fpoke to this purpofe, ' Give my dear ' love to friends, and tell them I die in the ' faith which I lived in, and firmly believe ' I fhall foon enter into the manfions of eter- ' nal happinefs prepared for the true believ- ' ers in Chrift; and altho' I never did much ' for the caufe and teftimony of truth, I ' fhall be with the believers, and that is ' enough;' foon after which he quietly departed this life, on the 6th day of the fifth month 1786, about the fiftieth year of his age; being the next day interr'd in friends burying-ground at Deer-Creek.

To which the Quarterly-Meeting held at London-Grove, *the* 21ft *of the eighth month* 1786, *add.*

THE foregoing account concerning our friend Jofeph Hufband, being communicated to us, was read here and approved; and from the knowledge and fenfe many of us had of him for a number of years, this meeting is free to add, that it appears he was born in Cecil county, Maryland, came into religious memberfhip with friends after he

he arrived to man's eftate, having been convinced of the principle of truth while young,
more by inward conviction than inftrumental
means, as he was educated in the way of the
epifcopal church (fo called) and even when
a lad, had to pafs through many trials under
his father, for declining that way of worfhip; and (as he related to his wife and
others) he frequently felt great tendernefs
towards the negro children with whom he
was brought up, from the profpect of their
ftate of flavery, which much affected him
at times before he was ten years of age.
He conducted with reputation and ftability
as a ufeful friend, manifefting a lively un-
fhaken concern for the maintenance of our
difcipline, the furtherance of our teftimony
againft an hireling-miniftry, and flave-hold-
ing, as well as for the doctrine of peace,
efpecially thro' the difficulties which occur-
red in the late times of public requifitions
for the purpofes of war; fhewing chriftian
fortitude, humility and refignation under
fufferings and clofe trials of different kinds
which fell to his lot. Sometime before his
deceafe he appeared in public teftimony, in
which he was not forward, but moftly brief,
pertinent and acceptable to friends; being
remarkably open to receive counfel as well
as to give; we find the remembrance of his
difpofition and fervice is fatisfactory, both
among the members of the monthly-meeting he belonged to, and this meeting.

Abftract

F f

Abſtract from the Teſtimony of Concord *Month-ly-Meeting as read and approved by* Cheſter *Quarterly-Meeting, held at* Concord *the* 14th *of the fifth month* 1787, *concerning our dear friend* EDITH SHARPLES, *deceaſed.*

S H E was born the 13th day of the fifth month 1743; her parents Nathan and Rachel Yarnall, members of Middletown particular meeting, having been careful to educate her in plainneſs and a diligent attendance of religious meetings, ſhe retaining a thankful remembrance of their care over her, has been often heard to bleſs the Lord on their account, as by their good counſel and wholeſome reſtraint, they contributed to her preſervation out of the vain faſhions and cuſtoms of the world.

By her own account, her mind was early in life accompanied with earneſt deſires after the knowledge of truth, and that ſhe might never do any thing to offend him whom ſhe often found near to her comfort, or that might bring a reproach on the profeſſion ſhe made; but giving way to her natural vivacity, ſhe frequently indulged herſelf in what with ſome is accounted innocent paſtime, for which ſhe was often brought under condemnation; and about the twenty-fourth year of her age was plunged into great diſtreſs, being cloſely beſet with the wiles of an unwearied adverſary; but the Lord, who will not ſuffer his people to be tempted

tempted beyond what they thro' his grace
are enabled to bear, made way for her escape
from under the power of temptation, for
which she had, in that day, as on the banks
of deliverance, to sing to the praise of his
holy name; saying, ' It is in my heart to
' praise thee O my deliverer! for thy ma-
' nifold kindnesses unto me a poor un-
' worthy worm; for altho', for disobedi-
' ence, thou hast seen meet to hide thy
' face for a moment; yet my soul is hum-
' bly bowed before thee, rendering unto
' thee the praise of all thy works; having
' witnessed the fulfilling of thy promise.
" But with everlasting kindness will I have
" mercy on thee saith the Lord thy re-
" deemer."

In the twenty-sixth year of her age she
was married to Joshua Sharples, settled
within the compass of New-Garden monthly-meeting, of which she became a useful
member, being qualified for service in the
church, whereto she attended with much
satisfaction to friends, filling the stations of
overseer and elder with diffidence under a
sense of the weight thereof.

In the thirty-first year of her age she appeared in the ministry, and being faithful,
grew in her gift, was found in doctrine,
accompanied with a degree of heart-
tendering authority to the careless and
indolent, yet edifying and consolatory to
the refreshment of the mourners in Zion.

In

In her approaches to the throne of grace in public fupplication, fhe was awfully attended with deep folemnity.

She was a great lover of the fcriptures, and well qualified to apply them to edification and inftruction, being concerned to invite friends and others to a more frequent reading of them. The doctrines of the principle of truth as held by friends fhe was fkilful in explaining, and was often exercifed therein in mixed auditories, endeavouring to lead out of forms to the fubftance of true religion. Much of her time was thus employed in the public fervice of her Lord and mafter, cheerfully giving up to his holy requirings, but carefully concerned to wait for his putting forth.

Having peculiar fervice in vifiting families, fhe was often ufefully engaged therein; and about the year 1778 with divers other friends under appointment from the Weftern quarterly-meeting, in a general vifit to all the meetings belonging thereto, fhe was exercifed under a deep concern to labour that a reformation in life and manners might be really effected amongft the profeffors of truth. Soon after, being removed within the compafs of our meeting, fhe engaged in a like vifit to the meetings in our quarter, wherein, as in other of her gofpel labours, fhe manifefted an ardent defire for the promotion of the caufe of truth, and that fhe might be favoured to do her days work in the day-time. And fince, with the concurrence

rence of friends, vifited moft of the meetings in the Southern governments; being diligent in the improvement of her
time for the fervice of truth, often drawn
into family vifits, and to the afflicted either
in body or mind, who experienced the con-
foling fympathy of her tender fpirit, in
which and other gofpel labours fhe reaped
the reward of peace and comfort to her own
mind. When at home fhe was not only diligent in attending meetings herfelf, but
careful to encourage and affift her family in
their duty therein; in herfelf an example of
plainnefs, and mindful to promote a like
fimplicity in thofe under her direction, manifefting much concern that her children
might be brought up in the truth, frequently retiring with them for their improvement,
her faithfulnefs againft wrong things in
them being confiftent with the tendernefs of
an affectionate mother. ' Great was her exercife for the rifing generation, that their
hearts might be early dedicated to the Lord,
and they thereby preferved in a conduct
confiftent with our holy profeffion. Open
and hofpitable in her houfe, a true help-
meet and affectionate wife.

Shortly after her return from a vifit to
friends on the Eaftern-Shore of Maryland,
in the fixth month 1786, fhe was brought
very low thro' bodily indifpofition, but favoured with inward confolation and true
peace, expreffing that fhe felt her mind
much weaned from the things of this world,

and

and if it fhould pleafe the Lord to call her
hence fhe found nothing in her way. On
a firft-day afternoon, divers friends being
prefent, after a time of filence, fhe fpoke to
this effect, ' I am glad of this opportunity;
' as I lay on the bed this morning, my mind
' was carried away to meeting with friends,
' and I thought if I had wings I could have
' flown thither for the great love I feel for
' the members of that meeting. Indeed we
' have had many favoured opportunities to-
' gether; and you fee I am in a poor weak
' way, and whether I fhall get out again I
' have not feen, but am refigned, and feel
' the reward of peace; but if fome friends
' of that meeting are not more faithful to
' the many gracious vifitations which have
' been in mercy to them extended, weak-
' nefs will overtake them, and they be in
' danger of miffing the anfwer of well done.'
She recovered and afterwards had many
heart-tendering opportunities with friends
there, and others not in memberfhip with
us, toward whom fhe was remarkably led
in teftimony, in order that they might be
gathered to the fold of reft.

About two weeks before her deceafe fhe
attended feveral of the neighbouring meetings, expreffing her fatisfaction therewith;
and on the firft-day before her departure,
was at New-Garden meeting and had acceptable fervice, having alfo a favoured opportunity the fame evening in a friends family where fhe lodged on her return home,

at

at which time fhe was concerned to revive
thefe expreffions of the Pfalmift, " Lord
" make me to know mine end, and the mea-
" fure of my days, what it is, that I may
" know how frail I am: Behold thou haft
" made my days as an hands breadth, and
" mine age is as nothing before thee."
Which fhe enlarged on to edification. Next
day fhe got home fomewhat indifpofed, but
held up till the day following in the evening
of the 16th of the firft month 1787, when
fhe was confined to her bed, and lay in a
fenfible refigned frame of mind, being, as
we believe, well prepared for her awful
change, appearing to have nothing to do
but to die. Some of the laft words fhe was
heard to fay were, ' I believe I am going,'
and in about fifteen minutes after, quietly
breathed her laft on the 18th, and on the
20th was interr'd at Birmingham, aged
forty-three years and feven months, a minifter upwards of 12 years.

F I N I S.

www.ingramcontent.com/pod-product-compliance
Lightning Source LLC
Chambersburg PA
CBHW031827270326
41932CB00008B/581